What Your Colleagues Are Saying . . .

This is the book so many of us in early childhood mathematics have been waiting for. It's practical, justice oriented, and, maybe most importantly, child centered. From lessons about representation in cartoons to differences in family structures to living through a pandemic, the book provides many detailed lessons that take up social justice concerns in ways that are real and relevant to young children while also providing ways to productively engage in grade-level mathematics.

—Amy Noelle Parks
Professor, Elementary and Early Childhood Education
Michigan State University, East Lansing, MI

Finally, a bold and beautiful mathematics resource for the early elementary educator that guides us to fully connect children's natural mathematical curiosity with their intimate sense of justice and humanity. In reading this book, I wanted to try out every single lesson immediately, just to see that look of joy when children truly read and write their own world with mathematics!

—Theodore Chao
Associate Professor
The Ohio State University, Columbus, OH

A wonderful collection of lessons, submitted by teachers, to help students of all ages see topics they care about, and use mathematics as a tool for progress in the world.

—Jo Boaler
The Nominelli-Olivier Professor of Education (Mathematics)
Stanford University, Stanford, CA

This book is a gift for early childhood educators, whether they are newly curious to social justice and mathematics or seasoned experts at implementing socially-conscious, mathematically rich experiences for their young learners. The authors invite readers in with their conversational and respectful tone, their attention to the specific contexts of the early childhood educator (such as discourses around "developmentally appropriate practice"), and their use of contemporary, research-based frameworks.

—Andrea McCloskey
Associate Professor of Education (Mathematics Education)
Penn State University, University Park, PA

Koestler and colleagues have curated a diverse set of lessons that invite children to "make sense of themselves and the world" through the lens of social justice mathematics. A particular strength of this book is the voices and experiences of the lesson authors, encouraging the reader to "trust in children" and allow the power of children's voices to guide this important and challenging work.

—Angela Chan Turrou
Senior Researcher
University of California, Los Angeles, CA

As a teacher educator for social justice, I am familiar with the near-constant refrain of "this isn't something you can do in math!" This book illustrates just the opposite. Indeed, not only is it possible to engage in social justice mathematics, but it is an educational imperative to do so. This much-needed and valuable collection provides practitioners with clear and compelling lessons that are grounded in theories of justice and equity. Especially timely in this text is the clear evidence that not only can early elementary–aged children engage in critical conversations, problem solving, and sociocultural analysis in their mathematics classes, but they must. The editors and contributors to this volume have curated a powerful resource that is a must-read for all mathematics educators and those who care about social justice teaching and learning.

—Alyssa Hadley Dunn
Associate Professor of Teacher Education
Michigan State University, East Lansing, MI

I imagine many people will purchase this book for the sample lesson plans. And you should; they're fabulous. But just as fabulous, and equally important, is the framework the authors lay out for a comprehensive, holistic, transformative approach to mathematics teaching—social justice at its core.

—Paul C. Gorski
Lead Equity Specialist
Equity Literacy Institute, Columbia, SC

This book is a must-read for all elementary educators. A call to action, this guide for teachers offers incredible resources, including powerful lesson plans, to engage readers in the practice of teaching mathematics for social justice in early childhood settings. This is an immense contribution to the conversation around social justice and mathematics in elementary education.

—Ruchi Agarwal-Rangnath
Assistant Professor
University of San Francisco, San Francisco, CA

A very compelling set of fresh ideas are offered that prepare educators to turn the corner on advocating for social justice in the mathematics classroom. Each book is full of engaging activities, frameworks, and standards that center instruction on community, worldview, and the developmental needs of all students—a must-needed resource to reboot our commitment to the next generation.

—Linda M. Fulmore
TODOS: Mathematics For ALL
Cave Creek, AZ

Early Elementary Mathematics Lessons to Explore, Understand, and Respond to Social Injustice is an outstanding addition to the growing number of texts and projects that weave the teaching of mathematics and social justice together. The authors go deep and broad to show how, why, and when this combination of curricular topics improves our students' mathematical understandings while honing their abilities and dispositions to promote social and environmental justice in their own lives and communities.

—**Bob Peterson**
Editor of *Rethinking Schools*
Editor of *Rethinking Mathematics: Teaching Social Justice by the Numbers*
Milwaukee, WI

Early Elementary Mathematics Lessons to Explore, Understand, and Respond to Social Injustice

at a Glance

In addition to pedagogical tools, additional resources, and voices from the field, this book delivers 14 lessons with extensive additional resources.

Notes tying each lesson back to Social Justice Outcomes, Mathematics Domains and Practices, and Cross-Curricular Connections.

General overview of the lesson describing the mathematical connection, learning goals, and needed materials and resources to complete the lesson.

LESSON 5.1 HUMAN DIVERSITY AND DISABILITY: DO WE ALL HAVE 10 FINGERS?

Jennifer R. Newton, Courtney Koestler, and Jan McGarry

BODY DIVERSITY AND DISABILITY

This lesson explores human diversity (i.e., different kinds of bodies), disability, and ableism. It is meant to be launched during or after a typical lesson found in many textbooks that assumes children all have "typical" bodies, such as having 10 fingers, and are able to participate in "typical" ways. Children can use critical literacy skills to examine the mathematics lesson as presented as usual (in many textbooks) as well as resources in their classroom to see how bodies, disability, and ableism are presented. Oftentimes the topic of disability in mainstream classrooms is invisible or explicitly not talked about unless absolutely necessary, and it is important for children to see others (both children and adults) with disabilities represented in their classrooms through empowering ways. Disabilities should be portrayed in ways that avoid deficits and stereotypes and instead accurately describe the disability and/or portray people with disabilities living their lives (whether or not disability is the focus).

DEEP AND RICH MATHEMATICS

This lesson engages children in using their bodies (i.e., their fingers) as a physical representation to support skip-counting groups of 10 and multiples of 10. Depending on the age and experience of the children, you may bring in concepts of doubling and halving.

ABOUT THE LESSON

This 1-day lesson includes ideas for continuing the work throughout the year, since talking about disability should not happen in just 1 day.

Resources and Materials
- Chalkboard/whiteboard, chalk/markers, or another way to record children's thinking

SOCIAL JUSTICE OUTCOMES
- I like being around people who are like me and different from me, and I can be friendly to everyone. (Diversity 6)
- I can describe some ways that I am similar to and different from people who share my identities and those who have other identities. (Diversity 7)
- I know everyone has feelings, and I want to get along with people who are similar to and different from me. (Diversity 9)

MATHEMATICS DOMAINS AND PRACTICES
- Number and Operations
- Patterns and Algebraic Thinking
- Make sense of problems and persevere in solving them. (MP1)
- Reason abstractly and quantitatively. (MP2)
- Construct viable arguments and critique the reasoning of others. (MP3)
- Look for and make use of structure. (MP7)

CROSS-CURRICULAR CONNECTIONS
- Language Arts (including Critical Literacy)
- Social Studies

167

Extensive facilitation notes help educators run through the lesson with their class in a thoughtful manner.

LESSON FACILITATION

Launch (10 minutes)

- A common elementary mathematics activity is to count by tens by counting all the fingers in the classroom. This implicitly makes an ableist assumption that all people have 10 fingers. This unit engages children in questioning those assumptions and thinking about different mathematical contexts we can use for making tens. Prior to implementing this unit, we recommend you consider your classroom and how you want to frame the topic. This is important for all classes, but it is especially critical if you have any children who do not have 10 fingers. The *Resources and Materials* section has several links that can be helpful in thinking about how to discuss these topics with children in your classroom. If you have a child in your class who does not have 10 fingers, we suggest you discuss the unit with the family and child to make sure you are approaching it in a way that feels inclusive and supportive to them. While we provide suggestions for some possible approaches to navigating this space, you should adjust based on your context.

- Begin the lesson by saying something like this to the children:

  + *I have been thinking a lot about today's activity and wanted to talk to you about it. It is an activity that is in a lot of math books because it is usually really good at getting kids to think about important math tools attached to our bodies (our fingers!) and patterns and numbers, but I also am wondering about some assumptions it makes about kids and bodies.*

  + *Let's talk about the task and think about some of the ideas in it before we start.*

- You may have to adjust what you would say depending on your context. For example, if you have already done work on critical literacy with the children in your classroom, the children may be familiar with the idea of how textbook authors' assumptions and biases can be analyzed. If not, you may have to discuss it a bit more, perhaps by asking if they know what an assumption is and if they can give any examples. For more information, see Vivian Vasquez's (2016) *Critical Literacy Across the K–6 Curriculum*. Also, you will want to be responsive to any needs the children have as well. For example, if you have a child in your class with a physical disability, you would want to exercise extreme sensitivity.

- Continue by using prompts and asking questions such as these:

  + *The activity that is usually in math books is to figure out the total number of fingers in our class counting by tens.*

  + *What does this problem assume about people's bodies? About their fingers?*

Many lessons have numerous online resources for students and teachers and are all available for educators to download on the companion website.

● ONLINE RESOURCE

Available for download at **resources.corwin.com/ TMSJ-EarlyElementary**

▼ Worksheet 1: *Recording Sheet*

Recording Sheet			

Find lesson background information and contributor bios at the end of each lesson to give you additional context of how this lesson came to be.

● BACKGROUND OF THE LESSON

Our classroom setting was composed of 3- and 4-year-old children from diverse backgrounds who were getting ready to enter the voluntary prekindergarten program in the fall (this work took place during the summer). Prior to this work, the children had been engaged in the creation of their own school garden and explored the location and number of community gardens nearby. From this work, the children learned of limited community gardens in our area and came to wonder about the ways in which people got fresh fruits and vegetables if they could not grow them or buy them from the local grocery store near campus, as well as what happened to the food they did not eat. This led to an inquiry into exploring what it means to lack access to food, food deserts in the area, and ways to take action against food insecurity.

In order to build my own understanding of these issues, I first needed to locate statistics about food insecurity for both our area and the state in general. I pulled up maps and looked for the location of various grocery stores (both chain and smaller, local grocers) to determine where areas of food insecurity were. I worked to develop a clear definition of a food desert for the children: a location where community members lack access to fresh and affordable food. I wanted for

Early Elementary
MATHEMATICS LESSONS
TO EXPLORE, UNDERSTAND, AND RESPOND TO
Social Injustice

Early Elementary

MATHEMATICS LESSONS

TO EXPLORE, UNDERSTAND, AND RESPOND TO

Social Injustice

Courtney Koestler · Jennifer Ward · Maria del Rosario Zavala
Tonya Gau Bartell · and Colleagues

Brian R. Lawler, *Series Editor*

Foreword by Julia M. Aguirre

A JOINT PUBLICATION

For information:

Corwin
A SAGE Company
2455 Teller Road
Thousand Oaks, California 91320
(800) 233–9936
www.corwin.com

SAGE Publications Ltd.
1 Oliver's Yard
55 City Road
London, EC1Y 1SP
United Kingdom

SAGE Publications India Pvt. Ltd.
B 1/I 1 Mohan Cooperative Industrial Area
Mathura Road, New Delhi 110 044
India

SAGE Publications Asia-Pacific Pte. Ltd.
18 Cross Street #10–10/11/12
China Square Central
Singapore 048423

President: Mike Soules
Associate Vice President and Editorial Director: Monica Eckman
Publisher: Erin Null
Content Development Editor: Jessica Vidal
Editorial Assistant: Nyle De Leon
Production Editor: Tori Mirsadjadi
Copy Editor: Christina West
Typesetter: Integra
Proofreader: Barbara Coster
Indexer: Integra
Cover Designer: Scott Van Atta
Marketing Manager: Margaret O'Connor

This book is printed on acid-free paper.

22 23 24 25 26 10 9 8 7 6 5 4 3 2 1

CONTENTS

Part III: Next Steps 229

Chapter 6: Advice From the Field 230

Chapter 7: Creating Social Justice Lessons for Your Own Classroom 236

Visit the companion website at
resources.corwin.com/TMSJ-EarlyElementary
for downloadable resources.

FOREWORD

Welcome to a new generation of social justice mathematics advocates.

I am very excited and humbled to be writing the Foreword to this series of books about teaching mathematics for social justice. Over the past 30 years, there have been very few teaching resources available in one place that support teachers to embrace children as mathematical problem posers, sensemakers, and community change agents. The volumes in this series provide teachers with pedagogical and curricular tools to create mathematical learning environments that invite curiosity, social consciousness and critique, and mathematical analysis and innovation—multiple paths that lead to challenging societal inequities and making mathematics a more humanizing and just experience.

Why have such resources taken so long? This is an excellent and complex question. In my over 25 years of experience as a mathematics educator and scholar with an explicit equity ethic (McGee, 2020), the mathematics education community has been slow to embrace an equity- and justice-centered approach to mathematics education. There has been a tremendous amount of emphasis on reform mathematics, mathematical thinking, and mathematical discourse. Yet that same approach has reinforced beliefs and structures about mathematics being universal and culture free. It was about making dominant mathematics—which emphasizes cisgendered male-centric and euro-centric values—accessible to more people, while failing to acknowledge that mathematics has been created and communicated by cultures and communities across the globe since time immemorial. Efforts to introduce mathematical investigations that center on community, family, and ancestral knowledge and uses of mathematics into schools—especially activities that mathematized fairness, representation, and power relationships—brought consistent criticism from mathematicians and mathematics educators, who asked, "Where's the math?" Ironically, it is the powerful mathematics inherent within these investigations that brought to light injustice, inequity, and a demand for change to make things right. Mathematics has always been created by us, with us, and for us. It is time that we embrace this idea fully.

The link between social justice and mathematics has strong roots in liberatory education as practiced by Brazilian educator and philosopher Paolo Freire, and connected to mathematics by American mathematics education scholars Marilyn Frankenstein, Arthur Powell, Eric Gutstein, Rochelle Gutiérrez, and Danny Martin. However, for me, another crucial link made between mathematics and social justice was the work of civil rights leader Bob Moses and the work of the Algebra Project. Bob Moses passed away in the summer of 2021 at the age of 86. He was the first mathematics educator to help me see mathematics as a civil rights issue. In his book *Radical Equations* (Moses & Cobb, 2001), he argued that "full citizenship" in the 21st century—including economic and political access as well as informed decision making and civic engagement—in our society is inextricably linked to mathematics literacy. We must remove the systemic barriers, beliefs, and structures that deny children the right to have a high-quality, nonviolent, and meaningful mathematics education. The guidance and resources found in this series support teachers to do just that.

I would be remiss if I did not acknowledge that this series was developed during the twin pandemics: COVID-19 and systemic racism. COVID only exacerbated systemic racism inherent in the education, economic, political, health care, and legal systems of the United States. Disproportionate deaths due to COVID in communities of Color; the deaths of Breonna Taylor and George Floyd, among countless other Black and Brown people at the hands of the state; the rise of hate crimes, domestic violence, and sexual assault; increased gun violence and homelessness; the opioid crisis; the separation of families at the border; the rise of suicide among young people and veterans; anti-Asian and anti-immigrant hate; and missing and murdered Indigenous women are some examples of the pain and violence we have endured. Our planet is on fire, and many of us lack access to clean water, air, and earth. We must change and we must look to the next generation of young people to lead this effort.

This series continues the work of social justice mathematics advocacy by providing classroom-based mathematics lessons that build children's empathy and analysis skills to connect mathematics to their own lives, their communities, and the complex world around them. Relationships among people, animals, and the planet are mathematized in various ways. The investigations are grounded in social justice and mathematics standards so educators can be confident that the work meets multiple teaching goals. But what I am really excited about is the amplifying of youth voice and activism through these mathematics activities. Bob Moses said,

> We don't listen to kids enough. Really listen. It is a difficult thing for grown-ups to do—listen and actually pay attention to what young people are saying. In the Algebra Project we are still learning how to do this also. It is the voices of young people I hear every day, more than anything, that gives me hope. (Moses & Cobb, 2001, p. 191)

We must listen and learn from the voices of young people. Children can grapple with hard topics because they understand ideas of fairness, sharing, love, and friendship. They are curious about the world and they reflect the world. They are complex human beings. They are our future. They are our hope. Welcome to the new generation of social justice mathematics advocates.

—Julia M. Aguirre, PhD
December 3, 2021

ACKNOWLEDGMENTS

The author team—Courtney, Jen, Maria, and Tonya—would like to first sincerely thank the lesson authors for their contributions to this book. We know that these past few months and years have made teaching (and life) especially complicated, and your willingness to develop, implement, and revise these lessons has made this book what it is. Your work is so important to the lives of the children in your classrooms and to the teachers in the early childhood and early elementary fields. Second, we would also like to thank the educators who field tested and reviewed all of the lessons in the book. We appreciate your time and expertise, which helped us refine the lessons. In addition, we wish to thank the reviewers who reviewed the manuscript for the entire book, helping us articulate key ideas and concepts important in early childhood mathematics and justice-oriented teaching.

While writing this book, we appreciated the thoughtful discussion and encouragement given from the author teams of the other books in the series. We especially want to thank the authors of the high school book—Robert Q. Berry III, Basil M. Conway IV, Brian R. Lawler, and John W. Staley—as their work greatly guided our process. We also wish to thank the authors of the upper elementary book—Tonya Bartell, Cathery Yeh, Mathew D. Felton-Koestler, and Robert Q. Berry III—as well as the authors of the middle school book—Basil M. Conway IV, Lateefah Id-Deen, Mary Candace Raygoza, Amanda Ruiz, John W. Staley, and Eva Thanheiser. Also, Series Editor Brian R. Lawler's guidance was invaluable. We appreciate your continued support throughout the entire process.

Thank you to Corwin and NCTM for making these books possible. Thank you to Erin Null and Jess Vidal at Corwin for all of your insightful and thoughtful feedback from start to finish. We appreciate you being able to guide us, using the high school book as a model, but making a book especially written for an early childhood and elementary audience. As you know, this kind of work is so important and necessary. Nyle DeLeon and Tori Mirsadjadi were also very helpful in getting our book together and out the door. And a special shout-out to Christina West, who made our writing even better!

And thank you to the artists, Cardon Smith and Wendy Minor Viny, who created *A Building Stands in Cardonia*, the cover art for the book. Cardon and Wendy are artists at Passion Works Studio (http://passionworks.org), an artists collaborative in Athens, Ohio. Directed by Patty Mitchell, Passion Works Studio invites makers, who may experience varying degrees of developmental differences, to work and thrive within partnerships celebrating the power of creativity, connection, and purpose.

Courtney's Special Acknowledgments

I give a very sincere thank you to Jen, Maria, and Tonya. The process of writing this book has been a very powerful one for me. You are all such smart and strong scholars in our field, and it has been an honor to be on your team and I appreciate you all so much. Thank you to Dawn Mooney for your assistance and experience with the preparation of the book. Thank you to my family (especially Parker) and my friends (TTT), who have heard me talk about this book so much. Your love and support is so appreciated. And finally, thank you to my former colleagues and the children and families at Bailey's Elementary School for the Arts and Sciences and Mt. Vernon Woods in the Fairfax County Public School District (2000–2005). It was in these communities that I was challenged and supported to think differently—professionally, politically, and personally.

Jennifer's Special Acknowledgments

To Courtney, Maria, and Tonya, I am honored to have been able to work and learn with you all throughout the writing of this book. Your work impacted my role as a teacher and teacher educator, and this was an experience I could have never imagined. Thank you to my family (Kevin, Chloe, and Rylee) and friends (especially my fellow soccer moms) for your support, listening to ideas, and encouragement to keep thinking and writing. Finally, thank you to the children and teachers I have been able to work with through the years. You have made me a better educator and I am forever thankful.

Maria's Special Acknowledgments

To Courtney, our fearless leader and due-date minder, I have learned so much from collaborating with you! To Jen, our resident expert, who quite honestly could have written this book without us because she is just that amazing and knowledgeable about young children and their mathematical and social justice brilliance. And to Tonya, who I have had the pleasure of working with before and whose clarity of thinking is always appreciated; I feel blessed to work with you three on this book, a dedicated, strong group of parents who believe in the brilliance and social consciousness of young children. I also dedicate the work here to Alejandro and Lucas—they informally field tested ideas in this book with me. And to my partner, Adam, for always standing firmly in my corner, especially when it comes to my radical ideas of teaching mathematics (xo—MZ). I want to also thank Olivia Udovic and the kindergartners who opened up their classroom to me, where the lesson I included in here was developed.

Tonya's Special Acknowledgments

To the mathematics teachers, educators, colleagues, and friends in my career—and especially to Courtney, Jen, and Maria—I have learned so much from you and am a better person and educator for it.

To my PK buddy Calum—this book is for your future teachers and your future. And to my family and friends, your love, support, and encouragement is so very much appreciated.

PUBLISHER'S ACKNOWLEDGMENTS

Corwin gratefully acknowledges the contributions of the following reviewers:

Angela Chan Turrou
Senior Researcher
University of California, Los Angeles, CA

Crystal Kalinec-Craig
Associate Professor
University of Texas, San Antonio, TX

Anita Wager
Professor and Associate Dean
Peabody College, Vanderbilt University, Nashville, TN

Isauro M. Escamilla
Early Childhood Educator
San Francisco Unified School District, San Francisco, CA
Lecturer in Elementary Education Department
San Francisco State University, San Francisco, CA

ABOUT THE AUTHORS

Courtney Koestler is currently the director of the OHIO Center for Equity in Mathematics and Science (OCEMS) and an associate professor of instruction in the Patton College of Education at Ohio University. Courtney earned a BS in elementary education with a concentration in mathematics at Ohio University, an MA in teaching at George Mason University, and a PhD in curriculum and instruction at the University of Wisconsin. Courtney began teaching in public elementary and middle schools as a classroom teacher in 1998, went on to serve as a K–5 mathematics coach, and then started working as a university-based teacher educator and researcher.

In addition to now teaching diversity and mathematics methods courses in an early childhood-elementary education program and graduate action research courses, Courtney spends time in classrooms alongside teacher colleagues teaching children and out in communities working with families. These experiences continue to guide Courtney in understanding teaching and learning as an equity- and justice-oriented endeavor.

Jennifer Ward is currently an assistant professor of elementary and early childhood mathematics education and the elementary undergraduate program coordinator at Kennesaw State University. Jennifer earned a BS in elementary and special education and an MA in Early Childhood Education from the State University of New York at Geneseo. During her PhD work in curriculum and instruction (with a dual focus in early childhood and mathematics education) at the University of South Florida, she became interested in social justice mathematics for young children. Her work centered around her experience as an early childhood teacher designing and teaching mathematics for social justice lessons with children ages 3–8. Jennifer has been a teacher in classrooms from prekindergarten to high school, with the majority of her work in kindergarten and first-grade classrooms.

As an instructor of PreK–2 methods, university supervisor, and mother of two young girls, Jennifer sees the ways issues of social justice and mathematics are taken up (or fail to be) in school spaces. These experiences help Jennifer to conceptualize ways that early childhood (mathematics) teachers can bring authentic, real-world issues and mathematics into classrooms where children can unpack them and use their voice and power to call for change.

Maria del Rosario Zavala is an American-born daughter of Peruvian immigrants, a mother, and an associate professor of elementary education at San Francisco State University. She studied mathematics at the University of California, Santa Cruz, and almost (!) became a high school mathematics teacher, before working in elementary education. Across her more than 20-year career in education, she has worked in classrooms across the K–12 spectrum and supported teachers' professional learning in a variety of contexts. During her PhD work in education with a focus on learning sciences at the University of Washington, she became interested in ethnomathematics and social justice mathematics, and in particular how topics like these can make mathematics classrooms welcoming spaces for Latinx students and other historically marginalized populations. In addition to work on the role of racial and other socially constructed identities in learning mathematics, a large part of her research agenda includes defining, expanding, and evolving ideas of culturally responsive mathematics teaching (CRMT)—in particular the impact of CRMT on both teachers and students. Maria believes mathematics teaching and learning are creative endeavors. She has unequivocal faith in teachers and the power of teachers, parents, and community members working together to make schools places worthy of our children.

Tonya Bartell is currently an associate professor of mathematics education in the College of Education at Michigan State University and serves as the associate director of elementary programs. Tonya earned a BS in mathematics from St. Cloud State University, an MA in curriculum and instruction from the University of Minnesota, and a PhD in curriculum and instruction at the University of Wisconsin-Madison. Tonya began teaching 25 years ago as a high school mathematics teacher, including 3 years as a founding teacher in an alternative high school to support students labeled as not succeeding by the system. For the last 15 years, she has volunteered in elementary mathematics classrooms and studies elementary mathematics education.

Tonya is passionate about learning about and supporting teachers in developing equitable mathematics instructional practices that recognize and transgress systemic inequity. She understands that issues of culture, race, ethnicity, identity, and power influence students' opportunities to learn and teachers' opportunities to teach mathematics and that these factors must be explicitly discussed and addressed if we hope to fully support equitable mathematics teaching and learning. Tonya is honored to have participated in the writing of this book and in continued efforts supporting mathematics education that explores, understands, and responds to social injustice and supports students' learning of mathematics.

INTRODUCTION

One of the things we love about early childhood and elementary spaces is the natural curiosity young children bring with them, including connections they build between school and their lives outside of school, the wonderings about their world they bring into conversation, and their sense and inclination for problem solving and exploration. Teachers bring their lives into the classrooms as well; their beliefs, values, and ways of learning and knowing are all reflected in curriculum, instructional design, implementation, and assessment of children. Teachers' desire to build on this knowledge and expertise in lessons can be stifled based on calls to use prepackaged materials, rigid timeframes for teaching (both during the day and throughout the year), and limited time to plan and collaborate around integrated lessons or units. Yet teachers push forward, mindful of what they know to be best for the groups of the young children in their care.

We know that when teachers can draw from the lives and interests of children, families, and communities, meaningful teaching and learning happens. This kind of work is rooted in contexts that are familiar, personal, and connected to the things that children in the classroom are experts in. This is an idea we share with teachers we collaborate with, preservice teachers we mentor, and policy makers we aim to inform. This work is hard; it takes time, persistence, and creativity. But it is also worthwhile and can mean the difference for children and grownups developing a passion for mathematics.

Our hope is that as you are reading and engaging with this book, you think of your own beliefs about teaching, the children in your classroom, and their ways of interacting with the world. We believe that you will experience several benefits:

- Acknowledge all children in your classroom as capable mathematics learners and social justice advocates, seeing their experiences and wonderings as opportunities to contribute their voice and agency with their communities.

- Recognize the ways in which you are already on this journey of teaching mathematics for social justice in your classroom and in your professional development, and identify ways to enhance what you are already doing.

- Know that you are not alone in this work and that there are other early childhood educators who exist to partner with, to share ideas with, or to lend support.

WHY IS TEACHING MATHEMATICS FOR SOCIAL JUSTICE CRITICAL?

As noted by Koestler (2012),

> *No content area, including mathematics, is neutral, and therefore teaching [mathematics] is not neutral. The topics teachers include (or do not include), the activities they ask students to do, and the forms of participation they demand, all send messages to students about what is important, valid, and valued in mathematics and in school. This lack of neutrality is true both with respect to what teachers value within mathematics—they can either emphasize memorization or they can emphasize learning with understanding through guided investigation—and with respect to the ways in which they present the role of mathematics in the world—they can emphasize oft-used contexts in elementary school such as apples, puppy dogs, and ice cream, or they can include problems that use mathematics to understand and analyze pressing issues such as environmental problems or democratic participation. (p. 84)*

Early childhood mathematics classrooms are ripe as a space for teaching mathematics for social justice because young children are interested in exploring topics related to fairness, equity, and justice.

Early childhood mathematics classrooms are ripe as a space for teaching mathematics for social justice because young children are interested in exploring topics related to fairness, equity, and justice. Using mathematics to do this supports children in using problem solving and problem posing skills in ways that help them understand their world, including social justice issues they encounter, and position them as active participants and agents in making their classrooms, schools, and communities more equitable and just places.

For decades, professional organizations like the National Council of Teachers of Mathematics (NCTM) have called for mathematics education to engage children in problem solving that involves real-life applications (e.g., see NCTM, 1989, 2000). More recently, there have been calls for teachers to support children in using mathematics as a tool in critical ways (e.g., Association of Mathematics Teacher Educators [AMTE], 2020; NCTM, 2020; NSCM & TODOS, 2016). Too often children get the message that mathematics is disconnected from their lives and are tasked with solving "fakey" problem after problem. Social justice mathematics is specifically connected to real-world cultural, social, and political issues that are related to learners' home, school, and community lives and to our broader society. We define teaching mathematics for social justice as engaging learners in using mathematics as a tool to understand life, power, and societal issues (Gonzalez, 2009).

In the early years, we envision teaching mathematics for social justice as children exploring characteristics of their lives, including their families, schools, and communities, and the ways in which mathematics can be used to engage with equity issues such as power, participation, and access. During the later years, teaching mathematics for social justice can help foster informed citizens who are empowered to identify and solve real-world problems. Children can see how mathematics can connect to their cultures and communities, both historically and in the present day. They can also begin to make sense of how mathematics can be used as a tool for social change in extensions that reach beyond the classroom setting. Besides being connected to our lives, we see other important aspects of this work. We argue that teaching mathematics for social justice is critical for four reasons:

1. It builds mathematical literacy.

2. It supports children to learn to use mathematics as a tool for social change.

3. It empowers children as agents of change.

4. It rehumanizes mathematics education.

THIS BOOK'S AUTHORSHIP

As former teachers, now teacher educators, part of our hearts will always be in the classroom. This identity permeates our work and our attempt to cultivate resources, curriculum, and stories that resonate with classroom teachers. Our role as mathematics teacher educators often takes us into schools and classrooms where we see children and teachers learning from one another and experiencing the joy and beauty that comes from mathematics. At other moments, we are in university classrooms, working with future teachers to think about the mathematics experiences they had as young learners. We also ask the future teachers with whom we work to consider how they might work to plan for and implement lessons to connect mathematics and social justice, recognizing for many of them this idea is new. We first offer them opportunities to engage in experiences that use mathematics to make sense of and critique injustices in our world.

We see the importance of having hard conversations with young children and encouraging them to "mathematize" their world. We want young children to continuously engage with mathematics that connects to the ways in which they, and their families, use mathematics outside of the school setting. We want them to see mathematics as a tool to make sense of the events and happenings close to them, using mathematics as a tool to critique their world and advocate for change when needed. We view children as an asset to our society, capable of great things. They push us to consider new ideas and to see the world from a different perspective. Their voices are powerful and deserve to be heard in spaces where adults are making decisions.

Lesson Authors

Our lesson author team is composed of early childhood teachers, early childhood teacher educators, mathematics teacher educators, undergraduate and graduate students, and children themselves. They live in various kinds of communities across the United States and have written lessons that support understandings of different kinds of topics and connect to different mathematics domains. Within each lesson, you will find out more about the lesson authors.

WHO IS THIS BOOK FOR?

This book welcomes those who are new to teaching mathematics for social justice and those who have been engaged in this work for some time. We envision early childhood educators (PreK–2), classroom support personnel, mathematics coaches, center directors, school and district leaders, and mathematics teacher educators to use this book as an entry point into thinking about teaching mathematics for social justice, as a wealth of ideas to modify for their classroom context, as inspiration for lesson design, and as confirmation that they are not alone in doing this critical work in the early years. Those outside of the PreK–2 grade band may find the lessons and guiding principles as important in their thinking about what precursory experiences children may come to their classrooms with, or as eye-opening highlights of the capabilities that young children bring with them to the classroom setting. Administrators may find reflection and lessons learned powerful as ways to provide conceptualizing support for teachers who are on this journey and needing a supportive community (whether on their teaching team, or when facing stakeholder pushback).

THE BOOK'S ORGANIZATION

This book is organized into three parts. Part I (Chapters 1–4) will lay the groundwork for teaching mathematics for social justice and what that means in early childhood and early elementary settings. In Chapter 1, we share our ideas of what we mean when we talk about teaching mathematics for social justice in early childhood settings, including ways in which these ideas are taken up in connection with the Social Justice Standards from Learning for Justice (formerly known as Teaching Tolerance). Chapter 2 illuminates ways to foster a classroom community that emphasizes social justice, for those who are new to this work to those who are looking to enhance the practices and pedagogies they are already using. Chapter 3 aims to provide insight into instructional approaches that you may already be using in your context and how they are connected to teaching mathematics for social justice. Chapter 4 transitions into thinking about how to design lessons that center both mathematics and social justice goals, before concluding with some reflection questions to prepare you for lesson planning and implementation.

Part II (Chapter 5) will feature lessons from our lesson authors. We wanted to create a book that could center the uniqueness of the early childhood–early elementary setting and the complexities that accompany being mathematics and social justice educators in an early childhood context. Because of this, there will be some lessons that span shorter amounts of time and others will take multiple days. Some lessons make connections to rich units of study or inquiries that center the children's own experiences. Lesson authors were encouraged to think about making connections to multiple subject areas and modalities of representing learning, a feature of early childhood classroom settings we dearly love. We invite you to look beyond those lessons that make connections to the grade level you are teaching and think about ways in which you might make modifications to the mathematics content for your grade level. We are confident every lesson we have included can be adapted up and down the PreK to Grade 2 spectrum, foregrounding a variety of appropriate mathematical ideas.

Part III (Chapters 6 and 7) concludes our book. Chapter 6 highlights some of the reflections and lessons learned from both our book and lesson author teams. We close with continued opportunities for reflection, growth, and development of your own lessons.

If you are like us, you might not read this book straight through from cover to cover. It might make sense to read the introductory chapters (Chapters 1–4), but then skip around Chapter 5 for lessons and topics that speak to you and may be most relevant to the children in your classroom. While we provide these lessons as templates to use in your classroom, as with any curricular resource, we assume that you will have to think through them and make minor (and maybe major) changes to meet the needs, interests, and backgrounds of the children in your classroom.

We hope that the resources in this book will help you create and focus energy on authentic experiences for children while also generating mathematical analysis or modeling to explore and take action upon issues of injustice to children's lives. We commend you for bringing your children's curiosities and concerns about their lives into your mathematics classroom. We hope that the lessons in this book help you to foster child-to-child interactions that move beyond the mathematics to be learned and into actionable change in children's lives and society.

PART
I

TEACHING MATHEMATICS FOR SOCIAL JUSTICE

WHAT IS SOCIAL JUSTICE AND WHY DOES IT MATTER IN TEACHING MATHEMATICS?

CHAPTER
1

For the past week, children in my classroom have been exploring data from the cartoons they watch at home to determine the prevalence of characters that represent attributes of their identities. Conversation around the characters and recent events had entered morning meetings, plotlines set the stage for play during indoor and outdoor recess, and children's writing set the characters in scenes with new problems to solve. The context of cartoons serves as a window for the children to continue thinking about issues of social (in)justice in their world. Wanting to capitalize on the interest of the children in mathematics as well, I began to visit the websites of the networks they were watching to learn more about the shows. Upon a quick analysis, I discovered that many of the characters being watched did not look like the children who were in my classroom every day. They did not have the same backgrounds, interests, and family dynamics as the children in my classroom. I longed for my children to be able to see characters they identified with on television, just as they did in the books they had access to in our classroom. Did they recognize this as an issue? How could we work to advocate for more diverse characters?

The buzz in the classroom slows as the first graders gather in our large group meeting area. One by one, each group shares their findings in the form of tally charts, snap cube towers, and graphs to show characters from their selected network. Children take time during the presentations to jot down notes from what was shared to refer to later. As the sharing culminates, the graphs from all the groups are displayed on the wall of the classroom. Children are invited to look across them and record what they notice and wonder. At first, there is conversation as children move among the graphs and review them. Slowly, a silence falls over the class. Eyes lock on the graphs, on their mathematics notebooks where they are recording ideas, and on the faces they see around them in the classroom. The silence lingers as the children are processing the information gathered and shared by their classmates, the information that is mathematically presented in front of them.

Across the sets of graphs, the children are beginning to notice what I saw during my initial exploration of the networks and cartoons they were watching—limited Black and Brown[1] characters, limited female characters, and male characters who exhibited stereotypical norms such as loving sports and being "bad in school." Eyes glance from one graph to the next, over and over again. After moments of silent analysis, one child speaks.

"Ms. Ward, where is the character like me?" inquires Genny, a girl whose family is from (and some still residing in) Puerto Rico. Others chime in—the boy who takes ballet and prefers to dance and sign on to a shared internet server with his friends rather than throw a football, the girl who lives with her step-brothers and step-sisters, and the boy whose dad is deployed in the military.

We talk over the children's noticings and how the graphs allow them to notice the lack of characters they could relate to. After the children have processed this information and the data presented, the conversation shifts to beginning to consider what could they do to get more characters like them for other children to see. We brainstorm ideas together and decide that we will present our findings for others, just as we had shared in class. We could share this information with the other classes at our school, our administration, and our families. A few children suggest using the school's Instagram and Twitter accounts (as we had for an earlier project), which the children decide is a good way to reach the networks and share our findings with them. The children then get busy. They create invites to come hear our presentation, practice filming each other with tablets and cameras to share on social media, and finalize their thinking about the data by turning their drafted graphs into beautiful works of art. They write scripts to present their findings. And by the time the presentation to the other first-grade classes comes, the children have become experts in graphing and sharing this knowledge.

This vignette comes from Jennifer Ward's first-grade classroom where children engaged in a study of the cartoon characters on the television networks they were viewing. As the vignette illustrates, children's lived experiences and interests can and should provide a context to engage in understanding, analyzing, and critiquing issues of social injustice. In this chapter, we begin by providing guiding principles of our work that underlie the concepts, lessons, and philosophies contained in this book. Then, we explore perspectives on teaching mathematics for social justice.

WHAT DO WE MEAN BY SOCIAL JUSTICE?

As you read in the Introduction, we define teaching mathematics for social justice as teaching that builds mathematical literacy, supports children to use mathematics as a tool for social change, empowers children as agents of change, and rehumanizes mathematics education. We draw this definition from an understanding

---

[1] Through this book and the lessons included, we have intentionally capitalized terms used for people of Color, such as Black and Brown, while leaving white written in lowercase. We follow Frances Harper (2019) in her rationale: "I chose to capitalize Color but not white to challenge the ways that these standard grammar conventions reinforce systems of privilege and oppression" (p. 268).

of social justice, which attends to key ideas of access, participation, empowerment, and human rights.

- **Access:** Ensuring access to and the fair distribution of human and material resources in society.

- **Participation:** Creating equitable opportunities for people to access information to be fully participatory in decisions that affect their and others' lives.

- **Empowerment:** Supporting people's sense of agency in taking advantage of opportunities society affords as well as working toward eliminating all forms of oppression.

- **Human Rights:** Acknowledging the rights inherent to each and every human being, regardless of race, sex, gender, nationality, ethnicity, language, religion, or any other status. Human rights include the right to life and liberty, freedom from slavery and torture, freedom of opinion and expression, the right to work and education, and many more (United Nations, 2006).

The Center for Economic and Social Justice (n.d.) situates social justice as a virtue that guides people as they institutionalize organized human interactions. Social justice instills within each person a responsibility to collaborate with others for the common good and to perfect institutions as tools for personal and social development. And while the United Nations (2006) has defined social justice as "the fair and compassionate distribution of the fruits of economic growth" (p. 7), social justice must also attend to the distribution of social and political rights. Feagin (2001) offered such a definition for social justice:

> As I see it, social justice requires resource equity, fairness, and respect for diversity, as well as the eradication of existing forms of social oppression. Social justice entails a redistribution of resources from those who have unjustly gained them to those who justly deserve them, and it also means creating and ensuring the processes of truly democratic participation in decision-making.... It seems clear that only a decisive redistribution of resources and decision-making power can ensure social justice and authentic democracy. (p. 5)

These definitions of social justice require us to think about how people connect to one another, how resources get distributed, and the meaning of fairness. For us, social justice emphasizes the relations between the individual and society, and the idea that they are to be fair and just, meaning that society has a responsibility to ensure equal rights, equal opportunity, and equal treatment for each and every individual. Living up to this responsibility means acting upon or responding to instances of injustice. This idea resonates with the joint position paper by the NCSM and TODOS: Mathematics for ALL (2016) as well as the position paper of the Benjamin Banneker Association (2017), both of which argue that embracing social justice moves us beyond noticing issues and concerns about societal inequities and requires actions that confront oppression and/or marginalization. This idea of taking action to confront oppression and/or marginalization may

Social justice emphasizes the fair and just relations between the individual and society, meaning that society has a responsibility to ensure equal rights, equal opportunities, and equal treatment for each and every individual.

feel like a big ask for young children to engage in, but we would contend that young children who are involved in taking action, even in small ways, can grow to become big agents of change in their local and global communities. We offer the following beliefs to frame our thinking about young children as social justice change agents.

Children are competent mathematical beings who come to early childhood centers and elementary schools already having mathematical knowledge that teachers can and should connect to and build on.

When children enter our preschool and early elementary classrooms, they already have been experiencing the world for years. They have engaged in a lot of mathematical experiences both formally and informally, from getting more food at a meal (joining/addition) to sharing their blocks at playtime (separating/subtraction). Many children have also heard the counting sequence when counting with their families or when watching children's media. It is important to notice and understand the different kinds of mathematical knowledge children bring so we can draw on and use them as resources in classrooms.

Children are capable of doing the intellectual work of problem solving.

We know from decades of research that children learn best when given the opportunity to make sense of early mathematics for themselves without first being told how, and they are capable of developing their own strategies to do so. We believe it is a teacher's role to support and facilitate their learning, not do the work for them. Teachers should provide multiple opportunities for participation in mathematical activities, so that children have independent thinking time, time to work in small groups with their peers, and space to hear from larger groups of children in order to hear diverse ways of thinking.

Children care about fairness, equity, and justice.

Some adults think that children may not be ready to discuss ideas related to injustice. However, we know that very young children come to school already thinking about fairness, equity, and justice (Derman-Sparks et al., 2020). They need opportunities and space to make sense of and work through these ideas with their peers and with adults. By allowing children to explore these topics in mathematics class, teachers send the message that they can "understand and critique the world through mathematics," a key recommendation by the National Council of Teachers of Mathematics (2020, p. 9).

Teaching is non-neutral.

Teaching is political. Teaching is non-neutral and can never be neutral. In fact, teaching is a political act. As teachers we make decisions based on our own backgrounds, which impact our teaching and children's school (and arguably life) experiences. We are pushed to follow policies, guidelines, and testing regimes that are infused with bias and used to label or categorize children. These are often used to determine who has access to additional educational opportunities, specifically in mathematics, but in other areas as well. We acknowledge the power and status teachers have and will always hold in classroom spaces, despite the real and perceived constraints they may feel given their relative power and status in society. Teachers must be aware that they send implicit and explicit messages to children about what counts as mathematics, what counts as doing mathematics, what counts as "good students," and a myriad of other ways children are positioned in relation to mathematics. For example, if we only engage kids in counting activities where the focus is on rote memorization and recall, children get a very narrow view into what counts as school mathematics. If, on the other hand, we engage children in real problem solving that relates to children's interests, that sends a different message about mathematics and doing mathematics. When we incorporate real-world issues that are important to children (like the one illustrated in the opening vignette and the lessons that follow in Chapter 5), that sends quite a different kind of message to children about what mathematics is. Given this, mathematics teaching can never be neutral, just as the mathematics we include or don't include in our classrooms, in textbooks, and in standards is not neutral.

Identity matters.

As teachers, it is important for us to understand the multiple identities children bring with them into classrooms that shape the way they experience school and their lives outside of school. It is also important to acknowledge that certain groups of children have been historically, and are currently, marginalized in our schools. Certain systems (e.g., ability grouping) will continue to foster inequitable and unequal circumstances for certain groups of children.

We also know that young children are already making sense of skin color, ideas of race and racism, gender and gender identity, and other aspects of what makes all of us similar and different. As children grapple with their multiple identities, it is up to early childhood educators to make spaces for them to make sense of themselves and the world. It is because of this idea that we assert attention to these big categories of identity as an essential aspect of teaching young children, including teaching children mathematics.

> As children grapple with their multiple identities, it is up to early childhood educators to make spaces for them to make sense of themselves and the world.

PAUSE AND REFLECT

What are some guiding principles that underpin your teaching philosophy?

WHAT IS TEACHING MATHEMATICS FOR SOCIAL JUSTICE?

In the education field, there are multiple—and sometimes contentious—conceptions of teaching mathematics for social justice. Those who choose to engage in this work do so from different perspectives that are informed by their own constellation of identities and experiences. Perhaps your definition will evolve through your engagement with this book.

This book connects the goals of teaching mathematics for social justice in early childhood settings with larger efforts focused on equity, such as the National Association for the Education of Young Children position statement:

> *Early childhood educators, however, have a unique opportunity and obligation to advance equity. With the support of the early education system as a whole, they can create early learning environments that equitably distribute learning opportunities by helping all children experience responsive interactions that nurture their full range of social, emotional, cognitive, physical, and linguistic abilities; that reflect and model fundamental principles of fairness and justice; and that help them accomplish the goals of anti-bias education. (NAEYC, 2019, p. 5)*

Nurturing children's "full range of ... abilities" can and should include mathematics. In some cases, mathematical explorations, such as counting and comparing, can lead to discussions of fairness and justice. In other cases, there may be hidden mathematical concepts that can be drawn out of discussions around fairness, justice, and bias.

We also want to consider how, for us, the term *social justice* involves a particular way of thinking about the world that is not always emphasized when talking about "equity." Paolo Friere's work in critical pedagogy has guided many educators who teach mathematics for social justice. Two key aspects of Freire's work that have been taken up in mathematics education are the idea of (1) *reading the world* and (2) *writing the world* with mathematics (e.g., see Gutstein, 2006). *Reading the world with mathematics* means using mathematics to critically understand our world and the way it works, from issues of power, resource distribution, systems of privilege, and oppression. When teaching mathematics for social justice, you can engage children to use mathematics as a tool to explore, understand, and analyze issues in their lives and broader society. *Writing the world with mathematics*, then, is a way to use this knowledge and take action and feel agency, individual or collective, over the world in which we live. Our goals for this book are to offer you community and ideas around facilitating this reading and writing of the world with the children in your classrooms. For our youngest learners, beginning to understand their world is a crucial component to feel a sense of belonging and connectedness with those around them. It helps them to build their own self-identity. When they write the world, that is where the magic happens. They see themselves as agents of change against injustice, able to share their voice and ideas with the world.

As Gustein (2006) notes in his book on teaching mathematics for social justice, critical consciousness is not just from theorists such as Paolo Freire. Black communities in the United States have long traditions of education for liberation. Murrell (1997) wrote that "the essence of a liberatory education project is the cultivation of a consciousness, and the development of children's identities, as well as academic proficiencies" (p. 28) (quoted in Gutstein, 2006, p. 23). Thus, when children are reading and writing their worlds *with mathematics*, they are developing new understandings of their own identities as well as gaining proficiency with mathematics.

Adopting a critical perspective on mathematics, and thus teaching mathematics for social justice, holds that mathematics itself is not a neutral subject but rather is steeped in bias and subjectivity. It is utilized as a tool for advancing social and political agendas, such that many educators are calling for the teaching of quantitative literacy for children, so that they can understand the ways in which mathematics and numbers are often used to advance perspectives of those in power. We've stated it before but it bears repeating: Mathematics is not neutral. Tate (2013) wrote:

> *Until recently, embedding mathematics pedagogy within social and political contexts was not a serious consideration in mathematics education. The act of counting was viewed as a neutral exercise, unconnected to politics or society. Yet when do we ever count just for the sake of counting? Only in school do we count without a social purpose of some kind. Outside of school, mathematics is used to advance or block a particular agenda. (p. 48)*

The understanding of the non-neutrality of mathematics itself is part of what it means to engage in mathematics for social justice.

As mathematics teachers, we must also include attention to culturally responsive and culturally relevant teaching (e.g., see Gay, 2000; Ladson-Billings, 1995). Common elements of this work include valuing and drawing on children's cultural backgrounds and identities, supporting children to succeed in formal and informal ways, and engaging children in taking up critical perspectives on social and political issues. For example, Aguirre and Zavala (2013) assert that mathematics lessons that are culturally responsive take into account how teachers are asked to make sense of and take action on an issue impacting the children in their classrooms. Their culturally responsive mathematics teaching tool provides a guidepost for lessons with strong connections to applications of critical knowledge and social justice in mathematics as having "deliberate and continuous use of mathematics as an analytical tool to understand an issue/context, formulate mathematically-based arguments to address the issues and provide substantive pathways to change/transform the issue" (Aguirre & Zavala, 2013, p. 187).

The interdisciplinary nature of mathematics in early childhood and early elementary education also means that you can look outside of mathematics for guidance around the approaches and pedagogies that constitute powerful lessons. For example, critical literacy has been at the heart of essentially all work on teaching mathematics for social justice, even if implicitly. In a critical literacy approach,

> *the world is seen as a socially constructed text that can be read. As such no text is ever neutral. What this means is that all texts are created from a particular perspective with the intention of conveying particular messages.*

> In traditional mathematics lessons, children are frequently asked to answer questions—questions that are often devoid of meaningful context for the children. Conversely, in mathematics for social justice lessons, children are asking the questions: they are engaged in problem posing as well as problem solving.

Such texts work to position readers in certain ways. We therefore need to question the perspectives of others. The earlier students are introduced to this idea, the sooner they are able to understand what it means to be researchers of language [and mathematics] and explore ways texts can be revised, rewritten, or reconstructed to shift or reframe the message(s) conveyed. (Vasquez, 2016, pp. 3–4)

Fundamentally teaching mathematics for social justice starts from asset-based perspectives where children are at the center. In addition, teaching mathematics for social justice tends to follow inquiry approaches, again rooted in Freirean traditions of problem posing and problem solving. In traditional mathematics lessons, children are frequently asked to answer questions—questions that are often devoid of meaningful context for the children. Conversely, in mathematics for social justice lessons, children are asking the questions: they are engaged in problem posing as well as problem solving.

While early childhood mathematics lessons might be easily adapted to be truly from asset-based perspectives, we recognize that some teachers may be unsure of how to open their mathematics spaces to involve children in problem posing and problem solving, where children are the ones both asking and answering the mathematics for social justice questions. They may believe that children's questions may distract from the "real" work of school mathematics, or fear pushback from those who hold power over their work as an educator. We argue that in a classroom where the goal is liberation, the cultivation of children to become active agents of their learning, allowing children's curiosities to guide exploration with and into mathematics, *is* the real work. At the very least, we argue for giving it a try and allowing yourself professional grace to get better at pursuing children's ideas with and through mathematics. As Dingle and Yeh (2021) assert, mathematics exists everywhere in our lives. As educators "we need only to look to current and historical moments of strategic, mathematical insurgence against structures of oppression as blueprints for liberatory mathematics education."

PAUSE AND REFLECT

Ask yourself: How do my own conceptions of social justice align with and differ from ideas shared here?

SOCIAL JUSTICE STANDARDS

In this book and the other books in this series for upper elementary (Grades 3–5), middle school (Grades 6–8), and high school (Grades 9–12), we draw from the four domains of the *Social Justice Standards: The Teaching Tolerance Anti-Bias Framework* (Learning for Justice, 2016). (Teaching Tolerance, now called Learning for Justice, is a project of the Southern Poverty Law Center and can be found at https://www.learningforjustice.org/.) These standards represent a social justice approach to teaching and learning that aim to reduce prejudice and bring about collective action for positive change. The four domains are Identity, Diversity, Justice, and Action, as shown in Figure 1.1.

Figure 1.1. Anchor Standards and Domains

Anchor Standards and Domains

IDENTITY

1. Students will develop positive social identities based on their membership in multiple groups in society.
2. Students will develop language and historical and cultural knowledge that affirm and accurately describe their membership in multiple identity groups.
3. Students will recognize that people's multiple identities interact and create unique and complex individuals.
4. Students will express pride, confidence and healthy self-esteem without denying the value and dignity of other people.
5. Students will recognize traits of the dominant culture, their home culture and other cultures and understand how they negotiate their own identity in multiple spaces.

DIVERSITY

6. Students will express comfort with people who are both similar to and different from them and engage respectfully with all people.
7. Students will develop language and knowledge to accurately and respectfully describe how people (including themselves) are both similar to and different from each other and others in their identity groups.
8. Students will respectfully express curiosity about the history and lived experiences of others and will exchange ideas and beliefs in an open-minded way.
9. Students will respond to diversity by building empathy, respect, understanding and connection.
10. Students will examine diversity in social, cultural, political and historical contexts rather than in ways that are superficial or oversimplified.

JUSTICE

11. Students will recognize stereotypes and relate to people as individuals rather than representatives of groups.
12. Students will recognize unfairness on the individual level (e.g., biased speech) and injustice at the institutional or systemic level (e.g., discrimination).
13. Students will analyze the harmful impact of bias and injustice on the world, historically and today.
14. Students will recognize that power and privilege influence relationships on interpersonal, intergroup and institutional levels and consider how they have been affected by those dynamics.
15. Students will identify figures, groups, events and a variety of strategies and philosophies relevant to the history of social justice around the world.

ACTION

16. Students will express empathy when people are excluded or mistreated because of their identities and concern when they themselves experience bias.
17. Students will recognize their own responsibility to stand up to exclusion, prejudice and injustice.
18. Students will speak up with courage and respect when they or someone else has been hurt or wronged by bias.
19. Students will make principled decisions about when and how to take a stand against bias and injustice in their everyday lives and will do so despite negative peer or group pressure.
20. Students will plan and carry out collective action against bias and injustice in the world and will evaluate what strategies are most effective.

Source: Reprinted with permission of Learning for Justice, a project of the Southern Poverty Law Center learningforjustice.org

It should be noted that the Social Justice Standards are explicitly written for Grades K–12. Therefore, PreK teachers can inform themselves from these standards but may have to adapt them for their particular context (see Chapter 3). The lesson authors in this book use these standards to identify the social justice component that is developed in the lesson. Let's look at both the roles of teachers and children in each domain, drawing on the work of Dingle and Yeh (2021), Learning for Justice (2021), and Yeh (unpublished data).

Domain 1: Identity

In the Identity domain, teachers provide children opportunities to learn about who they are and where they are from. This set of Social Justice Standards seeks to reduce bias as children learn about their own identities, privileges, and responsibilities. The goal is for children to develop positive social identities and to understand that multiple identities intersect to create unique and complex individuals. Children's sense of self is integral to their learning of mathematics. Banks (2004) explains, however, that oftentimes the knowledge possessed by some communities is not perceived as valuable in the dominant perception of schooling and education. Yet many of these rich and collective ways of knowing and being have not yet been made visible in mathematics education. Teachers can engage children in the process of honoring children's identities in mathematics by drawing on genuine problems from children's everyday lives.

Figure 1.2. Identity Domain in the Context of Mathematics Teaching and Learning

IDENTITY
Teachers
• Recenter identities, perspectives, and knowledge traditions that have often been silenced.
• Attend to and honor children's multiple social identities in curricular design and its implementation.
• View children as competent mathematical beings in which their lived experiences and community and cultural ways of knowing are leveraged during mathematics instruction.
• Deconstruct negative stereotypes about children's mathematical identities and about who can and cannot do mathematics.
Children
• Recognize that people's multiple identities interact and create unique and complex individuals that contribute to their learning of mathematics.
• Develop language and historical and cultural knowledge to affirm and describe their membership in multiple identity groups and their contribution to mathematics.
• Express self-love, pride, confidence, and healthy self-esteem about themselves and their community as mathematical thinkers and learners.
• Recognize the traits of the dominant culture, their own culture, and other cultures and understand how to negotiate their own identity in multiple spaces.

Source: Adapted from Learning for Justice (2021).

 Available for download at **resources.corwin.com/TMSJ-EarlyElementary**

A sense of pride in their culture, heritage, race and ethnicity, religion, skin tone, and gender should be cultivated in the mathematics classroom. Children develop language and historical and cultural knowledge about different aspects of their identity and the identities of their peers and the history associated with it.

For example, in Lesson 5.8 (*Seeing the Colors of Ourselves and Others*) by Sam Prough and Eric Cordero-Siy, children analyze the books in their classroom as they grapple with the meaning of different skin tones and how they see themselves represented in the books, or not. Within this lesson, emphasis is placed on children collecting data on this representation and comparing the prevalence of characters like and unlike themselves. Groups of children work to collect data to obtain a class result around the number of characters in books with a variety of skin colors, then link back to the main character in the story *The Colors of Us* by Karen Katz to think about how she would feel with the data presented. This creates a conversation around empathy and awareness of the feelings of others. When children have the opportunity to learn more about their own history and others', they are better able to identify, deconstruct, and challenge harmful stereotypes about themselves and others.

Domain 2: Diversity

Often, simply engaging in the Identity domain activities moves curriculum into the Diversity domain. The goal of this domain is to create a climate of respect for diversity. To do so, teachers need to recognize that all children are unique and have distinct differences (e.g., differences in children's thinking, backgrounds, and cultures) that should be leveraged to strengthen learning for all and create a multidimensional classroom that values and leverages many different ways of being mathematically "smart" (Featherstone et al., 2011) as well as children's cultural and linguistic background.

Figure 1.3. Diversity Domain in the Context of Mathematics Teaching and Learning

DIVERSITY
Teachers
• Design curriculum and implementation that honor diversity in mathematical reasoning, sensemaking, and engagement as strengths for individual and collective learning.
• Create multidimensional classrooms, raising classmates' expectations for contributions from each and every child in their classroom.
• Deconstruct stereotypes about children's mathematical identities and who can and cannot do mathematics.
Children
• Express comfort in working with and learning from people who are both similar to and different from them and engage respectfully in collaborative work and discussion.
• Express curiosity about the mathematical contribution and experiences of others and exchange ideas and perspectives in an open-minded way.
• Respond to diversity by building respect, understanding, connections, and empathy for different ways of knowing and being in mathematics classrooms.

Source: Adapted from Learning for Justice (2021).

 Available for download at **resources.corwin.com/TMSJ-EarlyElementary**

For example, in Lesson 5.1 (*Exploring Fairness Through Data and Numbers*) by Melanie Hollis, Marni C. Peavy, Anna Hayashi, Jane "Sissy" Poovey, and Sandra M. Linder, children explore instruments, sound, preference, and difference. They gather data about the instruments they prefer and reason about the data displays, exploring connections between their preferences along the way. In this lesson, children are able to explore how their preferences are part of their identity. They then extend on this understanding to explore how others in the classroom have similar and different preferences connected to our varying identities. From here, children are tasked to think about the multiple ways our identities co-exist within the classroom and community.

Mathematics teaching and learning is complex and embedded in a broader societal context of inequities in which implicit and explicit biases are pervasive. Significant and longstanding disparities in resources, access to cognitively rich and relevant tasks, and mathematics learning outcomes continue to perpetuate race, class, language, and ability hierarchies (Artiles et al., 2006; Flores, 2007; NCTM, 2020). Respecting diversity in mathematics requires explicit attention to deconstructing stereotypes about children's mathematical identities and who can and cannot do mathematics. Ability grouping and tracking practices are pervasive in elementary school classrooms (Loveless, 2013; NEA, 2015). The research is unequivocal; differential learning opportunities widen the achievement gap between groups (NEA, 2015) with harmful consequences that impact how children see themselves in relationship to mathematics learning—including their identity, self-confidence, and motivation toward mathematics (Boaler, 2015). Teachers that attend to the Diversity domain minimize separated instruction by designing mathematics curriculum and instruction that account for and leverage children's differences through an inquiry-based approach that encourages children to approach problems in a variety of ways that make sense to them, bringing to each task the skills and ideas they own. Infusing options in how children engage with and make sense of the mathematics content allows each learner to gainfully interact, learn from, and contribute to the learning environment (CAST, 2018). Options can be incorporated into a mathematical activity by giving children choices in how they communicate their mathematical thinking through talking, writing, or drawing and in the availability of visuals, manipulatives, and relevant contexts to build meaning of the mathematical concept. These examples serve as a glimpse into a multidimensional mathematics classroom that promotes children to express comfort in working with and learning from peers who are both similar to and different from them and valuing difference as strength.

Domain 3: Justice

The Justice domain moves from celebrating diversity to an exploration of how diversity has been used as a marker for oppression that has differently impacted groups of people. Teachers that attend to the Justice domain locate causes of inequalities in social conditions (e.g., tracking, ability grouping, and Eurocentric curriculum) rather than believe conditions are inherent within individuals. Teachers attending to the Justice domain reflect on how inequities in the larger society are replicated in common structures and practices that perpetuate disparities in mathematics learning opportunities based on race, class, language, gender, and ability status. Children are provided with learning opportunities to recognize that power and privilege influence relationships on interpersonal, intergroup, and institutional levels and to consider how they have been affected by those dynamics in their learning experiences and in the world using mathematics as a tool to identify unfairness on the individual, interpersonal, and institutional or systemic level. By helping children to understand how oppression operates both individually and institutionally, they are better positioned not only to understand their own lived experiences but also to develop strategic solutions based on historical and systemic roots rather than romanticized or missionary notions of social change.

Figure 1.4. Justice Domain in the Context of Mathematics Teaching and Learning

JUSTICE
Teachers
• Locate causes of inequalities in social conditions (e.g., tracking, ability grouping, Eurocentric curriculum) rather than believe conditions are inherent within individuals.
• Recognize that inequities of the larger society are replicated in common structures and practices that perpetuate disparities in mathematics learning opportunities based on race, class, language, gender, and ability status.
• Explicitly shift the power dynamic between child-and-teacher and child-and-child by centering identities, perspectives, and knowledge traditions that have often been silenced.
Children
• Recognize stereotypes and pervasive myths in mathematics around what mathematics is and what it means to know and be good at mathematics.
• Recognize that power and privilege influence relationships on interpersonal, intergroup, and institutional levels and consider how they have been affected by those dynamics in their mathematics learning experiences and in the world.
• Use mathematics as a tool to identify unfairness on the individual, interpersonal, and institutional or systemic level.

Source: Adapted from Learning for Justice (2021).

 Available for download at **resources.corwin.com/TMSJ-EarlyElementary**

The Justice domain is also about liberation. For example, in Lesson 5.2 (*Addressing Food Insecurity*), Jennifer Ward and Children of the Maple Classroom take us through an examination of who has access to healthy food. Using probability, children participate in a simulation of who gets to eat and how much. Through the simulation, they notice inequities that are beyond their control, questioning stereotypes they may have encountered about food access in their world. Children analyze the outcomes, and they are supported to call attention to the disparities they notice through connections to writing and communication as they collectively compose a letter to both their families and local government representatives to share statistics about local food insecurity.

Domain 4: Action

It is one thing for children to learn about social movements in books and videos and to tell others about it; it's another to participate in reading and writing the world. In the Action domain, teachers provide opportunities to move beyond raising awareness to supporting children to take action on issues that affect them and their communities. Children identify issues they feel passionate about and learn the skills of creating change firsthand using mathematics as a tool to analyze and create change. Children can learn how to improve the material conditions of their lives by learning how to do research, analyze who has the power to change particular situations, write letters and speeches, use new media (e.g., blogs, infographics, documentaries, and public service announcements about their cause), and learn other skills with which to work for justice.

Figure 1.5. Action Domain in the Context of Mathematics Teaching and Learning

ACTION
Teachers
• Engage in community- and place-based pedagogies and experiences that bridge mathematics classrooms with community and social movements.
• Understand that learning can emerge from a problem-posing pedagogy, designed around the ideas, hopes, doubt, fears, joy, and questions that occur when children use mathematics to develop "generative themes" about their world.
• Provide children consistent opportunity to recognize their own responsibility to stand up to exclusion, prejudice, and injustice.
Children
• Understand the nature and creation of social oppression and feel empowered to intervene and seek equity.
• Make principled decisions about when and how to take a stand against bias and status differences within the mathematics classroom and in their communities.
• Plan and carry out collective action using mathematics as a tool to address injustice in the world.

Source: Adapted from Learning for Justice (2021).

 Available for download at **resources.corwin.com/TMSJ-EarlyElementary**

For example, in Lesson 5.12 (*Respecting Our House: Protecting Our Salmon Neighbors*), Julia Maria Aguirre and Melissa Adams Corral describe a multiday lesson that involves children thinking about how they might take action to protect the natural home of salmon in their community. As children try out and clarify their suggestions, they mathematize these ideas in terms of time needed to clean areas, quantity of litter able to be collected, and ability of items collected to be easily sorted to preserve recycling efforts. Children then share their ideas for local government organizations and community-based efforts to support the cleanup and protection of the salmon home.

PAUSE AND REFLECT

Which of these roles in the four domains do you engage in with the children in your classroom? Which of these roles would you like to work on in a targeted way to continually improve your practice?

CONCLUSION

In this chapter, we have presented multiple perspectives that contribute to teaching mathematics for social justice and shown how the Social Justice Standards can be used to frame and inform social justice mathematics teaching. We need to emphasize that our view is much more than the lessons teachers might implement in their classrooms. It includes the relationships they build with and among children, the teaching practices that help them do that, and the goals to develop positive social, cultural, and mathematics identities with the children in their classrooms. Next, in Chapter 2, we discuss the aspects of developing and fostering a productive classroom community for social justice. Then, in Chapter 3, we discuss particular pedagogical approaches and instructional tools that are relevant to the early childhood contexts.

REFLECTION AND ACTION

1. Think back about why you became a teacher. How has this changed over the course of your teaching? Does this path draw on any of the perspectives discussed in this chapter?

2. Visit a colleague and initiate a similar conversation about why they became a teacher. Does the conversation draw on any of these perspectives?

3. Create your own definition of social justice. How might you help children develop their own definition?

FOSTERING A CLASSROOM COMMUNITY FOR SOCIAL JUSTICE

Teaching mathematics for social justice (TMSJ) in your classroom involves more than teaching and facilitating a series of tasks, activities, and/or lessons at opportune times throughout the school year. TMSJ is not simply a matter of method, but a process requiring you to adapt to the particular context of which you and the children in your classroom are a part. When we as teachers facilitate the co-creation of a classroom culture, it can empower children—helping them see, recognize, and value how mathematics supports them in understanding, critiquing, and changing their world. It is important to maintain connections with children and their social contexts while also building on their mathematics and social issue knowledge to co-create new knowledge.

To further consider what is important in the implementation of social justice mathematics lessons (SJMLs), this chapter is organized into five sections: *Context Matters*, *Content Matters*, *Who Matters*, *When Matters*, and *How Matters*. Each section provides guidance for you as you develop a plan to develop and justify the use of SJMLs in your classroom and foster a classroom community for social justice.

- *Context Matters* provides guidance for connecting with children's experiences and reaching out to families and communities to navigate your current school or district setting as you consider SJMLs that might involve potentially controversial topics in some communities, might result in children's responses leading to advocacy or other action, or might raise some parents/caregivers' or community stakeholders' concerns or opposition.

- *Content Matters* outlines the importance of making sure SJMLs focus on essential mathematics content, are part of a coherent learning experience for children, and balance the focus on both mathematical and social justice goals.

- *Who Matters* provides guidance for navigating assumptions that TMSJ is only or primarily about helping traditionally marginalized children see themselves in the curriculum. TMSJ is about learning mathematics through understanding the systemic oppression that affects us all and thus everyone, from positions of privilege and oppression, working to dismantle oppressive structures.

- *When Matters* considers the experiences and readiness of young children to engage with these topics and provides recommendations for ways to integrate SJMLs with other content area learning goals and classroom routines.

- *How Matters* highlights the fact that the SJMLs provided in this book have inquiry-based, play-based approaches and support you in choosing pedagogical strategies that will engage each and every child in the lesson. Further, this section provides guidance for anticipating and responding to children's myriad reactions to each SJML.

We present these five ideas, connect them back to the Social Justice Standards (Learning for Justice, 2016), and encourage you to consider them as you begin to plan the implementation of SJMLs in your early childhood classroom.

CONTEXT MATTERS

As a preview to this section, Figure 2.1 lists some guiding questions for you to ask yourself or your team to begin to consider how context matters when designing and implementing lessons that address social justice issues.

Figure 2.1. Guiding Questions for Context Matters

Context Matters
When considering any SJML, ask:
• What issues are of importance to children, families, and community members?
• What do I know about this social inequity/injustice and what do I need to know that intersects with local concerns and interests?
• How might this topic be received in my local setting?
• What is my purpose for including this social justice topic as part of my instruction?
• Who is on my team of allies ready to support me? How will I communicate both the social justice and mathematics goals to parents/caregivers, administrators, and other stakeholders?
• How does the SJML contribute to building children's mathematical and/or social agency and identity? How might this SJML allow children to share and develop an understanding of inequity or a sense of empowerment and liberation?

 Available for download at **resources.corwin.com/TMSJ-EarlyElementary**

A key purpose of schooling is to help young people become informed and active contributors to our society as well as critically thinking members of our democracy. As such, topics of social and political relevance must be a part of the early childhood and early elementary curriculum. Topics that seek to help children gain an understanding of inequities in their school, community, or society and which teach children to advocate for change may draw attention to those who wish to avoid controversy or seek to maintain the status quo. Topics themselves are not inherently controversial; however, the local sociopolitical context as well as ill-planned dialogue can create controversy around a topic. So, when we name a topic as controversial, we really mean to indicate that it has the potential to create controversy or disrupt a space of comfort (for some) or the status quo.

As you consider the context of your setting and classroom, it is important to work to know and understand the climate and culture of your classroom, school, and communities in regard to the teaching of controversial topics, especially those that people might not see as traditionally fitting into early childhood mathematics curriculum. Who children are, what they know, what they and their families have experienced, and what they care about matter in the classroom (Steele & Cohn-Vargas, 2013). The Identity domain of the Social Justice Standards describes outcomes for early childhood that focus on children knowing and liking who they are (Identity 1), feeling good about themselves without being mean or making other people feel bad (Identity 4), and seeing that the way their families do things is both the same as and different from how other people do things, and both are interesting (Identity 5).

Children in early childhood classrooms already possess experiential knowledge on issues related to identity, fairness, culture, and justice. Parents, grandparents, aunts, uncles, friends, cousins, caregivers, neighbors, and community members share stories about their lived experiences and perspectives—both about mathematics and social issues—and children carry this knowledge inside of themselves. Thus, it is our contention that *together* with children, families, and communities, you as a teacher identify issues to help children gain new or further understanding of injustice in their school, community, or society.

The overall goal in carefully connecting to context is to help plan for and anticipate possible opposition that might come during or after the lesson (e.g., parent or caregiver complaints to administrators, children believing their feelings have been hurt). Thus, as you plan for SJMLs, you need to consider recommendations, such as those in Figure 2.2, when pursuing topics of interest to children, particularly those that may be controversial in your community.

Figure 2.2. Considerations for Pursuing Controversial Topics in Early Childhood Classrooms

Considerations for Pursuing Controversial Topics in Early Childhood Classrooms

1. Consider what you have done (thus far), and may need to still do, to create an open, inclusive, respectful learning environment with children.

2. Consider what you have done to incorporate family and community knowledge into the curriculum or classroom (e.g., guest speakers, video projects, dialogue, using community reviews* or surveys).

3. Check to see if your school or district has policies or procedures for teaching controversial topics (e.g., rights of children who are transgender, politics, religion).

4. Look at cross-curricular connections to connect social justice goals with learning goals in literacy, science, social studies, art, health, and so on.

5. Identify community stakeholders (e.g., parents/caregivers, community organizations) who work with related issues and consider inviting them to be resources during lesson planning or teaching.

6. Be mindful of social injustices that are hot-button issues in your school, district, or community.

7. Determine if the social injustice is one that requires discussion with your administrator before teaching.

---

* In an effort to use more inclusive language, we use the term *community review* for what is commonly referred to as a "community walk."

To further think through your context and setting, also consider the purpose, audience, your allies, and the timing for the SJML you have selected.

Purpose

What is your reason for introducing social injustice during mathematics time? You need to consider any personal biases you have regarding the topic and any personal agendas.

Here's an example. If I identify as a white woman, I must approach topics related to race and racism thoughtfully and reflectively, realizing that my perspectives have been strongly influenced by the social context of my experiences (e.g., the invisibility of white privilege for white people), including the community in which I live and how I am responded to in public. It may require me to engage in my own learning both about myself (e.g., identifying and unpacking my personal bias and privilege) and the social injustice (e.g., What information do I need to know to make a principled decision about when and how to take a stand against this injustice? [Action 19] What are the different perspectives on this issue?). I must recognize that my actions—both intentional and unintentional—impact children's experiencing of the classroom community as well as shape the perspectives and beliefs of each and every child. I can ask myself, how does this SJML allow children to share and develop understanding of inequity or a sense of personal or mathematical empowerment?

You may also have to answer questions about why you chose this topic to include in your classroom routine or mathematics lesson. Thus, having a clear purpose that you can articulate will be helpful if you need to respond to questions and concerns.

PAUSE AND REFLECT

We all have biases; we are influenced by our feelings, opinions, and backgrounds. We have biases because we are human. Explore your own biases by engaging in the following questions (adapted from Nickel City Housing Coop, n.d.):

- Who are my three closest friends? What similarities do we share (race, class, religion, gender, etc.)?

- What is an environment I find myself most comfortable in? Who else is there?

- When did I last get uncomfortable or feel like I didn't fit in because I was a minority in some way?

- How am I reflecting on and addressing my own bias and positionality to create an anti-bias mathematics classroom?

Audience

Think about the children in your classroom and those with whom they will interact in other classes, extracurricular activities, and outside of school. Controversial topics have a way of reaching others, sometimes like rumors or bad press and other times as respectful curiosity about the world in which we live. With the children in your class, co-construct classroom norms so that all are comfortable expressing their individual perspectives on issues without fear of personal attack from their peers (see Figure 2.3). These norms should support all children in "respectfully expressing curiosity about the lived [social and mathematical] experiences of others" and to "exchange [mathematical and other ideas] and beliefs in an open-minded way" (Diversity 8). The art of teaching issues related to inequities and injustice involves co-establishing an identity-safe classroom where children believe their social identities are assets and diversity is a resource (Steel & Cohn-Vargas, 2013) as well as where acknowledgment and respect are a part of the culture. It is important to remind children of the importance of seeking to understand so they can "express comfort with people who are both similar to and different from them and respectfully engage with all people" (Diversity 6) and "respond to diversity by building empathy, respect, understanding, and connection" (Diversity 9) (Learning for Justice, 2016).

Figure 2.3. Possible Classroom Norms for SJMLs

Possible Classroom Norms for SJMLs
1. We listen deeply and carefully to what others say.
2. We know that other people may know things we do not.
3. We use our own experiences to share our ideas about the topic (*I* statements).
4. Although we do not necessarily always agree, we can understand more by learning together.
5. We can provide support (e.g., head nods, smiles) when someone is struggling to speak.
6. We can step out and back in if we need time and space to process. We can allow others the opportunity to step out and back in if they need to.
7. We disagree with ideas, not people.

Allies

Children, parents/caregivers, community members, colleagues, and administrators are all people whom you should consider when seeking allies in the planning process. Remember that children have knowledge and experiences, and many of them know a great deal about the social context you are considering for the lesson. Children may even know more about the school and community context, and they can play a key part in planning ideas for lessons. Also, consider parents/caregivers and community members who may work in a field related to or have experience with the social injustice at the center of the lesson to come in and observe your classroom and provide feedback. Similarly, consider providing your administrators and/or colleagues a brief overview of your lesson plan and invite them to your class to see it in action and provide feedback. You may also be less open for criticism when you have collaborated with others.

Timing

As the saying goes, "timing is everything," so consider when the SJML will be taught. For example, it is important to open up space to discuss and process events as they happen (Dunn, 2021). Think of the events of January 6, 2021, when the U.S. Capitol building was invaded, and teachers everywhere that night asked themselves, *So what will I do in class tomorrow?* We advocate for this kind of reflective questioning. And also, choosing to discuss a topic/issue immediately after a related incident in your school, district, or community (e.g., police brutality) is different than planning a lesson on how to utilize mathematics to examine the issue, which may not be best to do when events and trauma are fresh. For example, it may not be best to engage in a lesson on violence against people of Color shortly after a child has been attacked in your school or community. Waiting and allowing children to process what has happened might have more merit. On the other hand, children remember the silence, and not discussing a current event may communicate a lack of importance and/or avoidance of an issue children are already thinking about and affected by (Dunn, 2021). As the other saying goes, "There's no time like the present." Using a current event may very well be a powerful way for children to process the issues and for you to center the children and humanize them in the classroom. This decision relies strongly on consultation with your allies and the children in your classroom as well as on your personal expertise.

Ultimately, questions about timing lean heavily on the feel you have for the emotional state of your children and possibly on input from others closer to the experience than you may be. You have to make your best informed decision, and consider how the timing maximizes children's understanding and sense of agency.

CONTENT MATTERS

As a preview to this section, Figure 2.4 lists some questions for you to ask yourself or your team to begin to consider how content matters when designing and implementing lessons that address social justice issues.

Figure 2.4. Guiding Questions for Content Matters

Content Matters
When considering any SJML, ask: • How will the lesson contribute to the learning goals for the children in my class? • How does this lesson contribute to developing children's deep understanding of mathematics? How does the lesson empower children mathematically? • How does the lesson connect to an issue that is relevant to children? • How does the lesson promote anti-bias education by addressing prejudice reduction and/or collective action? Which domain of the Learning for Justice Social Justice Standards are addressed? Which standard? • How does the SJML allow children to use mathematics as a sociopolitical tool of analysis?

 Available for download at **resources.corwin.com/TMSJ-EarlyElementary**

We recognize that a lesson's content plays a major role in helping children make sense of both mathematics and their world by using mathematics in an authentic and empowering way. When selecting (or designing) a SJML, you should make sure that the lesson's content contributes to helping you achieve

1. The overarching goals you have established for the class (e.g., developing children who think critically as doers of mathematics and exchange curiosity about the mathematical contributions of others);

2. Mathematics goals related to required or recommended grade-level content standards; and

3. Deeper understanding of issues relevant to children's lived experiences *and* how children might advocate for change.

When you think about how the content of each lesson contributes to the mathematics story for the children in your classroom, the careful selection (or design) of lessons and associated tasks is critical. Lessons should be inquiry-, play-, or project-based, supporting children in making mathematical connections and deepening their understanding of mathematics.

> **Planning a SJML requires you to not only be thoughtful about the design and use of mathematics but also to think deeply about the context of social injustice.**

Planning a SJML requires you to not only be thoughtful about the design and use of mathematics but also to think deeply about the context of social injustice. There is often a tension when designing or implementing SJMLs between the mathematical goal and the social justice goal, where one may be foregrounded to the detriment of the other. You may feel nervous that you aren't an expert in certain topics—or may not feel expert enough. Part of your preparation should be learning all you can, both about the mathematics and the social issue. For the mathematics topic, engage in the mathematics yourself, consider how children might approach the problem solving, and ask yourself how the task or mathematical activity supports diversity in mathematical reasoning. Here are some questions for you to consider: What mathematics will children need to understand and examine this issue? What data or mathematics will they need to support particular conclusions, and why? For the social issue, learn all you can, not just from media and alternative media outlets but also from people closely involved who can provide the most insight. With respect to the integration of mathematics and social justice in your SJML, remember that for both mathematics and the social topic, one lesson is not sufficient for full understanding. Consider your SJML goals in relation to how you hope to adequately contextualize the social issue and develop mathematical understanding over time (Bartell, 2013). In any case, however, you will certainly not know everything there is to know or you may stumble on sensitive issues or an unexpected mathematical connection that a child makes. At that point, you can position children as competent mathematical human beings and collaborators (or allies) in the content and the social topic.

Having examined both the mathematics content and the social injustice, implementing a SJML implies that at the forefront of planning, you

- View children as competent mathematical beings in which their lived experiences and community and cultural ways of knowing are leveraged during mathematics instruction;

- Design lessons that help children see that they are knowers and doers of mathematics and which deconstruct negative stereotypes about who can and cannot do mathematics;

- Provide opportunities for children to use the mathematics they know and further grow their mathematical skills;

- Seek out opportunities to infuse topics that are relevant to children's background, culture, and lived experiences; and

- Guide children as they use mathematics as a tool to identify unfairness on the individual, interpersonal, and institutional or systemic levels.

When preparing the content of a SJML, you must also consider the age appropriateness of both the mathematics and the social justice content. In addition to organizations like NAEYC and NCTM, your state and local standards can likely serve as a guide to the appropriateness of the mathematics content. With respect to the social injustice, research documents that children ages 3–5 years have racial awareness (Goodman, 1952) and may begin to exclude their peers of different races from play and other activities (Winkler, 2009). Connections to ideas of fairness in elementary grades can support anti-bias curriculum in the classroom (Mistry et al., 2017). Young children rely on teachers (or other trusted adults) to help them make sense of the confusing messages the world sends them about race, fairness, diversity, and justice. For example, the racial stereotypes of how Asian and white people are supposed to be good at mathematics, and by association then Black, Latinx, and Native American people are not, starts early, with some research suggesting that children are aware of such academic stereotypes by second grade (Cvencek et al., 2011). They notice differences and need to feel safe and supported in asking questions about what they notice. Our recommendation is that you speak with trusted friends, children's families, community member allies, and possibly experts on the age appropriateness of the social content.

At any age, some information or discussions may be traumatizing due to children's personal experiences with the injustice. If this happens, be prepared to respond in humanizing and empowering ways; an important first step is to validate feelings and experiences. For some of you reading this book, your shared experience with children around a particular issue may be a wealth of support to them. For others, you may need to prepare more carefully for how you will be in potentially uncomfortable moments. Be sure to follow up with a school counselor or specialist to ensure children have an opportunity to find support.

WHO MATTERS

Figure 2.5 lists some questions for you to ask yourself or your team to begin to consider who you are designing and implementing SJMLs for and with.

Figure 2.5. Guiding Questions for Who Matters

Who Matters
When considering any SJML, ask:
• How are the children in my classroom similar to and different from one another across identity groups (e.g., race, class, gender, religion)?
• How does this lesson engage children in respectfully exploring the historical, lived, and mathematical experiences of themselves and others so as to exchange beliefs, ideas, and perspectives in an open-minded and respectful way?
• How does this lesson support each and every child in expressing pride, confidence, healthy self-esteem, and positive mathematical identity without denying the value and dignity of other people?

online resources ▶ Available for download at **resources.corwin.com/TMSJ-EarlyElementary**

TMSJ is about *all* children learning mathematics through understanding and working to dismantle systemic oppression and injustice.

Who children are, in a myriad of ways, should inform your SJMLs. Many people believe TMSJ is only or primarily about helping traditionally marginalized children see themselves in the curriculum, but this is not the case. TMSJ is about *all* children learning mathematics through understanding and working to dismantle systemic oppression and injustice. It is important, for example, for privileged (i.e., affluent) children to learn about injustice and social justice reform (e.g., Swalwell, 2013) as many, though they express concern about inequities, initially connect the problem to individual shortcomings rather than systemic disadvantages. Whether intentional or not, you likely hold stereotypes or biases about some of the children in your classroom and the knowledge that they bring to the classroom. Children, too, likely hold stereotypes or biases about other children.

The Social Justice Standards in the Justice domain can inform your selection and implementation of SJMLs. Think of who children are, and in your classroom engage in conversations that support children to

- Know their friends have many identities but they are always still just themselves (Justice 11)

- Know when people are treated unfairly (Justice 12)

- Know some true stories about how people have been treated badly because of their group identities (Justice 13)

- Know that life is easier for some people and harder for others and the reasons for that are not always fair (Justice 14)

- Know about people who helped stop unfairness and worked to make life better for many people (Justice 15)

It is critical that you understand who children are by working to understand each and every child as a whole child, including the world that the children are a part of outside of school. Knowing children well and deeply can keep you from succumbing to the reputations and biases some children carry that are assigned from other children, families, and colleagues.

Understanding each and every child as a whole child includes recognizing that some children have experienced trauma. Trauma can be defined as the reaction to a shocking or painful event or series of negative events. With TMSJ, it is important to engage without retraumatizing children. You can take some specific steps to mitigate the effects of trauma for children in your classroom.

Know Your Own Story

Teacher educator Yolanda Sealy-Ruiz describes how teachers should "dig deep and peel back layers of yourself and think about how issues of race, class, gender, religion, and sexual identity live within" (Dillard, 2019). Identify and confront your own biases—about yourself, children, colleagues, communities, and the world. What is beneath these layers that you peel back will affect your relationships with children. Worse, if these issues go unexamined, they may cause harm.

Learn From and For Children

It is important to learn both from and for children. Learn from children: What are children's needs? What are their struggles? Also, learn for children: Read literature to further your understanding of issues children face. Connect yourself with others who are doing this work to learn together. Increase your knowledge about trauma and how it may manifest for the children in your classroom.

Establish Social and Emotional Safety

Children who have and are experiencing trauma in their lives (or in their schools, including their classroom) have their sense of safety compromised. You can support children by working to establish a socially and emotionally safe classroom environment where you teach and model empathy, intervene in hurtful exchanges or prejudice and injustice, and establish connectedness with anti-biased and community-building curriculum and classroom routines.

When preparing the content of a SJML, explicitly consider what you do and do not know about the children in your classroom and how the SJML may, unintentionally, retraumatize some of them. Don't let the fear of harm stop you from engaging with important topics; rather, work together with others and engage in the steps described earlier to mitigate the effects of trauma for children in your classroom.

WHEN MATTERS

Figure 2.6 lists some questions for you to ask yourself or your team to begin to consider when to implement SJMLs.

Figure 2.6. Guiding Questions for When Matters

When Matters
When considering any SJML, ask:
• How does this SJML build on previous lessons or future lessons, both with respect to mathematics and social justice goals?
• How does the SJML integrate learning across content areas (e.g., art, social studies, science, literacy)?
• What might children already know about the mathematics and social justice topic of this SJML?

 Available for download at **resources.corwin.com/TMSJ-EarlyElementary**

> **Social justice mathematics cannot wait until children are "older." As we have argued, young children are both capable of and interested in engaging with issues of social justice and engaging in advocacy.**

Social justice mathematics cannot wait until children are "older." As we have argued in Chapter 1, young children are both capable of and interested in engaging with issues of social justice and engaging in advocacy. One of the goals of this book series is to lay a pathway from early childhood through high school to help children develop their mathematical agency in the world, to be critical creators of the mathematics needed to read the world, and to be empowered to take action. Our hope is that as children grow up in a world where, from a young age, they are encouraged to think interdisciplinarily, to connect issues of fairness to empathy and understanding, and to advocate for themselves and others, they will be strong advocates for justice—well-versed in the role mathematics plays in social action. We say this as the authors of this book and as parents who see social justice mathematics as part of a complete academic experience for our children.

Young children also bring mathematical knowledge to the classroom that can aid in making sense of big issues, while they also learn more mathematics. In our experiences, we hear from teachers that younger children may be interested in the topics, but they don't have enough mathematics skills in their toolbelt to engage in multistep mathematics problems on real-world topics. But the truth of the matter is they do, when the lesson is planned around mathematical sensemaking that leverages their prior knowledge and their vast wealth of community and cultural knowledge bases (e.g., their lived experiences.).

It is important to take up issues of social justice within mathematics instructional time. This helps to strengthen the experiences children have with mathematics and social justice as an integrated area, as opposed to separating it out in some attempt to keep mathematics "neutral." It's very possible that not every mathematics lesson in your classroom will have a strong social justice component; however, across a school year, many lessons can and should.

To aid teachers in this process, we advocate for blurring the boundaries between types of content lessons. Many of the lessons in this book explicitly incorporate literacy, science, art, and core mathematics content in the service of exploring and acting on a social justice issue. In addition to being good lessons to try, teachers can reflect on how lessons are structured to be interdisciplinary as a way to improve one's own lesson design skills.

HOW MATTERS

As a preview to this section, Figure 2.7 lists some questions for you to ask yourself or your team to begin to consider how you might implement lessons that address social justice issues.

Figure 2.7. Guiding Questions for How Matters

How Matters
When considering any SJML, ask: • What pedagogical strategies will I use to engage each and every child in the lesson with both the mathematics and social justice topic? • How am I reflecting on and addressing my own biases and positionality to create an anti-bias mathematics classroom? • What questions will I use to facilitate children's learning of both mathematics and the social injustice? • How might the children in my class react to this lesson, and how will I prepare for that? • How will we (children and I) assess the degree to which our mathematics and social justice goals have been met? • How will children communicate their learning of both social justice and mathematics to stakeholders? • What action will we take to make an impact on the social topic being investigated?

 Available for download at **resources.corwin.com/TMSJ-EarlyElementary**

The SJMLs provided in this book have inquiry-based, play-based, and project-based approaches and employ several different instructional models. We encourage you to thoroughly review each lesson, its instructional model, and the lesson goals (mathematics and social justice) to determine the appropriateness for use in your classroom, make adjustments and revisions as needed in order to localize the lesson so that it is relevant to children in your classroom, and plan for the appropriate level of guidance and support.

Figure 2.8. Social Justice Mathematics Lesson Planner

Social Justice Mathematics Lesson Planner

PART I

CONTEXT	
Purpose	
Audience	
Allies	
Timing	

CONTENT	
Mathematics Goal(s)	**Mathematical Content Domain**
Social Justice Topic and Brief Description	
Social Justice Outcome	

WHO	
Resources for Your Learning	Classroom Practices and Norms to Establish Social and Emotional Safety
How Your Lesson Supports Children in Recognizing Injustice at Both Individual and Institutional or Systemic Levels	

WHEN
Possible Interdisciplinary Connections

HOW
Instructional Model (e.g., Classroom Routine, Mathematics Task, Three-Act Task)

PART II

Launch	
What will the teacher do?	What will the children do?

Exploration	
What will the teacher do?	What will the children do?

Summarize	
What will the teacher do?	What will the children do?

Taking Action

Stakeholder Communication

How is the teacher communicating lesson goals?	How are the children communicating their learning?

You can draw on your professional knowledge to pull together the mathematical goals and the social justice goals to create a meaningful lesson for the children in front of you. As you do so, you should think about your class as a whole as well as the individual learners in your class and how they may take up certain elements of the lesson. As mentioned previously, you should also consider your own biases and positionality when preparing and planning the lesson.

As with any solid mathematics lesson that is child centered, you will want to plan and be ready for inquiry-based questions that you will use to support and extend children's learning of the mathematics and social justice goals of the lesson. Open-ended questions and prompts are a key feature of the lessons in this book, and they are important when engaging children's ideas at the center of any lesson. This also communicates to children that their ideas are valuable and valid and guide the lesson.

Next, we present a SJML Planner (Figure 2.8; also Appendix F) that the series team developed, attending to *Context, Content, Who, When,* and *How,* to help you organize information in your initial preparation for a lesson. Please note that the SJMLs in this book do not provide information on each of these sections, nor are they structured in this form. Some of the decisions that you need to make when planning are specific to your local and personal contexts. While this template can help with the planning that is needed when introducing issues of social injustice during mathematics time, additional questions are also provided in Figures 2.1, 2.4, 2.5, 2.6, and 2.7 to help you think through the elements of the SJML Planner. We close this chapter by providing guidance for anticipating and responding to myriad reactions of children and adults to each SJML.

RESPONDING TO WONDERINGS

As SJMLs are launched in early childhood classrooms, children may generate more wonderings as they begin to grapple with both their own interpretation of social issues as well as ways in which the narratives they may have heard outside of schools are different from those they are examining. Children may openly share their own wonderings and reactions to the issues being examined with mathematics, along with those expressed by parents/caregivers in their lives. As wonderings are brought up in the classroom setting (or beyond), think positively—the children trusted you enough to bring them up. They see this conversation as valuable; your classroom is a safe space to ask questions and seek answers. Follow up on these wonderings of children by asking for more information and finding resources for them to explore answers, including partnering with communities and families.

RESPONDING TO PUSHBACK

Planning for a SJML requires you to think about more than the mathematics goals; you also need to consider the social justice goals and thus the social injustices that might be addressed in the lesson. This chapter was designed to support you in the planning process. You must also consider the possibility that there may be pushback from both children and adults. Here are some recommendations for responding to this.

- *Seek to understand others' perspectives.* Ask questions to gain an understanding of any raised issues or concerns (e.g., Why do you say that? What would you like me to know more about?). Make a mental note of any power dynamics or biases that might be at play (e.g., Who is coming to you about the concern? Is it an administrator? A parent? An outsider not connected to your classroom community?).

- *Avoid responding from an emotional stance.* Monitor the emotional levels and try to take a break in the conversation when dealing with heightened emotions.

- *Share the rationale for integrating social justice topics into mathematics instructional time.* Use the guiding questions (Figures 2.1, 2.4, 2.5, 2.6, and 2.7) and the Social Justice Mathematics Lesson Planner (Figure 2.8) to prepare for the lesson and anticipate outcomes or reactions. Having a written plan to reference can show the thinking that went into the lesson planning. Connecting to standards is also very important to justify this work; we suggest you use professional organizations (such as NAEYC and NCTM), your state and local standards, and organizations such as Learning for Justice (http://www.learningforjustice.org).

- *Avoid sending lengthy responses through email.* People have very little control over the perceived tone of an email and how parts of a message will be interpreted or used. A timely response is needed, and keep it brief. For example, "Thank you for your email. When is a good time for me to call to discuss your concerns?"

- *Pick battles carefully.* Recognizing areas of compromise and noncompromise in the conversation is important. Refrain from getting caught up in small nuisances and details. Remember that the goal is to continue to use SJMLs during mathematics time, so retreat to teach another day when the opportunity presents itself.

CONCLUSION

For many teachers, the implementation of SJMLs in the early childhood and early elementary grades context is new. Much of what is required, however, is already in your repertoire. You have already implemented many aspects of TMSJ, such as organizing your curriculum around content standards and teaching in inquiry-based and child-centered ways. You use many strategies to engage children in meaningful discourse centered on mathematical ideas. You draw upon children's social, cultural, and academic resources in your instruction. For many of us, the aim to develop a critical consciousness in children is something we value and are ready to dive into. The SJMLs in this book can be an excellent starting point.

In this chapter, we asked you to consider five elements in preparation: *Context, Content, Who, When,* and *How.* Here are some questions to ask yourself: What social justice issues are of importance to children, families, and community members? Who is on my team of allies ready to support me? How will the lesson contribute to children's deep understanding of mathematics and/or empower children mathematically? What pedagogical strategies will I use to engage each and every child in the lesson, both the mathematics and social justice topics? Many of us feel expert in teaching, and sometimes expert in mathematics, but are quite wary of trying to teach about social injustice. Our experiences suggest that the best approach is to learn as much as possible, be open to learning more from and for children, and foster a classroom environment that both models empathy and views children as competent mathematical beings.

REFLECTION AND ACTION

Consider the following strategy for collaborating on the implementation of one of the lessons in this book or for developing your own. Working with a small team, organize your discussion using the following protocol:

1. Individually, on a note card or slip of paper, write down a topic of injustice that may be of interest to the children with whom you work. Create an additional note card for each topic. Spend several minutes identifying topics of interest for follow-up.

2. Place all the cards in a bag, then draw one card. Discuss this topic as a team.

3. Begin discussion by responding to the Context and Content questions from Figures 2.1 and 2.4.

4. Use all components of Part I from Figure 2.8, the Social Justice Mathematics Lesson Planner, to begin planning a lesson that might be used for this topic. (This begins to address the When and How questions in Figures 2.6 and 2.7.)

5. For your topic, identify any allies needed before teaching the topic. What information would each of these people want to know? What might be learned from them?

6. Pair up and role-play with a peer on how the topic/lesson idea can be shared with an administrator or colleague.

7. Finally, debrief with your team. What information do you need to move forward with your planning? Which section (*Context, Content, Who, When,* or *How*) was most difficult to complete?

INSTRUCTIONAL TOOLS FOR A SOCIAL JUSTICE MATHEMATICS LESSON

CHAPTER
3

As an early childhood educator, you likely have a robust toolkit of pedagogical approaches you draw from when designing and implementing classroom instruction. We intend to provide you with ideas that can enhance this toolkit, leveraging the tools you are already using to embark on your journey, new or continuing, when implementing social justice mathematics lessons (SJMLs). In this chapter, we provide you with a brief review of pedagogical approaches in early childhood and early elementary settings, attending to the tenets of each that can provide a pathway into SJMLs. Part of this pathway includes exploration of critical areas included in the other books in this series—goals, assessment, instruction, and discourse—while attending to the uniqueness of early childhood settings by considering how this area of study is taken up by our youngest learners in humanizing ways that honor their voice, agency, and identities.

PEDAGOGICAL APPROACHES IN EARLY CHILDHOOD SETTINGS

Work historically in early childhood settings has focused on *developmentally appropriate practice* (DAP), which is also often used as a means by which educators avoid conversations connected to social justice (Doucet & Adair, 2013). This approach is also often criticized as ignoring the sociocultural development of children, which relates to their membership in families, communities, and cultures. Because of these nuances, identifying what is "developmentally appropriate" cannot be reduced to a single idea (Ryan & Grieshaber, 2005), as this would not encompass the uniqueness of each child's experience as a member of their community. There have been changes and updates to DAP, most recently by the National Association for the Education of Young Children (NAEYC) in 2020. The current iteration of DAP has more emphasis on the social, cultural, and historical elements of child development. These revisions provide additional justification that the notion of DAP should not be used as an excuse to bar critical conversations with young learners.

Enter many early childhood classrooms and there will be a buzz about the room. Children will be engaged in conversation with each other, working with various mediums to create representations, immersed in dramatic play, and making sense of their world. How educators in early childhood settings describe their pedagogical approach to teaching often aligns with various types of experiential learning: a project approach, inquiry-based instruction, project or problem-based learning, or play-based learning.

Project Approach

Stemming from the interests of children, the project approach is a framework that emphasizes children's authentic construction of knowledge. The approach works in multiple modalities of representation, listening to and documenting children's voices as they interact with the curriculum (Katz & Chard, 2000). Occurring in three distinct phases, project work is crafted around a central question or wondering that emerges from authentic conversations with children.

- **Phase 1:** Children document their knowledge about the topic or question via webbing, where the teacher can gauge both background and interest level. Children share stories of experiences that connect to the project focus both to document their prior knowledge but also to position children as knowledgeable.

- **Phase 2:** Children begin to explore answers to the questions posed in Phase 1 through expert interviews, collection of artifacts, and field visits. These pieces require in-depth preparation on behalf of the children to develop questions and "look-fors."

- **Phase 3:** Children present what they learned during the project and prior phases. Presentations may vary in representation and modality with the aim to present the children's learning to others.

Inquiry-Based Instruction

The processes of questioning and collecting and making sense of information involve active, hands-on experiences.

Teachers using an inquiry-based approach in their classrooms acknowledge children's natural curiosity and design learning experiences, which provides an opportunity for children to uncover new knowledge through discovery. This approach allows children to have a sustained voice in their learning through identification of and work toward answering "need to know" questions about the world. By navigating the direction of their learning and how they will seek out information, children begin to determine more efficient ways in which they can learn information, taking an active role to collect and retain new knowledge (Nell et al., 2013). The processes of questioning and collecting and making sense of information involve active, hands-on experience aligning with constructivist approaches that value social interaction, discovery, and active engagement in learning.

Problem-Based Learning

Problem-based learning poses a problem to children, allowing them to explore, generate, and present possible solutions. Within this process, children spend time organizing their ideas, identifying causes of the problem, asking further questions, and researching responses (Svinicki & McKeachie, 2014). While often centered on a single subject, problem-based learning experiences tend to be shorter in duration, with solutions communicated via a presentation, written element, or constructed artifact.

Project-Based Learning

With the focus on a project at the end of learning, project-based learning rests on the three pillars of rigor, relevance, and relationships (Galindo & Lee, 2018). Learners support their recognition of the connection between the work they are about to embark on in the real world and mathematics. Within this type of learning environment, children work closely with one another to solve problems connected to real-world issues in their own lives and communities. Projects typically draw from multiple subject areas and often involve community elements in the form of expert speakers or professionals who provide insight into the topic being explored. At the culmination of the project, children are typically responsible for sharing a product of an artifact (project) they have developed in response to the topic posed. Emphasis in project-based learning is on developing 21st-century competencies.

Play-Based Learning

In play-based learning, children take the lead, which offers them a way to demonstrate their agency. It gives them the opportunity to explore complex topics, experiment with identity, and engage in thinking that helps them make sense of and interact with their surrounding world (Nell et al., 2013). Educators can use this pedagogy to bridge the gap between home and school, drawing upon the collective funds of knowledge children have.

During play, children make decisions around the elements of setting, actors, and plot. They are responsible for controlling the topics addressed and plotline. While adults may enter into this play, preservation of the children's voice and agency around both structure and content of play should be a priority. You can use this time to introduce diverse topics or connections to content through the inclusion of images, narratives, props, or other materials that can foster discussion, exploration, and inquiry. Parks (2015) reminds us that play has a purpose in the early childhood mathematics classroom, including problem solving, making connections to authentic mathematics content, and solving nonroutine problems as they occur.

MATHEMATICS CONNECTIONS

Of primary importance in each of these approaches to teaching and learning in the early grades is that the everyday events in the lives of children have meaning. We recognize that mathematics in many early childhood spaces likely takes place

While these approaches each promote opportunities for children to engage in exploration, discovery, and practical connection to content, they also open opportunities for teachers to begin to think about addressing social justice issues in the classroom.

in times beyond those identified as "mathematics" by sometimes rigid daily schedules. Routines in early childhood classrooms such as morning meetings, lining up, washing hands, and distribution of snacks offer opportunities for children to think about mathematics in ways that are relevant to their own lives. These routines also present opportunities in which teachers can capitalize on the authentic times that children are engaged in mathematical thinking, calling attention to the ways in which children are mathematizing their world. Furthermore, cultivating engaging experiences with mathematics at a young age supports the development of a positive mathematics identity.

Engagement in teaching mathematics for social justice shares many of the ideas central to these pedagogical approaches. You can look to expand work in this area by drawing from practices you are already using in the classroom. In each approach described, teachers work to leverage the voices and experiences of children in their classroom. Lessons presented in this text will cut across a range of these methods for teaching in early childhood contexts and highlight connections to the ways in which content (mathematics) and social justice can be infused into transitions and daily routines present in early childhood classrooms.

PAUSE AND REFLECT

Ask yourself:

- What pedagogical approaches am I currently using in my classroom?

- How might I work to center mathematics and social justice in these approaches?

- How will I communicate this to colleagues, administrators, and families?

PREPARING SJMLS

Preparing SJMLs may seem new, daunting, or exciting at first. It is important to remind ourselves that we are working to support the needs of children, their families, and their communities to help calm any nerves and silence critical voices (inside or outside our heads) that aim to perpetuate the narrative that teaching is (or should be) neutral. Hopefully, from reading Chapters 1 and 2 you can see that teaching is not, in fact, neutral but layered with decisions deeply rooted in our identities and politicized decisions often made within, outside of, and about schools. In this section, we provide insight into the preparation of lessons and the planning process. These revolve around ideas such as establishing goals, identifying and addressing mathematics content and practices, and attending to the social justice goals. While these ideas are centered in the chapter, as early childhood educators we recognize the need to tie in other subject standards as well as social emotional goals and motor development (NAEYC, 2002/2010).

Establishing Goals

What do I want children to know and be able to do?

As you are planning for instruction, one of the first steps is to ask, *What do I want children to know and be able to do?* The goals that are set for instruction will directly impact the approach, assessment, questions to facilitate discourse, and ways in which the children engage with the content. These goals should be lofty, but attainable. In many lessons, we do not provide children with goals that stretch them to reach new learning. We know that if we establish goals that reflect our high expectations and involve children in sensemaking, critical thinking, problem solving, and action, they will meet (or even surpass) these expectations. In the SJMLs in this book, teachers' goals were strategically designed for their unique groups of learners based on both the prior experiences of the children and possibly children's own input based on interest or area of need. You will see that when designing SJMLs, establishing mathematics goals is important, but of equal importance is the development of social justice goals that range from the development of awareness to taking an active role in addressing instances of injustice.

In Lesson 5.9 (*Human Diversity and Disability: Do We All Have 10 Fingers?*), lesson authors Jennifer R. Newton, Courtney Koestler, and Jan McGarry take a critical look at the concept of using 10 fingers, an anchor commonly used in many mathematics classrooms, and engage children in attending to and questioning the assumption that this model works for all learners. Within this lesson, children work on the mathematics goals of counting by tens and conceptualizing halving and doubling as they engage in skip counting and thinking about various scenarios involving groups of 10. At the same time, teachers are facilitating conversations around social justice goals centered on body diversity, disability, and ableism. Part of this conversation addresses the assumption that all people have 10 fingers (or toes) as teachers pose questions that introduce examples of people with less or more than 10 fingers and ask children to conceptualize other contexts for counting by tens that does not involve fingers.

Mathematics Content

What important mathematical ideas do I want children to understand and be able to use?

The decision around the content used to inform a SJML in early childhood will largely draw upon the early childhood mathematics standards provided by the early learning coalitions or state departments of education. These domains may vary, but most address key areas in early childhood mathematics thinking and learning. According to NAEYC (2002/2010), major domains in early childhood mathematics classrooms include number and operations, geometry, measurement and algebra, and data analysis. The Common Core State Standards of Mathematics (National Governors Association Center for Best Practices, Council of Chief State School Officers [NGACSB, CCSSO], 2010) use the domains of counting and cardinality, number and operations in base 10, operations and algebraic thinking, geometry, and measurement and data. A brief synopsis of each domain is provided in Figure 3.1 with points connected to children in PreK through Grade 2.

Figure 3.1. Mathematics Domains in Grades PreK–2

Content Domain	Children Need More Opportunities to . . .
Whole-number concepts and operations	• Read, write, count, create, and compare collections (up to 1,000) • Use symbols to compare • Subitize • Decompose and compose numbers • Understand place value units (up to hundred and thousand) • Use knowledge of place value to add and subtract
Fraction concepts and operations	• Partition shapes into equal parts • Use the terms *wholes, halves, thirds,* and *quarters*
Early algebraic concepts and reasoning	• Notice, replicate, and extend patterns • Represent and solve addition and subtraction problems using standard and invented algorithms
Data concepts and statistical thinking	• Sort objects; count, record, and compare groups • Construct simple graphs
Geometry and measurement concepts and spatial reasoning	• Match, name, and describe 2D and 3D shapes visually and by properties • Combine shapes • Create real-world models using shapes • Describe locations of objects with spatial terms • Recognize, label, compare, and sort by measurable attributes • Direct and indirect comparisons of measurement • Use standard and nonstandard units of measurement • Compare units of measurement • Estimate measurements • Tell time using digital and analog clocks

Source: NAEYC (2002/2010).

In Lesson 5.14 (*Journey for Justice: The Farmworkers' Movement*), Gloria Gallardo and Emy Chen examine disparities in pay, which contributed to the Delano Grape Strike. Children begin by creating a representation of Larry Itliong's life using Unifix cubes to represent the years on a timeline, equating one cube to 1 year. The color of the cubes can change in a pattern to support children in visually comparing the length of time and counting the number of years between key events. As children later model the pay of Filipinix and Latinx farmworkers with coins and dollars, they compose the amounts earned in various ways depending on the coins that they select.

Mathematical Practices

How do I want children to engage in mathematical activity?
The expertise that teachers aim to develop in children around their thinking and learning of and about mathematics is known as the Standards for Mathematical Practice (NGACSB, CCSSO, 2010). These standards draw historically from NCTM's process standards as well as the proficiencies outlined in the National Research Council (2001) text, *Adding It Up!* While the content standards center on what children are learning, the mathematical practices provide insight into the habits and dispositions children are developing through their engagement with mathematics.

Figure 3.2. Standards for Mathematical Practice

Standards for Mathematical Practice
1. Make sense of problems and persevere in solving them.
2. Reason abstractly and quantitatively.
3. Construct viable arguments and critique the reasoning of others.
4. Model with mathematics.
5. Use appropriate tools strategically.
6. Attend to precision.
7. Look for and make use of structure.
8. Look for and express regularity in repeated reasoning.

Source: Copyright © 2010. National Governors Association Center for Best Practices and Council of Chief State School Officers. All rights reserved.

In Lesson 5.4 (*Examining Air Quality*) by Maria del Rosario Zavala, children are asked to use real data about air quality from their neighborhoods and locations they visit or have knowledge of. Children use mathematics as a tool to make sense of their world and the experiences they have navigating air quality and a need to stay indoors. They engage in Mathematical Practice 4 (model with mathematics) as they notice the ways in which mathematics (number, measurement, and data) is used in their lives, specifically the current concerns around air quality. The use of these mathematics concepts provides a window in which they can begin to explore, question, and justify concerns around the need to stay indoors during recess.

Social Justice Standards

How do I want children to engage in anti-bias, multicultural, and social justice issues to develop knowledge and skills to reduce prejudice and advocate for collective action?
Learning for Justice (formerly Teaching Tolerance), a project of the Southern Poverty Law Center, lays focus on anti-bias education and social justice. Chapter 1 provides a substantial overview of the Social Justice Standards (Teaching for Justice, 2016) and how these might be implemented specifically in

early elementary mathematics instruction. Examples of how these domains were addressed in some of the lessons within this text are also included. Our decision to focus on the Social Justice Standards comes partially from our own experiences as parents with children in PreK–2 settings and beyond and from our work alongside teachers in classrooms. As educators, our aim is for children to have experiences from early on that center on understanding and addressing issues of injustice and positioning children as advocates for social action. Beyond this, we recognize that the Social Justice Standards and their domains of Identity, Diversity, Justice, and Action provide a clear structure for the ways in which educators can think about social justice specifically in the PreK–2 classroom. See Appendix E for a chart of the book's lessons correlated to the Social Justice Standards.

Figure 3.3. Learning for Justice Social Justice Standards, K–2 Outcomes

Anchor Standard	Grade-Level K–2 Outcome
Identity 1	I know and like who I am and can talk about my family and myself and describe our various group identities.
Identity 2	I know about my family history and culture and about current and past contributions of people in my main identity groups.
Identity 3	I know that all my group identities are part of who I am, but none of them fully describes me and this is true for other people too.
Identity 4	I can feel good about my identity without making someone else feel bad about who they are.
Identity 5	I know my family and I do things the same as and different from other people and groups, and I know how to use what I learn from home, school, and other places that matter to me.
Diversity 6	I like knowing people who are like me and different from me, and I treat each person with respect.
Diversity 7	I have accurate, respectful words to describe how I am similar to and different from people who share my identities and those who have other identities.
Diversity 8	I want to know more about other people's lives and experiences, and I know how to ask questions respectfully and listen carefully and nonjudgmentally.
Diversity 9	I feel connected to other people and know how to talk, work, and play with others even when we are different or when we disagree.
Diversity 10	I know that the way groups of people are treated today, and the way they have been treated in the past, is a part of what makes them who they are.
Justice 11	I try and get to know people as individuals because I know it is unfair to think all people in a shared identity group are the same.
Justice 12	I know when people are treated unfairly, and I can give examples of prejudice in words, pictures, and rules.
Justice 13	I know that words, behaviors, rules, and laws that treat people unfairly based on their group identities cause real harm.

Anchor Standard	Grade-Level K–2 Outcome
Justice 14	I know that life is easier for some people and harder for others based on who they are and where they were born.
Justice 15	I know about the actions of people and groups who have worked throughout history to bring more justice and fairness to the world.
Action 16	I pay attention to how people (including myself) are treated, and I try to treat others how I like to be treated.
Action 17	I know it's important for me to stand up for myself and for others, and I know how to get help if I need ideas on how to do this.
Action 18	I know some ways to interfere if someone is being hurtful or unfair, and will do my part to show respect even if I disagree with someone's words or behavior.
Action 19	I will speak up or do something when I see unfairness, and I will not let others convince me to go along with injustice.
Action 20	I will work with my friends and family to make our school and community fair for everyone, and we will work hard and cooperate in order to achieve our goals.

Source: Reprinted with permission of Learning for Justice, a project of the Southern Poverty Law Center. learningforjustice.org

 Available for download at **resources.corwin.com/TMSJ-EarlyElementary**

PAUSE AND REFLECT

Which elements are you already including in your plans? Which will require further refinement?

ASSESSING PURPOSEFULLY

As shared earlier, children are already involved in experiencing, exploring, and learning mathematics by the time they enter into a formal school setting. This itself demonstrates the idea that children are "ready to learn." Placing young children's mathematics development on stringent timelines and trajectories devoid of the assets and strengths children bring to the classroom is cautioned, as it can inadvertently result in teachers' increased emphasis on procedural fluency rather than conceptual understanding around mathematics content (NAEYC, 2002/2010). What needs refinement is the ways in which teachers and stakeholders uncover and explore the rich mathematical knowledge children enter school with (NCTM, 2020). Readiness assessments are commonly used as measures of school entry in the United States (Stipek, 2019). However, these assessments often do not measure what teachers would deem "readiness skills"; rather, they lead to labels, blame, and the perpetuation of deficit narratives around children, families, and communities (Adair, 2015). As a result, children are stifled from demonstrating their mathematical strengths in the school setting, as they are not seen as the norm. What positive mathematics identity was cultivated from early and exploratory mathematics experiences is often constrained or even eliminated in the first few years of school.

Assessment Strategies

Which strategies can children and I use together to monitor children's understanding of mathematics (content and practices) and social justice issues?

Given the emphasis on SJMLs and the element of children taking a form of action against injustice, along with assessment recommendations in the field of early childhood education, traditional assessment in the form of testing is not appropriate. The use of more authentic assessments in early childhood classrooms connects with many of the pedagogical approaches discussed earlier in this chapter. These assessments are not a one-time occurrence in the classroom but rather ongoing, multifaceted, and conducted both by you and children themselves (in the form of peer feedback and self-assessment).

Formative assessment tools are used during day-to-day interactions. These assessments offer a starting point for educators to build upon when designing classroom learning experiences by providing learners with feedback to move forward or activate children as knowledgeable contributors to classroom interactions. Figure 3.4, adapted from *A Fresh Look at Formative Assessment in Teaching Mathematics* (Silver & Mills, 2018), outlines some teacher supports of formative assessment strategies and connects them to discourse, which we'll discuss in the next section. We specifically identify strategies that support your actions to positively position your children and build their identity and sense of agency.

Figure 3.4. Assessment Strategies to Support Mathematics and Social Justice Discussions

Strategies for Supporting Formative Assessment	Connections Between Formative Assessment Strategy and Discourse
Providing feedback that moves learners forward	• Teachers are strategic about when to tell (e.g., when to show children what to do rather than letting them struggle through and figure it out).
	• Rather than rescuing their children when they are stuck, teachers have high expectations for how children should work with their groups.
	• Teachers sometimes explore incorrect answers.
	• Teachers monitor the room as their children are working.
	• Teachers use what they learned during monitoring to plan for productive discussions.

Strategies for Supporting Formative Assessment	Connections Between Formative Assessment Strategy and Discourse
Activating children as the owners of their learning	• Teachers invite children to share their ideas. • Teachers position children as having the right to evaluate the reasonableness of one another's mathematical ideas. • Teachers position children as authors of mathematical ideas. • Teachers facilitate a growth mindset through discourse.
Activating children as resources for one another	• Teachers have children talk to one another in mathematics class. • Teachers make strategic use of group work. • Teachers use the think–pair–share strategy to give children an opportunity to think individually and to give all children opportunities to discuss their ideas. • Teachers provide children with accountable talk stems (Michaels et al., 2008).

Source: Adapted from Silver and Mills (2018).

 Available for download at **resources.corwin.com/TMSJ-EarlyElementary**

Formative assessment tools in early childhood classrooms may include observations, anecdotal notes, interviews, and work samples. Emphasis is placed on the strengths children demonstrate during an assessment rather than the deficits. Additional examples of assessments may include documentation boards, children's portfolios, performance-based tasks, or projects shared in a range of modalities. These assessments, while summative in nature because they capture a culmination of learning and thinking over time, provide space for children to share their unique voices, perspectives, and emerging ideas. There is an opportunity for children to be positioned as experts in their learning and for their ideas to be listened to. They are seen as people who can self-reflect and share their own analysis of how they are growing over time.

Beyond this, children are positioned as sensemakers and doers of mathematics. Picower (2012) describes six elements of social justice curriculum for teachers: self-love and knowledge, respect for others, issues of social injustice, social movements and social change, awareness raising, and social action—the final element being the taking of action against the injustice. As children navigate their role as activists in SJMLs, they begin to explore the ways that they are able to take action in their world (facilitated by their teacher as needed) and can be closely aligned with the assessments teachers are already using in their classroom settings. Figure 3.5 provides a description of the above assessments and how they may be used to examine learning of both mathematics and social justice goals.

Figure 3.5. Holistic Approaches to Assess Children's Mathematics and Social Justice Understandings

Formative Assessment	Brief Description	Assessment of Mathematics Goals	Assessment of Social Justice Goals
Observations, anecdotal notes	Informal and targeted observations of children engaged in mathematics learning. Teachers constantly gather evidence of a child's progress as they engage in the mathematics and social justice task.	Take time to record a few "look-fors" for the mathematics. For closed mathematics tasks, develop an answer key with anticipated answers. For open mathematics tasks, create several solution pathways or key features you expect to see in a solution.	Take time to record a few "look-fors" for the social justice issue. Anticipate multiple perspectives and various points of view. Monitor children's emotions during small- and whole-group discussions.
Interviews	Brief, informal conversations between a teacher and a child or small group of children that provide a "deep dive" into thinking and understanding. Teachers continuously monitor a child's progress and look for opportunities to support children.	Write questions that push and probe children's thinking. Include questions that address anticipated misconceptions and suggestions to build from children's strengths.	Write specific questions that address the lesson's social justice goal or standards. Develop question prompts to connect the mathematics and social justice issue.
Work samples, documentation boards, portfolios	Hard-copy or electronic work samples, portfolios, or documentation boards can document children's growth and learning over time. All may be collected throughout a unit of study, whereas portfolios may be ongoing throughout the school year. These may also include written, artistic, and digital media and can be easily shared with stakeholders and through various media outlets (Twitter, Instagram, Facebook, emails, websites, blogs, etc.).	Children and teachers can work together to select samples that reflect their growth and understanding about the mathematics standards in the lesson or unit. Language or coding from the standards can be included to enhance ongoing review throughout the school year.	Children and teachers can work together to select samples that reflect their growth and understanding about the social justice standards in the lesson or unit. Language or coding from the standards can be included to enhance ongoing review throughout the school year. These pieces can be largely used in early childhood classrooms as a way to promote action and communication with key stakeholders, including families and community members.

Formative Assessment	Brief Description	Assessment of Mathematics Goals	Assessment of Social Justice Goals
Performances	Children demonstrate their learning using multiple modalities that involve dramatization of their learning and experience. Children or groups may also engage in tableau to share, discuss, and become immersed in varying perspectives related to the social justice concepts in the lesson (e.g., Branscombe, 2019).	Children and teachers work together to co-construct and assess performances related to mathematics content and practices based on criteria. These could be in the form of checklists, rubrics, or anecdotal notes.	Children and teachers work together to co-construct and assess performances related to social justice outcomes based on criteria. These could be in the form of checklists, rubrics, or anecdotal notes.
Projects	Children are provided with, or develop, a culminating project idea to share their thinking and learning about the concept being addressed.	Children and teachers work together to co-construct and assess projects based on criteria indicated on rubrics. Criteria would involve demonstration of mathematics content mastery and use of the mathematical practices.	Children and teachers work together to co-construct and assess performances based on criteria indicated on rubrics. Criteria would involve demonstration of connections to the social justice standard, domains, and key ideas being explored.

online resources Available for download at **resources.corwin.com/TMSJ-EarlyElementary**

In Lesson 5.7 (*Activism Through Art*), lesson author Lauren Murray incorporates geometry and geometric reasoning standards as children identify and describe attributes of shapes as well as compose and create shapes of their own. Murray uses current events surrounding Black Lives Matter (BLM) to center conversations around activism in the mathematics classroom. By exploring street murals created to depict BLM advocacy, children identify the shapes used in the murals and the attributes of these shapes. As a culminating project, children are tasked with creating their own mural and describing the message that the mural is communicating. During this creation, the teacher facilitates thinking and is able to document children's knowledge of shapes and what attributes they will need to use when drawing the shapes on their murals through a series of prompts. After the creation of the final products, children display their murals for their classmates and present them through a gallery walk. As a follow-up to the public share in the classroom setting, children record how their mural design advocates for their self-selected advocacy topic. In this way, Murray uses the project as a means to assess both children's knowledge of the mathematics topic (shapes) and their knowledge of the social justice topics (justice and action).

Asset-Based Assessments

How might I consider what children do not yet understand in ways that view them as sensemakers rather than deficient?

In educational spaces, we are often trained to seek out and name the deficits of our children. We are asked to do this when we unpack test data and errors children make, when we are told to share with families where children need to develop in relation to grade- or age-level standards and norms, and when we make comparisons between children and their placement in trajectories of learning used in a one-size-fits-all context. While knowing this information may be important to consider for planning purposes, naming the strengths and unique insights and assets of our children is a far more powerful tool. Referred to as a *funds of knowledge* approach to teaching (e.g., González et al., 2005), educators recognize and draw upon the experiences of children in and outside of school as members of a community. This recognition leverages knowledge connected to children and families' social and cultural backgrounds as well as the content knowledge with which children enter into school.

Within the landscape of addressing issues of social (in)justice, accessing and attending to knowledge children enter school with is critical. This background offers a lens in which children see the world and places them as experts of their learning. It allows us as teachers to see the assets children enter into our classrooms with, providing new perspectives relevant to children and situated within a community of which we may not be members. As former teachers, we recognize that some solution pathways may be more desirable in terms of efficiency or feasibility in the mathematics classroom. Using effective questioning and discussion strategies can help in drawing out children's thinking and their justification for such thinking in productive ways. This places the emphasis on children sharing their knowledge openly, providing opportunities for teachers to examine their current understanding and where it comes from in their rich history.

TEACHING EQUITABLY

Chapter 2 speaks to the specifics of fostering a classroom community for social justice and, as that is happening, equitable teaching practices need to be considered during instruction. Children who have the opportunity to critically examine issues of social injustice become informed citizens and active participants in a diverse society. However, this only happens with intentional instruction. When topics and voices are expressed that do not reflect the dominant or majority view, many children have the opportunity to feel recognized, opening the potential to develop a sense of empowerment. These voices, however, can easily be shrouded by the dominant view—that which is assumed to be normal in the local setting. TMSJ teachers can draw upon equitable teaching practices to prevent this from happening.

The NCTM publications *Principles to Actions* (NCTM, 2014) and *The Impact of Identity in K–8 Mathematics: Rethinking Equity-Based Practices* (Aguirre et al.,

2013) identify research-based instructional practices that exemplify the qualities of mathematics instruction. *Principles to Actions* provides a set of eight mathematics teaching practices. The *Impact of Identity* names five equity-based instructional practices that support teachers in the use of these eight equitable mathematics teaching practices. Figure 3.6 outlines these practices side by side for review.

Figure 3.6. Mathematics Teaching Practices (NCTM, 2014) and Equity-Based Mathematics Teaching Practices (Aguirre et al., 2013).

Mathematics Teaching Practices	Equity-Based Practices
1. Establish mathematical goals to focus learning.	1. Go deep with mathematics.
2. Implement tasks that promote reasoning and problem solving.	2. Leverage multiple mathematical competencies.
3. Use and connect mathematics representations.	3. Affirm mathematics learners' identities.
4. Facilitate meaningful mathematics discourse.	4. Challenge spaces of marginality.
5. Pose purposeful questions.	5. Draw on multiple resources of knowledge (math, culture, language, family, community).
6. Build procedural fluency from conceptual understanding.	
7. Support productive struggle in mathematics.	
8. Elicit and use evidence of student thinking.	

Beyond these strategies, NCTM's (2020) recent publication *Catalyzing Change in Early Childhood and Elementary Mathematics* acknowledges the need for a variety of groupings and perspectives in mathematics classrooms. It has become commonplace in some early childhood classrooms in elementary schools for children to be grouped by "ability" in connection to reading and mathematics assessment scores. In this form of destructive tracking, children are quickly positioned in categories according to their level of "smartness" as perceived by expectations that are often normed to white, affluent children. Children's identity in mathematics is determined *for them* instead of *by them*. They are left feeling powerless and "othered" because their ways of thinking and learning are not represented in education.

Proponents of leveled groups perpetuate the idea that this type of grouping supports children in getting needed supports (rationalizing the tracking as needed of "scheduling" of services) and provides enrichment for those who need to be "challenged." However, its enactment typically results in inequitable and unjust instruction. Groups labeled as "low ability" are given prescriptive, low cognitive demand tasks with repetition and focus on procedural fluency, whereas "high ability" groups are afforded opportunities for problem solving, reasoning, and

NCTM's *Catalyzing Change in Early Childhood and Elementary Mathematics* (2020) has a section devoted to problematizing ability grouping and reflection questions to consider when thinking about beliefs around ability grouping.

integrated learning experiences. In other words, some groups of children never get access to rich and engaging mathematics. We ask you to challenge these groupings in a variety of ways; allow children to self-select groups to work with or place them in groups with varying strengths in mathematics, prepare supports for children in the moment to use as they are needed, and utilize mathematics tasks that are open enough to provide multiple methods of entry, engagement, and participation. This can include providing a variety of opportunities for children to communicate their thinking and learning.

PAUSE AND REFLECT

Ask yourself:

During my instructional planning, what are some of the equity-based practices that I readily attend to and consider in lesson and classroom design? What are some that I need to focus on more carefully?

NAVIGATING DISCOURSE

In Lesson 5.10 (*Feeding Ourselves and Others*) by Elizabeth Barnes, Jordan Barnes, Natalie Uhle, and Sandra M. Linder, teachers navigate discourse around both the mathematics concept of number and operations and social justice standards related to diversity and action. During the lesson, children are introduced to the book *Uncle Willie and the Soup Kitchen* by DyAnne DiSalvo-Ryan. Discourse in the lesson not only allows children to enter into a conversation around hunger and soup kitchens, but it also helps them to make sense of why soup kitchens are used by some and how they can take action to support a local soup kitchen in their community. Discourse is used to facilitate children's explanations of mathematics strategies used to problem solve in both verbal (discussion and questioning) and nonverbal (using thoughts to connect to mathematics and social justice, tasks with multiple entry points) patterns.

Discourse to Enter In

How can I ensure that mathematical discourse—children actively speaking and being heard—is a prominent and equitable part of our classroom culture?

As early childhood teachers, we know that the culture we create in the classroom setting permeates everything we do with children. In spending time to actively learn about the children in our classrooms and their ways of communication, we can both use and attend to these preferences and encourage others in the classroom to do the same. We work with children in the classroom community to model and set the tone for establishing a classroom culture that nurtures acceptance, respect, and justice. The manner in which you speak and listen to your children in whole-class, small group, or child-to-teacher settings establishes the model children will follow. Figure 3.7 suggests ways that the teacher may promote or discourage discourse during a SJML. Children who feel a sense of respect, acceptance, power, and value from their teacher are more likely to behave similarly toward their peers. Modeling and encouraging equitable speaking and listening skills with children will help establish a classroom culture that makes room for discourse about sensitive and controversial topics as part of lessons. You can be intentional in highlighting when children demonstrate speaking and listening skills that are productive to fostering respectful discourse.

Figure 3.7. Strategies to Promote Discourse in Mathematics Classrooms

	Promotes Discourse	**Discourages Discourse**
Verbal Patterns	Facilitates and referees debate between children in a way that promotes children's identity	Allows children to use language and tone that reduce the voice and experiences of other children
	Uses questioning probes and revoicing strategies that ensure equity and children's development of thought	Moves from one mathematical or social discussion to the next without ensuring the child's voice was understood by others
	Uses open questioning to facilitate discourse, which allows children to create and maintain development and voice	Uses closed questions, which often include one-word responses that funnel children into a preplanned thought pattern
	Uses good "wait time" to promote discourse among children	Answers children's questions quickly in group and classroom discussions without seeking children's voice
Nonverbal Patterns	Uses tasks with multiple entry points, pathways to a solution, or differing solutions	Uses tasks with one solution or one potential pathway to a solution often found in the directions of an activity or scaffolded exercises
	Uses body language such as head nodding, eye contact, and other strategies to affirm children's voice	Uses head turns, lack of eye contact, crossing arms, eye rolling, and other body language that devalue children's voice, perspective, or thought
	Chooses and uses children's thought and perspective to ensure connection to social justice and mathematics	Does not seek equitable participation by calling on children and/or purposefully disregards children's solutions, voice, and/or perspective

 Available for download at **resources.corwin.com/TMSJ-EarlyElementary**

Discourse to Make Sense

During my instructional planning, how can I design opportunities and use specific structures for meaningful discourse that engages all children?
Emergent Bilingual children—a term we prefer over English Language Learners because it assigns competence rather than deficit and leverages the asset of knowing multiple languages—benefit from guided activities that allow for personal inquiry as well as opportunities to express mathematical ideas with a language that makes sense to them. It is important to engage Emergent Bilingual children in child-child and whole-class discourse so that they can practice shifting from natural to academic language structure as well as develop mathematical concepts. In fact, this value of discourse benefits all children in your classroom.

As emerging navigators of a language (even one dominant language), early learners benefit from many of the strategies for discourse that are supportive for Emerging Bilingual children. Opportunities for young children to learn and use discourse that is specific to the academic content can be achieved by associating motion (gestures) and terms together through total physical response, development of child-friendly definitions, and unpacking Tier Two vocabulary with concrete examples. We encourage teachers to use language that is complex and pushes the boundary of what teachers may think children are capable of understanding. Oftentimes, we have found our children learn far more quickly and use more advanced terms in their discourse than we give them credit for.

Discourse to Take Action

How can I support children in using their voice to support their agency and action?

As indicated earlier, for young children, engagement in conversation around a topic can be a strong method of formative assessment. During these conversations, teachers can gain a glimpse into children's thinking around both mathematics and social justice topics. Additionally, this discourse can serve as a mechanism for young children to think about developing an action orientation to social justice. For the youngest learners, written, verbal, and pictorial communication can serve as a mode of action when addressing issues of social (in)justice. Within Picower's (2012) framework of six elements for social justice design, the author calls attention to element 5 (awareness raising) as an opportunity to reconceptualize previous activities to create movement toward raising awareness. Taking these ideas public to stakeholders and other public audiences (via social media, for example) offers opportunities for children to engage in element 6, social action. Figure 3.8 offers strategies for you to support conversation around difficult topics.

Figure 3.8. Strategies to Support Conversation on Difficult Topics

When You Want Children to . . .	Try This Strategy
Discuss a contentious topic	**Solo Writes/Draws:** Invite children to draw or write about their knowledge and feelings about a topic independently. Variations might include these: <ul><li>Writing or drawing on a sticky note to collect</li><li>Posting or sharing a video for the class or teacher</li><li>Using a chalk talk or graffiti wall</li></ul> **Four Corners:** Children move to a corner based on their agreement/disagreement on a given statement. Variations could be done in a line, or using tools like Pear Deck where children might move a dot to show their thinking virtually. **Inside/Outside Circles:** Children make two circles while facing each other. Children take turns actively speaking and listening about a topic. Variations might include a turn and talk, or two parallel lines.

When You Want Children to . . .	Try This Strategy
Process an emotionally difficult event	**Solo Writes/Draws:** Invite children to draw or write about their knowledge and feelings about a topic independently. Variations might include these: • Writing or drawing on a sticky note to collect • Posting on a flipgrid or sharing a video for the class or teacher • Using a chalk talk or graffiti wall **S-I-T:** Read, observe, listen, or watch and then identify one **S**urprising fact or idea, one **I**nteresting fact or idea, and one **T**roubling fact or idea.
Understand/consider diverse perspectives	**Learn to Listen, Listen to Learn:** Children reflect on a topic in journals, share reflections in a small group, and then present ideas to the whole class.

Encompassing all of the strategies listed earlier is creating a classroom environment in which children feel in community with one another—safe to speak and challenge ideas, and safe to enter into discourse where they are at and move forward. Teachers need to consider the names and terms being used in lessons; do these names and terms continue to marginalize populations? Are there alternatives to be used or introduced during discussions? Other elements for consideration include giving children the ability to take space and moments in which they may need to disengage from conversations, allowing that to happen, and providing space for them to re-enter the discussion.

PAUSE AND REFLECT

Ask yourself: How can I ensure that mathematical discourse—children actively speaking and being heard—is a prominent and equitable part of each child's experience of our classroom culture?

CONCLUSION

Our emphasis is that you may already possess many of the skills to implement a SJML effectively, and you may already be using instructional pedagogies from early childhood that align with the key tenets of TMSJ. You might learn some additional strategies to support child-to-child discussion about sensitive or emotional topics, or you might refine your formative assessment strategies to focus on your social justice goals in addition to your mathematical goals. Ultimately, TMSJ presses you to be a more effective teacher of young children. Mathematics doesn't have to be the only thing foregrounded in this work. Children's interests and concerns about their lives, their community, and their world can provide you with rich context to develop informed and active citizens who are able to participate in and shape a diverse society. As early childhood teachers, we have found that the more ways we can aim to integrate content into our lessons, the more children find themselves entering into complex learning.

REFLECTION AND ACTION

Before you continue to read through the remainder of this book, consider the following guiding questions and how the responses to these might guide your interaction with both the forthcoming lessons and advice from the authors in your journey.

1. In what ways do I consider mathematics and social justice goals in my lesson planning already? What areas can I build upon? Who might serve as critical friends and resources to support me in planning and instruction? Who is already doing this work that I might go to for advice and support?

2. How are children in my classroom currently involved in the planning and design of lesson content? How might you work to involve them more in this process so that they have a voice in the curriculum? What challenges might be presented by doing this? What might be some of the successes?

TEACHING SOCIAL JUSTICE MATHEMATICS LESSONS

CHAPTER 4

Now that we have provided some background on the purposes, approaches, and pedagogical tools for teaching mathematics for social justice (TMSJ) in early childhood and early elementary settings, you may be ready to dive into the lessons provided in Chapter 5. This chapter is a guide to what you are about to see. It will provide an overview of the overall structure and format of the social justice mathematics lessons (SJMLs). While we had a variety of lesson types submitted—activities, lessons, and units of varying scopes—you will notice a common structure to the lessons in the book. We asked lesson authors to follow a Social Justice Mathematics Lesson Planner format (Figure 2.8) we provided to illuminate important key features that will be described next.

When implementing a SJML, teachers should ask children questions to get at their understanding and children should be encouraged to wonder and ask questions themselves, providing opportunities for them to create a meaningful and personal connection to the issue. This begins an authentic, sustained inquiry into the tasks at hand. Although most of the lessons in this book are designed for 2–3 days, some could be extended even further. Each lesson closes with children taking action, a form of a public product, and includes ways for teachers to communicate with various stakeholders. In this chapter, we will provide you with details about the overall structure of the SJMLs in this book. It is our hope that understanding elements of the structure will not only help you think through the lessons as you plan to use them, but also support you to develop your own SJMLs. We hope that you will look at these lessons, review them to understand how they were implemented, and envision what they could look like in your own context, making any necessary modifications to meet the needs of the children in your classroom.

PLANNING TO IMPLEMENT A SJML

The elements of the SJMLs we have included in this book were designed to help teachers think through different, important aspects of mathematics lessons designed to explore, understand, and respond to social injustices. As mentioned previously, the lessons in this book were not meant to be picked up and followed exactly; these lessons were meant to be examples of what is possible in early childhood and early elementary classrooms. Like any curricular resource, you will likely read through the lesson and see parts of the lesson that speak to you that you can use as is and others that you may have to modify to reflect your context.

The lessons in this book are designed to engage children in meaningful mathematics to more fully understand issues of social injustice and be able to act. As with any mathematics lesson, we encourage teachers to be ready to support multiple ways of thinking about solutions, both in terms of mathematics and thinking about responding to the social justice issue at the center of the lesson.

We encourage you to structure your lessons in a way that helps you enact the equitable mathematics practices introduced and discussed in previous chapters. These practices are foundational to teaching mathematics for social justice and help teachers establish a classroom culture and environment that is ready to take on the challenge of integrating social justice lessons in the mathematics classroom. We encourage you to revisit them when thinking through your lessons.

How you implement a lesson is not a linear, predictable, or systematic process, as the structure of the SJMLs we present in this book may suggest. Many excellent SJMLs arise in classrooms in which teachers listen to and are involved with children and have established a culture of facilitating social justice goals that integrate mathematical standards. Reflections on these experiences and recommendations from the lesson authors, field testers, and reviewers are provided in Chapter 6.

COMMON STRUCTURES FOR ALL SJMLS

As you prepare to implement any of the SJMLs provided in this book, we recommend that you start by carefully reading through the materials provided by the lesson author(s). Most lessons require preparation of materials, choosing from and acquiring an anchor text, or tailoring materials for your particular context. Each SJML begins with a brief description and overview of the lesson describing the social justice topic that the lesson investigates.

Social Justice Topic and Brief Description

In this section, the lesson author(s) introduce to you what the social justice topic is and the connection and significance of the topic to them and the children in their classroom. The topics in our book are grounded in various issues important and relevant in early childhood education. In some instances, they could arise from questions or concerns from children. They might provoke or connect to their prior knowledge and understandings, allowing for authentic and challenging learning. The social injustices explored in the SJMLs include food insecurity, air quality and pollution, disability, social movements, the pandemic and illness, diversity of families and of our world, and poverty and homelessness, among other topics. These contexts can help children to learn about themselves, learn about the children in their classrooms and communities, learn about the world around them, learn mathematics, and learn about important issues related to (in)justice. These lessons also provide opportunities to observe patterns, to critique information, to learn to ask questions, to reflect, and to act for the common good.

As noted, the contexts of the lessons here may be less authentic to the children in your classroom given that they were written by other people. You may need to adjust the lessons to include a local context, data, or resource. Another strategy is to ask children if there is a similar concern that they are familiar with in the community and then to use this to lead the modification to the SJML. The local, authentic context can serve as a powerful way to increase their engagement and motivation to learn mathematics, to understand the social injustice, and to plan and carry out collective action. Further, the knowledge of the local context also helps position children as experts in the mathematics lesson, creating another avenue for validating children's funds of knowledge within schools and helping broaden what counts as important knowledge in the classroom. Curriculum can and should serve as "windows, mirrors, and sliding glass doors" (Bishop, 1990, p. ix) for children to experience and understand the world. In other words, our teaching, including our mathematics lessons, should reflect children's lives and experiences, give them insight into others' perspectives, and allow them to enter into new spaces and understandings.

Mathematics Standards, Social Justice Standards, and Cross-Curricular Connections

Each of the lessons identifies and provides an opportunity to support, challenge, and expand children's knowledge of three goals:

1. *Mathematics Domains*—what we want children to know and be able to do

2. *Mathematics Practices*—how we want children to show what they know and can do

3. *Social Justice Standards*—how we want children to demonstrate their understanding of and response to an issue (Learning for Justice, 2016)

In addition, we have noted the cross-curricular connections, as many of the lessons have natural connections to other content areas beyond mathematics.

We especially encourage you to return to the Social Justice Standards, and specifically the Grades K–2 Outcomes, developed by Teaching Tolerance (now called Learning for Justice, 2016) to consider how you might refine the learning goals you have for the children in your classroom. As you have a better understanding of the social justice goal(s), you also have a foundation from which to decide what courses of action to pursue.

With practice, you will get better and better at noticing how you can mathematize a variety of social justice topics, and children in your classroom will too. So many of the questions children ask about the world have a mathematical component, from counting to pattern noticing to fairness. We encourage grace and patience while you learn how to coordinate social justice and mathematical goals and to support the development of both kinds of learning within your lessons. You may notice that sometimes the social justice goals may be foregrounded, and that's fine. Not every lesson can perfectly attend to every objective every time. However, it is important to be clear about your goals and objectives and to think about the development of the mathematical thinkers in your classroom.

It is also important to note that while a lesson may be noted as having specific grade-level standards, we believe that any lesson in this book could be adapted for any classroom at the PreK–2 level. Please be willing to consider each and every lesson as appropriate for PreK–2 classrooms with modifications.

Deep and Rich Mathematics

Although we asked the lesson authors to state the mathematics domains that their lesson was aligned to, we also asked them to describe more fully the mathematics in the lesson, unit, or activity and the ways in which the lesson could empower children mathematically. It is in this section that teachers may also see the connections to their grade level and be able to envision modifications to meet the needs of children in their classroom based on children's experiences.

Resources and Materials

Like most curricular resources, the lessons in this book list materials you need for the lesson, including handouts, children's books, mathematics manipulatives, and other kinds of materials. Handouts and other kinds of resources are available for download at resources.corwin.com/TMSJ-EarlyElementary.

About the Lesson

In this section, you will find an overview that provides a big-picture description of the lesson(s), including the total amount of time that it typically takes and across how many days if it is a multiday lesson. As with any lesson, we trust you as experts to make decisions about planning, and these are simply given as suggestions based on the lesson authors' experience and expertise and on the field testing and review. This will be one adaptation for many of you. Each day of the lesson is structured most typically with three phases: a launch to the lesson, then a time to explore the mathematics and social justice topic, followed by a summary and conclusion.

Lesson Facilitation

In this section of the lesson, you will find detailed procedures that walk you through how the author(s) implemented the lesson. We recommend that after you review the Lesson Facilitation section once, you identify the social justice goals and the mathematics goals for yourself, and then map the overall structure of the lesson onto the context of your classroom. Determine how the lesson might work with the children in your classroom, and what kinds of materials you might need.

Next, consider any modifications you might need to make to the lesson to allow you to support and achieve your teaching and learning goals for children, which adjustments to best match their interests, meet their learning needs, and match your instructional goals. In addition, you may want to revise the lesson's context to localize it to your school setting where appropriate. For example, Lesson 5.4 (*Examining Air Quality*) might be modified to change the locations to look at air quality in areas meaningful to the school community. Lesson 5.5 (*Family Counts! Mathematics, Family, and the Diversity Across Our Homes*) might be reframed to look at the number of people in children's buildings, rather than just homes. Lesson 5.6 (*Learning From Our Animal Friends*) might use varying artwork from a local artist or murals found within the community that children see daily.

The SJMLs included in this book provide opportunities to build on the individual, family, cultural, and social knowledge that children bring to your class and to challenge spaces of marginality, specifically by centering children's experiences and knowledge as legitimate intellectual spaces for investigation of mathematical ideas. Ensuring that the SJMLs provide opportunity for these equitable mathematics teaching practices is a fundamental step toward achieving Gutstein's (2006) mathematics and social justice goals: to read and write the word of mathematics, to read and write the world with mathematics, and to develop positive social, cultural, and mathematical identities. As you read through the Lesson Facilitation, be intentional in thinking about the children in your classroom and their individual and collective strengths and knowledge, and how you might leverage those to strengthen the learning experience.

Finally, a well-planned lesson is an important quality of effective, child-centered instruction, and a carefully thought-through plan provides the greatest opportunity for powerful improvisation. In other words, be ready to improvise in order to be responsive to children's ideas. When you have a strong sense of the learning goals, have considered at least one pathway to those goals, and have predicted how children may engage in that pathway, you can make sound decisions based on their interests, experiences, or questions. Establishing goals and strategies to assess ensures you maintain a focus as the pathway changes.

Taking Action

An important and intentional element in the SJML format in this book is the Taking Action piece. It is important for teachers to consider and make space for children to have opportunities to take action when making justice-oriented pedagogies a focus in their teaching. We asked that each lesson include a Taking Action component as a way for children to use the information that they were learning to express empathy, to recognize their own responsibility, to speak up with courage and respect, to make principled decisions about when to take a stand against bias, or to plan and carry out collective action.

We see the Taking Action piece as an important part of each lesson that provides possible actions for you to introduce to the children in your classroom, and it often serves as a culmination of the lesson. The suggestions in the lessons are just

> It is important for teachers to consider and make space for children to have opportunities to take action when making justice-oriented pedagogies a focus in their teaching.

that—a list of possible actions to get you and children thinking about next steps. The lesson may be even more relevant and meaningful if you and the children in your classroom develop your own actions as you seek to create positive change around you. It will also help determine the level of involvement with other children, teachers, administrators, community members, and other stakeholders in your sphere of influence. You may also want to consider different levels at which one could take action and articulate short- and long-term goals at the individual and classroom level, school level, local school community level, and beyond. Not every lesson will have multiple levels of action, but children should have opportunities to engage and to develop their sense of agency.

Attending to the various levels of social action and considering what is appropriate for your grade and context is essential. For young children, the Taking Action piece may also take the form of family-supported action or a similar experience to aid in the development of the children's sense of social justice. For example, kindergarteners might participate in their own march around the school or neighborhood in support of climate justice to learn more about engaging in protest and civic action.

Such experiences are both authentic in some ways and constructed in others, for example creating the opportunity for developing the understanding of participation in a protest with or without the presence of an actual protest. Certainly, there is no substitute for an authentic experience; however, each community is different in the opportunities for action available and the risks families or teachers can take. We suggest you trust your professional knowledge in this case and consult with trusted colleagues about how to engage in meaningful action with children in your classroom and create experiences that seed ideas as they grow and develop into even more powerful young people.

Communicating With Stakeholders

As with any PreK–12 lesson, but particularly important in early childhood and early elementary education, it is always wise to communicate regularly with important stakeholders, especially when teaching about social (in)justice. Because each context is unique, it is important for you to know the children in your classroom, their families, your administrators, and the greater community to anticipate how and what you should communicate about the lessons you teach.

In this section of the SJML plan, you will find suggestions on how a teacher might communicate about the social justice goals, the mathematics goals, and other pertinent information to families, administrators, and other stakeholders. Authors of the lessons might also include how children communicate their learning of both social justice content and mathematics to various stakeholders.

Teacher Resources

As mentioned earlier, each lesson will provide a list of any materials and resources needed for the investigation. Previews of some of the resources, such as worksheets, are provided in this book to help give context as you read the lesson plan.

In order to allow you to modify or contextualize the lesson to your local setting, the lesson worksheets are provided in Word format on the book's companion website (resources.corwin.com/TMSJ-EarlyElementary).

Background of the Lesson

This section gives the reader background on why the lesson was initially developed. In some cases, this is where information about the specific context for which the lesson was developed is contained; in other cases, information about how the lesson has gone when taught in the past by the authors is contained in the section. Because of the variation in submissions, this section is nonstandard and readers can expect to get different information out of the background of the lesson section. Nevertheless, the goal of including a section like this is to provide a bit more contextualization to readers and to better understand why a particular lesson was developed.

About the Author(s)

This section is provided so you will know a bit about the lesson author(s). Each author has provided a brief biography and describes how they became a social justice teacher.

CONCLUDING THOUGHTS BEFORE YOU GO TEACH

Early childhood and elementary teachers have experience in planning lessons that incorporate mathematics content and practices. You may also have experience with lessons that focus on social (in)justice, but not necessarily including mathematics. How might you get started working at the intersection of social justice and mathematical goals? We offer a simple recommendation: allow yourself to be a learner individually and alongside children as you implement these SJMLs.

Focus first on the development of the social justice goal; be a problem-poser with the children in your classroom. Also, resist the urge to force particular mathematical standards to fit with your social justice goal. Instead, view the landscape of mathematical knowledge as all potentially connected to the issue. The mathematics the children work on may not be aligned to where you are in the standards progression for the school year, but will connect mathematics they have learned or be a preview for mathematics they are yet to formalize. Second, as you listen to how children respond to the social justice learning goal, you likely will better understand the goal yourself.

We hope that these introductory chapters have formed a groundwork for you to further advance your efforts to teach mathematics for social justice. We have attempted to provide frameworks and connect to strategies you already know well in order to create some comfort—both competence and confidence—to implement some of the SJMLs in this book, modified to fit the children in your classroom and the context in which you teach.

> How might you get started working at the intersection of social justice and mathematical goals? We offer a simple recommendation: allow yourself to be a learner individually and alongside children as you implement these SJMLs.

As we end this chapter, we send you forward to examine the SJMLs that come next in Chapter 5. In this chapter, we described the SJML format we used in this book. Understanding this will be useful for your SJML implementation. However, more importantly, we hope that this lesson structure will propel you into the development of high-quality mathematical investigations into issues of social injustice that the children in your classroom are passionate about and will engage them in investigation and action.

REFLECTION AND ACTION

It's time to dive in and plan and teach a SJML. For some of us, it is a significant step—a sort of leap into trying out this kind of teaching and building on children's interests and connecting to families. Others may already have experience doing this work, and these lessons may further enhance that work. The following steps can help you get started:

1. Return to the previous chapters, which ground the big ideas of teaching mathematics for social justice in early childhood education. Commit to enhancing your teaching in alignment with ideas, or frameworks, related to TMSJ. Teaching is, for us, the most important aspect of TMSJ.

2. Review the SJMLs in the next chapter and select one to teach in your class. Think through the lesson carefully, and modify as needed, recognizing that you might need to make changes to make the topic or questions a bit more relevant for young children, to make the mathematics more accessible or challenging, or to pose prompts to connect to local issues.

3. Invite a "critical friend," a trusted colleague, to help you think through, plan, and even watch you teach and help you reflect on the lesson.

As you begin or continue your journey to integrate SJMLs into your mathematics classroom, we invite you to share your story. Together, we can all make a difference in the lives of children. The website of support materials for this book (resources.corwin.com/TMSJ-EarlyElementary) offers a space to share your experiences implementing one of the SJMLs in this book. Please consider sharing your experiences with the lessons in this book or contributing anything else related to teaching mathematics for social justice. The lesson authors have shared their thoughts—including successes, challenges, and advice—regarding this work, which we provide in Chapter 6.

PART II

SOCIAL JUSTICE MATHEMATICS LESSONS

SOCIAL JUSTICE MATHEMATICS LESSONS

CHAPTER
5

In this chapter, you will find lessons written by a wide variety of lesson authors in and for different kinds of early childhood and early elementary settings. Each lesson has materials and resources that you may need to prepare and look at ahead of time. For example, as always, you should preview and read any children's books that are included in any lesson, and make any adjustments needed for your class. Also, as we have said previously, these lessons were developed, and many were taught, with a particular group of children in mind, but we believe they can be used in other contexts. While these lessons were taught in a specific grade level or with a certain age group, the lessons contained in this chapter are appropriate for early childhood and early elementary children. Please use these lessons as models to envision what they could look like, using your professional expertise to make any revisions needed to be appropriate and relevant to the children with whom you work.

To organize the mathematics content found in the lessons, we have developed a framework of mathematical content largely based on the domains found in the National Association for the Education of Young Children Learning Paths (2002/2010) and the Common Core State Standards Mathematics (CCSSM) (National Governors Association Center for Best Practices, Council of Chief State School Officers, 2010). In addition, you will find Learning for Justice Social Justice Standards and CCSSM Standards for Mathematical Practice at the start of each lesson to further guide your planning and enactment of the lesson.

The following chart shows the primary focus of each lesson; there may be secondary focuses already in some lessons or ones that you may draw out and extend since early mathematics concepts are interconnected. Our intention with this chart is to help you understand the big ideas of each lesson.

LESSONS

Lesson No.	Lesson Title	Mathematics Focus Areas	Grade	Social Justice Topic	Authors
5.1	*Exploring Fairness Through Data and Numbers*	• Data Collection and Analysis	PreK–K	Diversity and Empathy	Melanie Hollis, Marni C. Peavy, Anna Hayashi, Jane "Sissy" Poovey, and Sandra M. Linder
5.2	*Addressing Food Insecurity*	• Number and Operations • Measurement • Data Collection and Analysis	PreK–2	Food Insecurity	Jennifer Ward and Children of the Maple Classroom
5.3	*Same and Different: An Exploration of Identity Through Geometry Shapes*	• Geometry	PreK–2	Exploring Identity	Heather Winters and Juan Manuel Gerardo
5.4	*Examining Air Quality*	• Number and Operations • Measurement • Data Collection and Analysis	K–2	Air Quality	Maria del Rosario Zavala
5.5	*Family Counts! Mathematics, Family, and the Diversity Across Our Homes*	• Number and Operations • Measurement • Data Collection and Analysis	K–2	Family Diversity	JaNay Brown-Wood
5.6	*Learning From Our Animal Friends: Mathematizing With the Artwork of Ricardo Levins Morales*	• Number and Operations • Data Collection and Analysis	K–2	Taking Care of Ourselves and Others	Courtney Koestler and Anita Wager
5.7	*Activism Through Art*	• Geometry	1–2	Activism Through Art	Lauren Murray

Lesson No.	Lesson Title	Mathematics Focus Areas	Grade	Social Justice Topic	Authors
5.8	*Seeing the Colors of Ourselves and Others*	• Number and Operations • Patterns and Algebraic Thinking • Data Collection and Analysis	1–2	Skin Tone Representation in Picture Books	Sam Prough and Eric Cordero-Siy
5.9	*Human Diversity and Disability: Do We All Have 10 Fingers?*	• Patterns and Algebraic Thinking	1–2	Body Diversity and Disability	Jennifer R. Newton, Courtney Koestler, and Jan McGarry
5.10	*Feeding Ourselves and Others*	• Patterns and Algebraic Thinking	1–2	Poverty and Homelessness	Elizabeth Barnes, Jordan Barnes, Natalie Uhle, and Sandra M. Linder
5.11	*Representation Matters in our Mathematics Class*	• Number and Operations	1–2	Mathematical Access and Identity	Amber Beisly and Brandy McCombs
5.12	*Respecting Our House: Protecting Our Salmon Neighbors*	• Number and Operations • Measurement	1–2	Protecting the Watershed	Julia Aguirre and Melissa Adams Corral
5.13	*Early Elementary Mathematics to Explore People Represented in Our World and Community*	• Patterns and Algebraic Thinking • Data Collection and Analysis	2	The Diversity of the "Global Village"	Courtney Koestler, Eva Thanheiser, Mary Candace Raygoza, Jeff Craig, and Lynette Guzmán
5.14	*Journey for Justice: The Farmworkers' Movement*	• Number and Operations	2	Workers' Rights and the Delano Grape Strike	Gloria Gallardo and Emy Chen

SOCIAL JUSTICE OUTCOMES

- I know that all my group identities are part of me— but that I am always ALL me. (Identity 3)

- I see that the way my family and I do things is both the same as and different from how other people do things, and I am interested in both. (Identity 5)

MATHEMATICS DOMAINS AND PRACTICES

- Data collection and analysis

- Construct viable arguments and critique the reasoning of others. (MP3)

- Attend to precision. (MP6)

CROSS-CURRICULAR CONNECTIONS

- Language Arts

- Music

- Art

LESSON 5.1 EXPLORING FAIRNESS THROUGH DATA AND NUMBERS

Melanie Hollis, Marni C. Peavy, Anna Hayashi, Jane "Sissy" Poovey, and Sandra M. Linder

DIVERSITY AND EMPATHY

The topic addressed within this lesson sequence focuses on developing empathy, through establishing relationships between diverse groups of children. The social justice–focused objective in this lesson is as follows: *Children will recognize the value of developing relationships with people who are different from themselves and engage respectfully with all people.* According to the Collaborative for Academic, Social, and Emotional Learning (CASEL, 2022), a national leader in social-emotional learning, empathy is a key part of social awareness, or one's ability to recognize the value of others around them. We believe that empathy is posited to be essential to cultivate in all people, to overcome differences and create space for collaboration and mutual understanding, if not agreement and collective action. We believe that empathy is something learned, not something we should expect will develop on its own.

If we expect children to develop the needed dispositions to respond to injustice as they get older, we first must support early development of a sense of empathy. In the multiday lesson presented here, we begin this journey for PreK and kindergarten children early in the school year through an exploration of similarities and differences as identified at first through a sorting task using instruments and then making connections to similarities and differences between groups of people. Through an interactive read-aloud, instrument sort, instrument design and creation, and finally composing a song, children can compare, contrast, and connect through difference. This exploratory lesson acts as a springboard toward engaging in continuing experiences around understanding others and building a sense of empathy toward others.

When discussing some of the overarching concerns of the community, topics such as extreme poverty, hunger, inequitable access to technology, and mental health emerged as critical areas of need. It is difficult to engage in conversations around these topics at the early childhood level, as young children are often still exhibiting high levels of egocentrism and only an emerging sense of empathy.

To begin these explorations (which would occur throughout the year), this lesson experience focuses on examining one demographic within the community (those considered elderly). We hope this lesson helps teachers catalyze a year-long examination of the needs of others and supporting these children's ability to empathize and identify strategies for supporting their community.

DEEP AND RICH MATHEMATICS

The mathematics content for this lesson focuses on sorting at the PreK or kindergarten level. As a critical component of many early explorations, sorting allows children multiple entry points for examining collections and opportunities for varied discourse between children and their teacher. The sorting lessons depicted in this chapter are built largely on the mathematical processes and are grounded in problem solving and play.

ABOUT THE LESSON

This is a multiday experience that incorporates read-alouds, interactive writing, mathematics, music, and social/emotional concepts. This lesson sequence culminates with reflective discussions focused on connecting the content of the read-aloud with the creation of instruments, while also emphasizing connecting the lesson experience to real-world contexts of empathizing with the needs of others. Suggestions for extending the learning are included.

Resources and Materials

- *Miss Tizzy* by Libba Moore Gray

- A variety of musical instruments (for example, rhythm sticks, tambourines, kazoos, and bells)

- Assorted counting materials (e.g., beans, beads)

- Other materials for the lesson include string, rubber bands, tubes, paper or plastic plates, boxes or containers with or without lids, tape, glue, scissors, and craft sticks

LESSON FACILITATION

Day 1

Launch (20 minutes)

- Begin an interactive read-aloud of *Miss Tizzy* by Libba Moore Gray, by presenting the cover of the book and asking what the children notice about the characters on the cover. (This read-aloud may occur over several days based on the stamina of your class.)

- Allow children to share their noticings. They may notice that some characters may be girls, some may be boys, and some may be other kinds of children; some of the people are old, some are young. They may also notice the expressions and interactions of the characters; they are smiling, touching, and/or seem to know one another well.

- **Note:** You should read the book ahead of time and strategically plan opportunities for questioning and discussing throughout the book relating to developing relationships with people who are different from themselves and engaging respectfully with all people.

- Continue to have the children share noticings and wonderings as you picture walk through the book. Be sure to comment, if necessary, on how we might make assumptions about some of these groupings as we discuss (for example, we might not be able to immediately tell gender based on the picture in the story).

- After the picture walk, read the story using the interactive read-aloud format. We have included suggested questions, but feel free to develop your own as you plan your read-aloud. If you feel as if any of the vocabulary in the book needs to be discussed, please do so as needed. Suggested questions for the read-aloud include the following:

  + *As the children are picking flowers, how are they arranging the flowers in the vases?*

  + *Why do you think they are choosing these arrangements?*

  + *The story says, "And they loved it." What do you think it is that they love?*

  + *Why do you think the children love?*

  + *How do you know the children loved making cookies with Miss Tizzy?*

  + *In the story, every child got a turn. How would you feel if you did not get a turn?*

  + *Why do you think the people have stopped smiling?*

  + *How would you feel if you couldn't leave your house?*

  + *How can we tell that the children love it?*

+ *When Miss Tizzy got sick, predict what you think their ideas may be.*

+ *Why do you think the children are sad?*

+ *Why do you think the children did all of those things for Miss Tizzy?*

+ *What do you think Miss Tizzy loved? Why?*

+ *What are ways we could show older adults we care about them?*

Explore (20 minutes)

- Show the children a collection of instruments and allow them to explore the instruments like the children did in the story. Encourage the children in your classroom to play with the instruments and share them with their classmates so everyone has the opportunity to explore a variety of instruments.

- Allow children to make sounds, sing, dance, and so on. You can circulate during the play to confer with children about what they are noticing.

- Ask questions such as these:

  + *What do you notice about the shape of the instrument?*

  + *What do you notice about the sound the instrument makes?*

  + *How does playing the instrument make you feel?*

Debrief (10 minutes)

- Bring the children back together to share their exploration experiences. Allow the children to tell what they may have noticed about the instruments (shape, color, sound, etc.) as well as how they felt as they explored the instruments (excited, happy, frustrated, etc.) and why.

Day 2

Note: This lesson may take place over the course of several days depending on the age of the children in your classroom.

Launch (10–15 minutes)

- Revisit the "Wednesday" page of the book *Miss Tizzy*. This page highlights the playing of instruments. Talk about this part of the book with the children in your classroom.

- Tell the children that as partners they will explore a set of instruments (or pictures of instruments) and identify attributes (such as shapes, sound, etc.).

- Next, have the children find different ways to sort the instruments. Encourage them to identify their own rules for sorting and to sort more than one time.

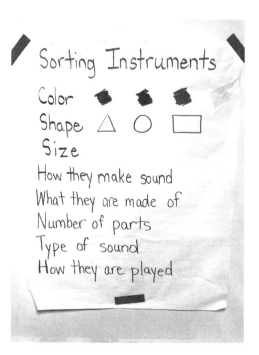

- After about 10 minutes, bring the children together to share all the ways they have sorted the instruments so far. Create a class sort chart to organize their thinking (e.g., see the "Sorting Instruments" image). After all sorting suggestions have been shared, challenge the children to find another way to sort their instruments that is not on the class sort chart. After about 5–7 more minutes, add the new ways children discovered to the chart.

Explore (45+ minutes)

- Tell the children that they will work with partners to invent an instrument.

- Show them a variety of materials for the instruments (beans, beads, string, rubber bands, tubes, paper or plastic plates, boxes or containers with or without lids, tape, glue, scissors, craft sticks, etc.) and allow them to explore for a few minutes.

- Children will then work with partners to draw a plan in their mathematics journal for an instrument they will create. The plan should specifically identify an attribute or attributes the class recognized from the previous sorts they have done that they will include in their instrument.

- Possible questions you could ask children as they are previewing and planning are as follows:

    + *How will your instrument make sound?*

    + *How will you hold the instrument to play?*

    + *(In reference to specific material) Why did you choose . . . ?*

    + *How are you feeling about planning your instrument?*

    + *How do you feel about your plan?*

- Children will use the plan they developed in their mathematics journal to create the instrument. The children worked as partners to develop their plan, but they will now support each other as they create individual instruments following their plan.

- As children build their instruments using the materials they selected, visit the groups and ask questions. You should ask them to explain their ideas (such as why they chose specific materials, what is or is not working the way they planned, what changes have they made to their plan and why, etc.).

- Even though partners developed one plan for their instruments, you should expect that each child's instrument will be unique.

- Next, provide opportunities for pairs to discuss their instruments, focusing on attributes as well as how their instruments are alike and different. Suggested techniques for partnering children to share are as follows:

    + Have children in two lines facing their initial partner. After each partner has a turn to talk about how their instruments are alike and different, one line shifts to the right so they are now facing a new partner. The child at the front of the line moves to the rear. Have children share similarities and differences with a variety of partners.

+ Play music. Have children find a new partner before the music stops, making sure no one is left out.

+ Make two circles (inner and outer). The inner circle shifts to the right to create new partnerships.

• Repeat this process with multiple partners in the class. The idea is to give children several opportunities to recognize similarities and differences in their instruments with as many different people as they can.

• After some time is allowed to create the instruments using the given materials, have the instruments created by the children on the carpet in the center of a class circle. Using the class sort chart, have the children sort the instruments using the previous sort suggestions or come up with new ways to sort. You can add any new ideas to the class sort chart. For example, children may suggest sorting by shape (rounded, straight, etc.). Have each child place their instrument in the corresponding group. Possible questions that you may ask are as follows:

+ *Why do some groups have more than others?*

+ *Why is this instrument not in a group?*

+ *Is there an instrument that could be in more than one group? Why?*

+ *Which group has the most?*

Final Day

• Reread a section of the book *Miss Tizzy* to specifically highlight the relationship between Miss Tizzy and the children. For example, look again at the section in the book where people had lost their smiles. You may ask the children:

+ *Sometimes people get lonely. Describe a time you have felt lonely. What helped you feel better?*

+ *Why do you think it is important to visit or spend time with older people?*

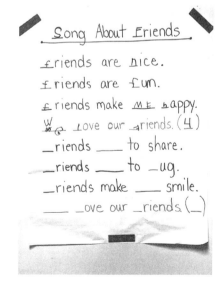

+ *We tend to spend time with people who are like us. What do you think you could learn/gain from having friends of many ages? What about people who are different than you?)*

- Next, together with the children, write a simple song using words and their instruments. The song can incorporate patterns, numbers, and so on.

- This provides an opportunity to highlight rhythmic and auditory subitizing as well as focus on the principles of counting. See the image for an example of what this interactive writing might look like in an early childhood setting.

- Children can practice and perform the song and share the process (reading, mathematics, creation, writing, etc.) through a video or live in-person performance with a selected group of older friends from the community.

Other Children's Literature Suggestions
- *Wilfrid Gordan McDonald Partridge* by Mem Fox

- *Come With Me* by Holly M. McGhee

- *All Are Welcome* by Alexandra Penfold

- *The Push: A Story of Friendship* by Patrick Gray

- *Happy in Our Skin* by Fran Manushkin

- *Giraffes Can't Dance* by Giles Andreae and Guy Parker-Rees

- *Mango, Abuela, and Me* by Meg Medina

Center/Learning Labs Connections
- Have a dress-up/tea party, encouraging children to pretend they are someone else.

- Make cookies, while allowing children to discuss times they have connected with family members through cooking or baking and practicing measurement skills.

- Make puppets, while writing and telling stories focused on characters that they have met in their lives.

Other Lesson Possibilities That Connect Mathematics and Early Social Relationships
- Collect canned foods, coats, gloves, or other items to donate to an older population. These items can be used for activities in class such as sorting, graphing, counting, and comparing amounts.

- Write and illustrate a book about numbers, sorting, and so on and share with an older population. Then ask them to write and/or share a book with the children.

- Develop or make mathematics games to play in class and then share those games with an older population (e.g., visit a retirement center or host a *Games With Grown-ups* event at school). These discussions act as a vehicle for supporting children's empathy toward others (especially elderly populations).

- Begin to explore similarities and differences between other groups using sorting, counting, and comparing as the primary mathematics content. Such groups might include jobs in the community, types of transportation within the community, or types of living spaces within a community.

- Think about exploring similarities and differences within the classroom as well, for example, around the holidays. Instead of teaching about different types of celebrations, focus lessons on the traditions that are important for the families in your class and extend these conversations into the community by having children visit local stores, libraries, and other community spaces to ask the people there about their own family holiday traditions.

- As you notice children becoming more at ease with sorting, counting, and comparing within the context of examining different groups, begin to pose the question: *Why do you think these differences exist?* For example, a lesson focused on sorting types of living spaces or jobs within a community might lead to a discussion of income levels and inequities. While these discussions may not be the focus of a lesson, they are an important byproduct that forms the foundation for future grade levels to explore injustices in a more substantive manner.

TAKING ACTION

As this lesson focuses young children on examining sets to determine similarities and differences, you can encourage children in your class to develop a sense of empathy for those around them. This emerging understanding of a world beyond themselves is critical to support future action against the injustices present in their immediate community and beyond. As early childhood and early elementary years really focus on the notion of community and the needs within a community system, you can limit extensions geared toward developing empathy to examples within their immediate community (as described next). These extensions could be implemented over a period of months at this age, as children require time to reflect and assimilate/accommodate these experiences into their schema in order to fully transition from an egocentric to an empathetic point of view.

COMMUNICATING WITH STAKEHOLDERS

Communication plans are implemented in these classrooms that promote two-way communication and build on asset-based framing for the mutual respect and value of both home and school environments. In addition to concrete strategies (e.g., newsletters, texting apps, or formalized systems such as Canvas or Schoology) for weekly communication of school-based tasks, teachers in this district also implement weekly communication systems focusing on connecting home and school environments by providing support for families. This support may look like a document or weekly video explaining why children are doing certain tasks at home and what they look like in school or providing example questioning strategies or home extensions that promote mathematical play between parents/caregivers and children. These systems are established in the beginning of the year to encourage a positive discourse between parents/caregivers and teachers that focuses on children's needs. Once these systems are established, teachers are able to traverse conversations about social justice issues and how they are examined within an early childhood setting.

For this particular lesson, teachers communicate the goal of the overall unit (promoting empathy and examining needs within the community, with a particular focus on how certain groups are disadvantaged and how to approach helping the people around them). They begin this conversation by explaining how children at this age often display egocentric tendencies and how this unit will help children to develop a sense of empathy toward the world around them. Supporting this sense of empathy in early childhood settings can lead to multiple interactions around social justice issues. In terms of connecting with the community outside of the immediate families of children in each class, the lesson calls for the children to create a video or host an in-person performance (hopefully engaging with elderly members of the community) where they would show their instrument plans and creations, discuss what they learned, and perform the song they wrote together.

BACKGROUND OF THE LESSON

Lancaster School District is a rural district in the midlands of South Carolina (see the state-level map at bit.ly/3ltF45c). According to recent South Carolina census data, Lancaster County currently has more than 13% of the population living in poverty and a per capita income in 2018 of just under $30,000 (see U.S. Census data at https://bit.ly/3EgUwsL). Currently, over 50% of students are not meeting expectations in mathematics, as determined by the SC Ready Assessment administered in third grade. Additionally, on the mathematics portion of the state-mandated Kindergarten Readiness Assessment (KRA), only 21.3% of Lancaster children demonstrated "readiness" when entering kindergarten (South Carolina School Report Card, 2022). Given this reality, looking at the community needs near some of the elementary schools in this area, discussions among teachers we work with (including some authors of this lesson) turned to the amount of poverty, hunger, and homelessness among community members. Through these discussions, the mathematics coaches and teachers struggled with the innocence of children at the PreK and kindergarten levels and the reality that it is critical for these children to understand the world around them in a developmentally appropriate manner to ensure their ability to advocate for and support those around them as they grow. Teachers were also struggling with what they perceived to be a lack of engagement or involvement from parents/caregivers. However, through the exploration of the current community contexts, teachers moved past a deficit orientation toward parent involvement and began to focus on the strengths that families within these communities were showing in terms of supporting their children.

Although initially developed in a rural county experiencing deep economic and educational divides, this lesson can apply to a variety of contexts. Where originally implemented, the lesson also supported deeper connections between teachers and parents and cultivated empathy between families and school personnel. While shedding light on issues of inequity is difficult to imagine within an early childhood setting, introducing the concept of attributes and sorting as a means to discuss similarities and differences provides an entry point for future discussions of demographics within the community.

Children at this age are still largely egocentric and lessons such as these provide experiences that explicitly support them to see beyond their own needs. These experiences take time and likely will form the basis of instruction across the curriculum throughout the year. By beginning with sorting experiences connected to concrete objects (e.g., instruments), early childhood teachers are then able to move to more visual indicators (e.g., age, hair color). Once we begin these explorations, we can then extend them to look at differences such as skin color, income inequities, accessibility, and even status within communities.

In order to fully support the children and families within our community, it is vital to teach all subject areas from a social justice lens. We strive to find the balance between ensuring children's positive growth and development through play-based experiences and introducing sensitive topics that require substantive exploration. While there is not a current focus on social justice at the school or community level in this area, conversations around teaching for social justice have emerged through professional development and coaching sessions. Creating classroom mathematics environments that foster an equitable approach to understanding mathematics content, processes, and value is a priority for teachers in this district. As such, part of the discourse around the classroom environments includes a productive struggle from teachers, coaches, and facilitators of professional development, related to how to best support children's needs within the context of their own experiences and allow for the connection building necessary to broaden their experiences and come to fully understand the world around them.

ABOUT THE AUTHORS

 **Melanie Hollis** is an instructional specialist for mathematics in South Carolina. Her work focuses on growing teacher knowledge and clarity around early mathematics and creating mathematics-rich learning environments. She began her teaching career in a Title I school. As a teacher of upper elementary students, she recognized that strong foundational skills often coincided with her students' success. Quality early childhood instruction has become her focus as a district instructional specialist based on her experiences in the classroom. As an instructional specialist for an extremely diverse district, she works to support all primary teachers in their instructional practices and content knowledge so strong foundational skills can be established for all children.

 **Marni C. Peavy** is an instructional mathematics coach at an elementary school in South Carolina. Her work focuses on developing a deeper understanding of mathematics instruction by recognizing teachers' strengths, building upon those strengths, and elevating teacher capacity. Marni Peavy started her teaching journey because she recognized early that certain populations were educationally disenfranchised. Her focus at that time was in the area of special education services, but as her teaching career continued and diversified, her eyes were opened to the widespread marginalization in our education system. As an instructional coach, Marni continues to advocate for equity in education through her work with teachers and students and strives to be a change agent.

 **Anna Hayashi** is a kindergarten teacher in South Carolina. She is working to develop strong practices around early mathematics by incorporating mathematical play. She is also working to incorporate more cross-curricular opportunities for her students. She recognized the importance of providing deeply enriching, diverse experiences early in her career. As a teacher of early childhood education, she began to explore new ways to provide opportunities for students. Her experiences in the classroom have motivated her to promote academic equality and diversity. Anna strives to grow in her knowledge of early childhood instruction. She hopes to continue spreading awareness of the importance of quality instruction for students.

 **Jane "Sissy" Poovey** is an early childhood educator in South Carolina. She is working with 4-year-old students and their parents to develop connections between mathematics and their world through mathematical play. Jane began her career in teaching with a concentrated interest in early childhood education. As a teacher of young learners, she saw firsthand how many students come to school with varied preschool

experiences. Those prior experiences carry much weight in building solid foundational learning skills that lead to success. Conversely, young learners entering school with no preschool experiences often encounter difficulties that challenge them academically long after they leave the PreK and kindergarten classrooms. Early in her teaching career, she became aware of the importance of fairness and equity in the early childhood classroom. As a result, she has worked to advocate for quality early childhood instruction for all children.

 **Sandra M. Linder** is a professor of early childhood mathematics education at Clemson University. Her research focuses on increasing parent and child interactions around mathematical play and supporting teacher practices around early mathematics. She started engaging in teaching through a social justice lens after realizing that while her teacher preparation included a focus on culturally responsive practice, it did so in a passive way. While part of teaching through social justice is certainly focused on teaching children to respect and honor other cultures, there is also a more active lens grounded in preparing children to become advocates for themselves and for those around them as they grow. It is with this lens that Sandra strives to support both preservice and in-service teachers as they implement instruction.

- I want to know about other people and how our lives and experiences are the same and different. (Diversity 8)

- I know everyone has feelings, and I want to get along with people who are similar to and different from me. (Diversity 9)

- I know when people are treated unfairly. (Justice 12)

- I will join with classmates to make our classroom fair for everyone. (Action 20)

MATHEMATICS DOMAINS AND PRACTICES

- Number and operations

- Measurement

- Data collection and analysis

- Make sense of problems and persevere in solving them. (MP1)

- Reason abstractly and quantitatively. (MP2)

- Construct viable arguments and critique the reasoning of others. (MP3)

CROSS-CURRICULAR CONNECTIONS

- Language Arts

- Science

- Social Studies

- Art

LESSON 5.2 ADDRESSING FOOD INSECURITY

Jennifer Ward and Children of the Maple Classroom

FOOD INSECURITY

The main social justice topic in this lesson is food insecurity. According to the organization Feeding America (http://www.feedingamerica.org/), millions of children and families in the United States face food insecurity and hunger every day. In the wake of the COVID-19 pandemic, it is estimated that 42 million people experience food insecurity, which is defined as a lack of consistent access to enough food for every person in a household to live an active, healthy life. Feeding America also notes that every kind of community, be it rural, suburban, or urban, is impacted by food insecurity. However, in the United States, it is Black, Latinx, and Native American communities who are at higher risk for food insecurity due to systemic racism.

Regular access to nutritious food is a social justice issue that young children can explore through seeing how this issue impacts their own families and communities as well as by learning about local organizations working to end food insecurity. Children can draw on their knowledge of gardens—for example, a school garden—to consider how people access fresh fruits and vegetables. They can reflect on the food they eat across various meals of the day. They can also grapple with leftovers (including food waste). The way that this exploration is structured, children learn more about what it means to experience food insecurity and how they can take action to fight food insecurity in their own neighborhoods. By having them construct letters to stakeholders in the school along with their own families, the children are positioned as both knowledgeable about issues in the community and also powerful in taking steps to address the issue.

DEEP AND RICH MATHEMATICS

Within this lesson, children are involved in making sense of the ratio of children in our community who are food insecure (1 in 5). Children are provided with manipulatives to make sense of this ratio in a concrete way, visually seeing one item out of five as a different color. Following this, children engage in a simulation with a spinner of the numbers 1–15 where they are asked to identify the number they spun. Depending on what they spin, children are able to add a manipulative to their bucket, which is counted at the end of the lesson. Children are involved in comparing their quantities with one another, using various methods to determine who has more and who has less and providing models and justifications for why they feel that is the case.

ABOUT THE LESSON

This 3-day lesson is designed for a small group setting and can be modified for a whole group by providing each student with their own bag of numbers (see the *Resources and Materials*). You are encouraged to modify the numbers to reflect the right level for your children's needs.

Resources and Materials

Prior to teaching the lesson, here are suggested resources to develop background knowledge on food insecurity for yourself:

- Website: Visit FeedingAmerica.org for general information, research, and statistics on the United States food insecurity issue as a whole. You can also use their national registry of food banks to find a food bank in your area.

- Blog post: "Food Equity: Our Social Awakening" by Jaclyn Bowen, *Clean Label Project Blog* (https://bit.ly/3xR15zJ)

- Website: "Food Deserts" by the Food Empowerment Project (https://bit.ly/3I9tLc3)

- Blog post: "Food Deserts in the United States" by The Annie E. Casey Foundation, February 13, 2021 (https://bit.ly/3IczSft)

Other Materials Needed
- Chart paper

- Markers

- Index cards

- Masking tape/painter's tape

- Sticky notes

- People connectors in two colors (one color to represent food secure, and one to represent food insecure) or other similar manipulatives in two colors

- Images of local grocery stores

- Snap or Unifix cubes

- Location to collect cubes labeled "Breakfast," "Lunch," and "Dinner." Examples may include the following:

    + Three clear plastic cups per child (1 label per cup)

    + A three-section plate (1 label per section)

    + A piece of paper folded into thirds (1 label per section)

- Random number generators, one per child. Examples may include the following:

    + Brown bags with number cards with 1–15 inside for children to pull (numbers can vary in representation; for example, tally, ten-frame, dot image, digit)

    + Spinners labeled with the numbers 1–15

    + 15-sided dice

- Worksheet 1: *Recording Sheet* (1 per student)

- Tools to compare quantities (as needed)

    + Number lines (0–20)

    + Hundreds chart variation (grade-level dependent: 0–20, 0–30, 0–50, 0–100)

The following items are recommended:

- Computer with a camera and speakers to videoconference with a representative from a local Feeding America branch (or similar organization)

- Representative from a local food bank to provide an overview, give a virtual tour, and answer questions

LESSON FACILITATION

Day 1

Launch (15–20 minutes)

- To elicit children's thinking, invite them to share places in the local community where they get food and how often. Questions may include these:

  + *Where do you typically eat every day?*

  + *Where does your food come from?*

  + *Where does your family purchase or grow food?*

- Encourage them to share orally or use invented spellings to record their locations on a sticky note. As children are sharing, encourage ideas connected to not only large-scale grocery stores but also small, family-owned grocers, restaurants, farmers markets, and others.

- Next, prompt children to consider how they decide to get food from the places they name. You may have to prompt them about cost, proximity to home/school/family member's work, as well as specific brands or specialty shops (in-store sandwich station; coffee, tea, or sushi bar) and other aspects that influence their families' decisions.

- Continue by asking children to think about what kinds of food they eat and why that might be. Pose various kinds of questions to have children share ideas about eating foods. For example, you might say:

  + *Let's share some of the foods your family makes at home for special occasions that connect with your background.*

  + *Let's share some of the food you eat all the time.*

  + *What's a food you could eat all day every day?*

  + *What about foods you eat on special occasions?*

- Finally, ask the children to consider why we need to eat food.

  + *Why do we need to eat food?*

  + *How does eating food help or hurt our bodies?*

- List student ideas in a two-column chart under the labels "help" and "hurt."

Explore (20 minutes)

- In this part of the lesson, you may be introducing new information.

- Present the local ratio of food insecure children (in the initial implementation of this lesson, it was 1 in 5) using the people connectors manipulatives (or something similar).

- Ask children to brainstorm what they notice and what they wonder about the visual they see with the manipulatives.

- Record children's thinking on chart paper with their name next to their contribution. Use this to display for a documentation panel later in the lesson with a photograph of the people connector–created ratio.

- Explain the statistic to the children. Share that food insecurity means that these children do not have access to fresh food close to their home. They often are only able to access food from small convenience stores, like gas stations.

- Show children images from local food stores/markets and images from local smaller convenience stores and gas stations (preferably those they noted in the initial question).

- Highlight some of the product nutrition labels in these images.

- Ask and record on a Notice/Wonder chart what children notice and wonder about these images. Prompts may include these:

  + *What do you notice?*

  + *What types of food do you see here?*

  + *What do you notice about the number or amount of vitamins/fat/calories/sugars in these foods?*

  + *What do you notice about the cost of foods in these places?*

  + *What do wonder?*

  + *How long would you be able to keep foods from each location in your home and still be able to eat them?*

  + *How do you feel about what you are thinking?*

- You should take care to not shame children who may be food insecure or those who frequently rely on food from convenience stores and gas stations. You can choose to emphasize ideas such as these locations allow families to obtain more food and/or more calories for the price. These foods are often more shelf-stable for longer amounts of time, so they can be purchased and stored in larger quantities than fresh foods as well.

Summarize (5 minutes)

- Share with children that over the next few days, you all will be thinking more about what it means to be food insecure and how we can take action to raise awareness about food insecurity in our area.

- Allow for any further comments or questions.

Day 2

Launch (15 minutes)

- Prepare children to participate in a "Food Insecurity Simulation" by telling them that you will be using materials to explore the idea of food insecurity that you discussed the previous day.

- Briefly review the discussion and the Notice/Wonder chart from Day 1 with the image of the people connectors. Ask:

  + *Who can remind the group what this image represented?*

- Review the 1-in-5 statistic (or a context-specific statistic) from the prior day.

- Distribute snap cubes and three cups (or a sectioned plate or paper folded into thirds) to each child. Explain to children that this will represent their breakfast, lunch, and dinner.

- Show children the brown paper bags and explain that they will be pulling a number from the bag one at a time. Depending on the number they select, it will determine if they are able to put a cube into their cup for that "meal." There will be three meals during a day, and they will pull enough numbers to represent 3 days.

- Spend time reviewing the numbers (1–15) and how they might be represented on the cards in the bag.

- Review the representations the children may encounter for each number, such as the digit form, tally marks, ten-frames, or dot images. (Word form could be used for older grades, along with base-10 block notation.) Numbers may be differentiated based on children's need to include greater or lesser values.

Explore (20 minutes)

- Invite children to select a number from the bag to simulate Sunday breakfast.

  + If a child selects a 1, 6, or 11, they cannot place a snap cube in their cup.

  + If they select any other number in the bag (2–5, 7–10, or 12–15), they can add a snap cube to their cup.

  + Periodically ask children questions about the numbers they are selecting:

    - *How did you know what number that image represented?*

    - *Where might we see that number in our world?*

    - *How might you show that number in another way?*

    - *What would be one more/less than that number?*

- Repeat the last step for each child in the group to see if they get "breakfast," then proceed for "lunch" and "dinner" for Sunday.

- At the end of Sunday (breakfast, lunch, and dinner), ask children:

    - *What do you notice about your cups and those of others?*

- On the recording chart, have children fill out the row for Sunday, using an "X" or "1" to denote they had a cube in their cup for a given meal and leaving the space blank if they did not.

- Have children remove the snap cubes from their cups and link them together to create their own personal train.

- Repeat the simulation for Monday and Tuesday, recording on their chart and adding the cubes they receive to their cube trains.

Summarize (5–10 minutes)
- Debrief the simulation with the children, asking questions such as these:

    + *How did you feel when you did or did not get a cube?*

    + *How did it feel when there were multiple times you did or did not get a cube?*

    + *How did it feel to see someone not able to get a cube for their cup?*

Day 3

Launch (<5 minutes)
- Briefly review the previous day's work and ask for brief comments or questions.

Explore (20 minutes)
- Repeat the simulation with children, this time completing more days or a week or more (if time permits).

- Continue to ask questions related to number representation and identification.

- Continue to probe children about the social issue and idea of fairness in the simulation:

    + *Is it fair that you got a cube and someone else did not?*

    + *Is it fair that you did not get a cube and others did?*

- Invite children to share their cube trains with the group.

- Chorally count the cubes in each child's cube train, recording their name and their total on chart paper.

- Label each cube train with the associated child's name using an index card, tape, or a sticky note.

- Lay cube trains flat on the carpet adjacent to one another so that children can begin to visually see size differences. Ask children to share with a partner:

    + *What do you notice about the size of some of our cube trains?*

    + *Who has the longest train(s)?*

+ *Who has the shortest?*

- Have children share their noticings and ask something like this:

  + *Why might some cube trains be longer or shorter than others?*

- If appropriate, ask children to use number lines and number charts to locate the number of cubes in their cube train compared to a partner's to determine who had more and less through both indirect (by the size of the cube train) and direct (using a number line or chart) comparisons.

- Link the cube train comparisons back to food insecurity. Ask children a question such as this:

  + *Why might it be problematic that some people got fewer meals that others (as shown by those with shorted cube trains)?*

- Encourage children to link back to their understandings of why we need food from the building background conversation. Topics could include growing bodies and healthy development, alertness in school and other activities, and so on.

Children's Literature Suggestions

- *Maddie's Fridge* by Lois Brandt

- *Lulu and the Hunger Monster* by Erik Talkin

- *Uncle Willie and the Soup Kitchen* by DyAnne DiSalvo

- *The Ugly Vegetables* by Grace Lin

- *The Have a Good Day Café* by Francis Park and Ginger Park

Possible Lesson Extensions

Science and Mathematics

- Record observations of fresh vegetables versus canned when left at various temperatures. Chart observations over time.

- Examine the length of time it takes to prepare canned food versus fresh food. Graph and chart various foods and look for trends.

Art and Social Studies

- Examine maps of the area and locations of local food access. Determine where additional locations are needed. Draw, sculpt, and construct potential new food stores.

- Observe, draw, and sculpt food locations within the community. Use these to create a model of the community to display to stakeholders when advocating for more access to fresh produce.

TAKING ACTION

Suggestion 1

- Remind the children of the simulation and some of their responses to getting and not getting "meals" during it.

  + Attempt to use the words and language shared by the children as much as possible.

  + Invite children to reshare their ideas to the group around how it felt to not get a "meal" or have a cube train that was shorter than others due to lack of food.

- Share with children that there are organizations in our local community that help children and families who are food insecure, such as Feeding America.

- Pull up an organization's website and review it with the children. Ask them to generate questions based on what they see as well as what they learned so far. Record these questions on chart paper. Ask children to think about issues such as, "What might be some reasons families need to visit an organization like this beyond not having a grocery store near them?"

- Set up a videoconference call with an organization representative to provide a virtual tour of the facility and allow children to ask the questions they have generated. Record responses on the chart paper below the question for later reference. Be sure to ask the representative some of the reasons why families need to utilize the organization.

- After the call, review the response to the children's questions and think about ways in which you and the children in your class might help develop awareness around the issue.

- Children could also participate in a shared writing experience, where they contribute ideas and help with pieces such as punctuation, spelling of grade-level high-frequency and consonant-vowel-consonant words, while you do the formatting of the letter itself to the organization. The children then sign the letter and work with you to deliver it to the mail drop site on campus.

Suggestion 2

- Using their understanding of the number of children that are affected by food insecurity in their area, the children in your classroom can write to local and state representatives and encourage them to visit their area and learn more about the families impacted.

- Invite children to consider that there is a way you and the children in your class can encourage other people (e.g., their representatives) to visit the local Feeding America group. Explain that you and the children can write a letter to share what we learned through our project, simulation, and virtual tour with others.

- Ask children to share ideas for the letter. Ask questions such as these:

    + *How would we want to begin our letter?*

    + *What did we learn about being food insecure?*

    + *Who can restate what we did in our simulation?*

    + *What did you learn from our videoconference?* (if you completed Suggestion 1)

    + *Why is this a problem that needs to be addressed in our area?*

- In a shared writing experience, the children will share their ideas and you will form the words and letter. Record on chart paper or display on a screen for all children to see as the letter is composed.

    + Once complete, reread the letter and have the children sign their names. Send the letter to local representatives.

    + Share the letter on school social media pages and with families.

Suggestion 3

- Have children create informational posters and flyers to place around the school for various stakeholders to see when they visit the school. You can invite similar processes utilized to create the letter, with a focus on visually impactful works of art. Additionally, these flyers or posters can be featured on the school's social media pages. You can also work to have them shared on the district or university's social media or webpage.

COMMUNICATING WITH STAKEHOLDERS

Prior to the lesson, it is recommended that you communicate with your school director around the potential topic (food insecurity) that you would try with children. Sharing the idea and rationale for taking on this topic will also help you decide if it was a trauma-inducing discussion for the children in your class due to their personal connections with food insecurity in their homes. As you launch into the lesson, you can communicate information about the social justice topic and simulation to families through your school's preferred mode of communication. Follow-up items such as work samples, photographs, and final products can be shared with the broader school community, including your director and parents/caregivers.

ONLINE RESOURCE

 Available for download at **resources.corwin.com/ TMSJ-EarlyElementary**

▼ Worksheet 1: *Recording Sheet*

Recording Sheet

Day of the Week	Breakfast	Lunch	Dinner
Sunday			
Monday			
Tuesday			
Wednesday			
Thursday			
Friday			
Saturday			

BACKGROUND OF THE LESSON

Our classroom setting was composed of 3- and 4-year-old children from diverse backgrounds who were getting ready to enter the voluntary prekindergarten program in the fall (this work took place during the summer). Prior to this work, the children had been engaged in the creation of their own school garden and explored the location and number of community gardens nearby. From this work, the children learned of limited community gardens in our area and came to wonder about the ways in which people got fresh fruits and vegetables if they could not grow them or buy them from the local grocery store near campus, as well as what happened to the food they did not eat. This led to an inquiry into exploring what it means to lack access to food, food deserts in the area, and ways to take action against food insecurity.

In order to build my own understanding of these issues, I first needed to locate statistics about food insecurity for both our area and the state in general. I pulled up maps and looked for the location of various grocery stores (both chain and smaller, local grocers) to determine where areas of food insecurity were. I worked to develop a clear definition of a food desert for the children: a location where community members lack access to fresh and affordable food. I wanted for children to see that these areas did exist and that children, like themselves, were often impacted so that they could understand the issue in their community and take action against it. They should have a voice and feel empowered to have difficult conversations and challenge stereotypes about food access.

Based on the initial teaching of this lesson, I was able to make modifications to teach it in a multiage setting for kindergartners to second graders in a non-Title I setting. We extended our thinking about numbers to enact the simulation out across longer time spans, from 2 weeks up until 1 month. We were also able to reach out to additional food banks in our area that were lesser known and to hear their insight. This led to more comparisons of quantities as we explored the volume of donations various food banks in our area received and discussed why (ideas related to location in the community) these places were in areas of high or lower need as well as the national versus local view of the organization. Children in this group organized a schoolwide food drive for a smaller, local food pantry that served the local school by providing food for weekend backpacks and holidays. Some of the children in the group shared that they had used the services of this food pantry prior to the project as well and offered to share their experiences with food insecurity with our group.

ABOUT THE AUTHOR

 Jennifer Ward is a first-generation college student who was an early childhood and elementary school teacher. She is now a faculty member at Kennesaw State University in Georgia, focused on teaching early childhood mathematics methods. As part of this work, she encourages preservice teachers to find ways to address social (in)justice through their teaching of mathematics. She continues to work toward using mathematics to teach social justice as a result of experiences learning about the world of social justice mathematics in graduate school. She noticed a gap in early childhood and wanted to address it. Based on her experiences as an early childhood educator and mother of two young children, she knew that children had the capacity to engage in deep mathematical thinking along with complex conversations and ideas. She positions her work as a way to merge advocacy efforts with mathematics and help young children be able to share their voice loudly and strongly with adults, using mathematics as a means to do so.

- I know and like who I am and can talk about my family and myself and name some of my group identities. (Identity 1)

- I can describe some ways that I am similar to and different from people who share my identities and those who have other identities. (Diversity 7)

- I know everyone has feelings, and I want to get along with people who are similar to and different from me. (Diversity 9)

MATHEMATICS DOMAINS AND PRACTICES

- Geometry

- Construct viable arguments and critique the reasoning of others. (MP3)

CROSS-CURRICULAR CONNECTIONS

- Art

- Language Arts

LESSON 5.3 SAME AND DIFFERENT: AN EXPLORATION OF IDENTITY THROUGH GEOMETRY SHAPES

Heather Winters and Juan Manuel Gerardo

EXPLORING IDENTITY

Across this multiday lesson series, children discuss the importance of the "empathy, respect, understanding, and connection" the children and teachers have to each other in a diverse classroom, which aligns with the Learning for Justice Standards. As noted in Lesson 5.1 (*Exploring Fairness Through Data and Numbers*), cultivation of empathy is central to fostering community across diverse cultures, languages, traditions, and beliefs. Cultivating empathy aids in understanding and respecting differences, while also encouraging connections among different communities and identities. Therefore, in this lesson series, children are supported to note similarities, as well as differences, among and across children's social identities.

The exploration is mainly through polygons, sorting, categorizing, and comparing. You are encouraged to align the lesson to the geometry standards you are working with (for example, shape names, properties of different quadrilaterals). In this way, children engage in mathematical analysis drawing on mathematical argumentation as well as personal knowledge of self and others. Along the way, we emphasize having "pride, confidence, and healthy self-esteem" in who we are. By engaging children in conversations about diversity and identity, we hope to foster resilience and positive self-image in our children of Color as well as curiosity, understanding, and a positive self-image from white children.

DEEP AND RICH MATHEMATICS

In this lesson, similar to a lesson from Gerardo and Winters (2018), children will be able to identify and describe shapes (specifically the triangle, square, and circle). Children will also analyze and compare shapes. Children will have opportunities to describe, make claims, and justify their responses as they identify similarities and differences across shapes, as well as opportunities to create and compose shapes.

ABOUT THE LESSON

This is a 6-day lesson with an average of 45 minutes per lesson each day (time can vary). The first day serves as an introduction to shapes. The second day involves further exploration of geometric shapes. Days 3–5 discuss the topics of diversity, identity, and immigration (inclusion/exclusion) as well as scaffolding connections between these topics and geometry shapes. The sixth and last day is the culmination of the lesson with the construction of a Friendship Quilt.

Resources and Materials

Across the lesson series, the following materials will be utilized:

- Pattern blocks (per table) or other polygon tiles as appropriate to your grade level

- Teacher Resource 1: *Pattern Blocks Template* (available in English and Spanish)

- Stencils (per table)

- Mirrors for each child

- Flesh-colored crayons

- Slide deck that includes images of shapes (e.g., triangle, square, circle) and photographs of quilts and tapestries reflective of diverse cultures that have examples of geometric qualities

- Teacher Resource 2: *Shape Portrait Template* (triangle, circle, square) printed on 8 × 8 pieces of paper (available in English and Spanish)

- Teacher Resource 3: *Shape Portrait Examples*

- 5 × 5 pieces of paper (that could be used as a border for the Friendship Quilt)

- Poster paper and markers

- Books

  + *Shapes That Roll* by Karen Nagel

  + *Color Zoo* by Lois Ehlert

  + *I'm New Here* by Anne Sibley O'Brien

  + *I Am America* by Charles R. Smith, Jr.

  + *The All-Together Quilt* by Lizzy Rockwell

- *Optional:* Teacher Resource 4: *Example Letters to Stakeholders* (invitations for administrators/teachers, family members, and community members)

LESSON FACILITATION

Day 1

Launch (20 minutes)

- Begin by activating children's prior knowledge of shapes by showing a prepared slide deck of images of shapes.

- For example, show an image of a purple triangle, and ask questions such as these:

    + *Can someone describe this shape for me?*

    + *Can you tell me more?*

    + *Does someone else notice anything about the shape?*

- Ask various children to share their thoughts, and probe with clarifying questions so that the triangle's attributes are described. And if it has not been mentioned, ask:

    + *What do we call this shape?*

- You may also ask questions like these:

    + *Where have you seen this shape before?*

    + *Can you find this shape anywhere in our room?*

- Repeat this inquiry for a gray square and then a light gray circle.

- Finally, show the initial shapes in pairs. Ask the class to compare the triangle and square, then the triangle and circle, and then the square and circle. Ask questions about each pair, such as these:

    + *What do you notice about these shapes?*

    + *How are they the same?*

    + *How are they different?*

- Next, introduce the book *Shapes That Roll* by Karen Nagel. Explain to the children:

    + *As I read the story, I want you to pay attention to how circles, triangles, and squares come together to make different shapes and pictures.*

- As you read the book, stop to ask questions to check for understanding. Allow for opportunities for the children to make predictions, describe what they see, and review the names and attributes of the shapes on the pages.

- When finished, ask children to identify with and imagine themselves as one of the characters in the book. You may ask:

    + *Are you more like the Circle, the Triangle, or the Square?*

    + *Turn to a buddy and tell them why.*

- After they have had a chance to share, you may ask a few children to share with the whole group and discuss what they notice as similarities and differences they have with their classmates.

- **Note:** During this time, you may notice their creativity, but you should also encourage empathy as they think about themselves and others' ideas.

Explore (10 minutes)

- Since this is an introductory geometry lesson, have children explore pattern blocks at their tables (which include shapes other than those discussed).

- Encourage children to compare and contrast the shapes, to create new shapes, and to describe shapes. If children are not familiar with the shape names, you can support them by cueing them with the shape and color names. For example, you could say:

    + *Did anyone notice how all the yellow hexagons have six sides?*

    + *I see that three green triangles fit inside the red trapezoid.*

- Some prompts and questions you could ask children include the following:

    + *Tell me about your creation.*

    + *What are those shapes called?*

    + *How did you make that? Which shapes did you use?*

+ Why did you choose these shapes? Why did you not use other shapes?

Summarize (10 minutes)

- To end this lesson, ask children to share some ideas discussed during the lesson. (You can show the slide deck from the launch with images of the triangle, square, and circle and review attributes such as the number of sides, angles, and vertices.)

- You could end the lesson with a chant or song about shapes.

Day 2

Launch (15 minutes)

- Briefly review with the children the shapes that you discussed on Day 1 (circle, square, triangle, and other shapes in the pattern block set). Remind children to use terms such as *sides* and *vertices*.

- Tell the children that today they will be going on a Shape Tour in the classroom (and/or in the hallway or the playground). You may say:

  + *Shapes are all around us. Do you think we could find shapes in our classroom?*

  + *Let's spend the next 5 minutes moving around the classroom, looking for circles, squares, and triangles.*

- As the children identify shapes in the classroom, you can encourage them to compare and contrast these shapes. They may see that the clock is a circle. They might notice that the calendar is like a square, and the cubby is a square. You might ask: *How are they the same and different?*

- After the Shape Tour, reconvene as a group on the carpet.

- Introduce the book *Color Zoo* by Lois Ehlert. As you read the book with the children, ask what they notice about the animal portraits. Be sure to point out and discuss any new (unfamiliar) geometric vocabulary and highlight important attributes of the shapes (e.g., an octagon is a shape with eight straight sides and eight vertices).

Explore (15 minutes)

- Tell children that they will have an opportunity to create a whole-body portrait of themselves, perhaps doing a favorite activity, with pattern blocks, just as Lois Ehlert did in *Color Zoo*.

- **Note:** You may want to have a model of your own whole-body portrait using pattern blocks as an example.

- Give children time to create their whole-body portraits.

- As the children are creating portraits of themselves, encourage them to use geometric vocabulary (shape names, *sides*, *vertices*). You may ask:

  + *What shapes are you using?*

  + *Have you created new shapes?*

- Encourage children to talk at their tables and have them compare and contrast their portraits. You can suggest that they ask each other questions such as these:

  + *What are you doing in your portrait?*

  + *How is your portrait the same as mine? How is it different?*

  + *How many triangles did you use? Did you use more triangles than I did?*

- You may want to display photographs of their work in order to compare and contrast portraits as a whole class.

Summarize (10 minutes)

- To end this lesson, have children reconvene as a whole group and ask them to share what they learned during their exploration of pattern blocks. You may ask:

    + *How did you create your bodies?*

    + *What activities were you doing in your picture?*

    + *Why did you choose that activity?*

    + *What did you notice about your classmates' portraits?*

    + *Did any of your classmates choose the same activity as you?*

    + *What do you have in common? Did you notice any differences?*

- You can record the children's answers.

Day 3

Launch (15 minutes)

- Begin the lesson with all of the children together. Ask children to recall any of the shapes they have been learning about.

- Then show them the slide deck from the first day that includes the purple triangle, the gray square, and the light gray circle. Except this time, also include images of additional images of a different-sized triangle, square, and circle, and change the orientation of the new triangle and square.

- Similar to the previous days, ask children to describe, compare, and name the shapes. Some possible prompts and questions include:

    + *What do you notice about these shapes?*

    + *Let's compare and contrast these shapes: How are they the same? How are they different?*

    + *Look at the two triangles. The second triangle is rotated and a different size. Is it still the same shape? Why or why not?*

- With the children, define and list different types of attributes of the shapes (e.g., size, type, color, shape) and record them.

- Begin a discussion with the children about how people have different attributes too, just as shapes do. You may say something like:

    + *We also come in different shapes, sizes, and skin tones. Just as there are similarities and differences between shapes, there are similarities and differences between people.*

- Introduce the book *I Am America* by Charles R. Smith, Jr., and tell children to pay special attention to the children's attributes in the story.

- As you read the book, you may have children point out different attributes such as hair type and color, skin color, and eye color. After you finish, you may ask:

  + *What do you notice about the children in the book?*

  + *How are they the same and different?*

  + *Do you have any similarities and differences with the children in the book?*

  + *What do we have in common with these children? How are we different from them too?*

- **Note:** It may be important to note attributes that are not included in the book, whether or not they are in your classroom (e.g., children with physical disabilities, atheists), and to share with children that your classroom, your school and community, and our country have even more diversity than is included in the book.

Explore (15 minutes)

- To elicit a conversation about diversity, ask children:

  + *Why did the author, Charles R. Smith, Jr., include so many different kinds of children in his book* I Am America?

  + *What is diversity?*

  + *How does diversity help the United States?*

  + *How does diversity help our school?*

- To support the discussion, we may add something like:

  + *The United States is composed of all different kinds of people. The children in Smith's book look like our country.*

  + *Does our classroom look like our country? In what ways?*

  + *We have similarities and differences too. These make our country and our classroom more interesting. It's important to learn about different kinds of people.*

- Create a Diversity Poster with the children titled, "What Is Diversity? How Does Diversity Help Us?" Use their responses from the previous discussion to add to the poster. You may add some ideas such as these:

  + Learning about diversity can help us respect and celebrate the differences in all people.

  + Learning about different cultural aspects offers new experiences for us.

  + Diversity helps us realize that we're all humans, despite differences in how we look or dress or what we eat or celebrate.

Summarize (15 minutes)

- Have children get up and stretch if needed.

- Introduce and play the game *Sort and Guess the Attribute*. Say:

  I am going to choose several children who have the same attribute. You will guess which attribute I am sorting by and it will be something that is easily apparent (e.g., hair color, long-sleeve shirt, gym shoes, earrings, brown skin, short hair, blue eyes).

- Children can take turns sorting one another. A group of children may share more than one attribute.

- **Note:** It is important when playing this game that the "sorter" uses readily apparent attributes (e.g., hair color, long sleeves), and not assumed attributes (e.g., soccer skills, gender identity), in case children might not all have the same shared assumptions.

Day 4

Launch (10 minutes)

- Recall with children the previous day's activities and review a few images from the book *I Am America* (or create a slide deck of diverse children). You can say something like:

  + *We learned that just like shapes have different attributes, similarities, and differences, so do people.*

  + *Our different attributes are part of our identity. Our identity is who we are. We are going to draw our own portraits, paying close attention to our attributes.*

  + *We will proudly display our portraits as Charles R. Smith proudly displayed children from our country.*

Explore (30–40 minutes)

- Give each child a mirror so they may closely examine their face and their features.

- You should also have a mirror, and begin describing your own characteristics that you are observing: your eye color, skin color, hair color and style, and so on.

- Ask the children to do the same and to pay close attention to their facial features. Have them observe themselves and think quietly to themselves.

+ *Look carefully at your skin color. How would you describe it?*

+ *What about your hair color and texture? Is it straight or curly? Long or short?*

+ *What about your eyes? Look carefully at the shape and color.*

- After some time, you can ask children to share with a partner or ask some to share with the whole group.

- Be sure to emphasize the beauty in our differences, even the differences in our shades of skin color, eye color, style, and hair color. You can remind children:

  + *Like the photographs of the children in* I Am America, *our class too is a reflection of the school, city, state, and country; it's okay to be different and unique.*

- Probe children about how they feel about their self-image. Ask:

  + *What do you like about yourself?*

  + *What similarities and unique qualities do you notice about yourself?*

  + *What makes you special?*

- Next, introduce the Shape Portraits activity to children (refer to the *Shape Portrait Template* in the online resources).

- Still with the whole group, model how to begin your self-portrait by drawing, with a pencil, a large oval inside the shapes (square, circle, or triangle) of their choosing. This oval represents the child's head.

- Then show children how they might draw each part of their face and head, asking the children to name these parts (eyebrows, eyelashes, nostrils, lips, etc.) while emphasizing to the children that there is no one way to draw their self-portrait. Their Shape Portrait will be unique as they are unique.

- Model how to use the skin tone–colored crayons to color our skin. You may say:

  + *Maybe you can find a crayon that matches your skin tone or maybe your skin is a blend of colors.*

  + *Your eyes and hair may be a blend of colors too. Look closely at your attributes.*

- Next, say:

  + *Now you are going to have a chance to draw your own self-portrait.*

  + *Do you remember when we read the book* Shapes That Roll, *and you chose a shape that was most like you? Today you will choose one of those shapes to use as your frame for your Shape Portrait. Do you still want to use the shape you chose or do you want to choose another?*

- Allow children to choose any of the shapes—a circle, square, or triangle— that is "most like them" or their "favorite" shape. Assume that children will select different shapes, and encourage a variety of the three shapes if possible.

- Children should pick up the corresponding 8×8 square piece of paper with a large square, triangle, and circle printed on it. (This shape will serve as the frame for their portrait.)

- After getting the paper, they will use their mirror to begin drawing their portrait, paying close attention to their features (hair, eyes, nose, etc.). They will use skin tone–colored crayons to match themselves as closely as possible.

- You can assist them as necessary, asking questions and prompting them to describe their portrait and the choices they are making (skin tone, eye color, hair style), complimenting their efforts, and instilling a positive sense of self-image. You should be sensitive and thoughtful in your comments to make them feel comfortable with themselves (as sometimes can occur, children of Color might draw themselves with traditional white features).

Summarize (10 minutes)

- Either later in the day or immediately after completing their Shape Portrait, children can decorate the border of their Shape Portrait. You can encourage them to use geometry shape cutouts (or stencils). They can either be creative and make visually pleasing designs or you can suggest they make the shapes to reflect something special that reflects something from their culture, family, or home. For example, a teacher sample might include a circle representing the Aztec Calendar (sketch), an oval as a calavera (skull representing Día de los Muertos, or the Day of the Dead), or rectangles to represent paint brushes and writing utensils.

- Depending on time, you can briefly revisit shapes by sharing, describing, and comparing the Shape Portraits. Children could also listen to an online video of Charles R. Smith, Jr. read his book *I Am America*.

Day 5

Launch (15 minutes)

- Begin by rereading the Diversity Poster as a class. You may start by saying:

  + *Our country is composed of all kinds of people from many countries and cultures who speak many different languages.*

- Entertain any connections to the past few days with children.

- Introduce and read the book *I'm New Here*, by Anne Sibley O'Brien.

Explore (20 minutes)

- Pose the following scenario for the children to consider about when they may have felt excluded and/or included:

Source: JackF/iStock.com

One day when I was watching the kids on the playground, I saw a group of kids talking about a new child named Selma. She was new to our school and didn't know much English. She was all by herself and looked very lonely. I saw that group of kindergartners point at Selma and say, "That new kid is weird. She can't speak English. Don't ask her to play!"

- Next, facilitate a conversation.

    + *What do you think about that?*

    + *Why do you think that group of children wouldn't include Selma?*

    + *How would that make you feel?*

    + *Those children "excluded" Selma.* [show gesture of pushing away]

    + *They did not "include" her.* [show gesture of pulling toward self]

    + *What would you do if you saw a new child at our school who was so sad and lonely?*

- You can create a Friendship Inclusion Poster to display in your classroom by recording answers to questions and prompts such as these (and anything discussed above):

    + *How would you include that child?*

    + *What could you do to make the child feel welcome?*

Summarize (10 minutes)

- Ask children to notice how they are playing at recess that day (or the next) and to include someone at recess. You may say something like,

    + *Remember how the new children felt in* I'm New Here? *Keep your eye open for someone who looks lonely or may feel excluded. What can you do to include that person?*

- After recess, revisit the poster and have children share how they included someone. The class can add to the Friendship Inclusion Poster throughout the year.

Day 6

Launch (15 minutes)

- Begin by asking the whole group:

  + *Who knows what a quilt is? Who can describe a quilt?*

- After a brief discussion, show a slide deck of images of bedding and blankets that are reflective of diverse cultures, emphasizing geometry (patterns, shapes, symmetry, tessellations, etc.)

Source: Rebecca Burnett/flickr.com

- Ask children to describe what they notice and how they call these things/concepts (quilt, shape, color) at home and/or in their home language and culture. You can record these new words on the board so that all children see and understand this discourse.

- Introduce and read the story *The All-Together Quilt* by Lizzy Rockwell by saying something like:

  + *This is based on a true story in which a community came together to create a quilt. We are a community, and we will create our own quilt with our Shape Portraits after we read the story.*

Explore (20 minutes)

- Tell children that they will now be creating a Friendship Quilt with their Shape Portraits. You can emphasize that the Friendship Quilt will be special because it will include everyone in the class.

- Develop a way to choose children to participate in the creation of the quilt, using some sort of random process (e.g., choosing names out of a hat) so that all children can be included and don't feel left out.

- You can model the process by choosing a name and saying:

  + *I'd like to include you in our Friendship Quilt.*

- That child will tape or glue their Shape Portrait somewhere on the butcher paper/Friendship Quilt. That child will then randomly choose another child and invite them to place their Shape Portrait on the Friendship Quilt. This process continues until everyone is "included."

- As you accompany the child to the Friendship Quilt to place their Shape Portrait, you can support them and ask them about its position. For example:

  + *Why did you choose to place your portrait there?*

  + *Who is to the left (or the right) of you?*

  + *Who is above you or below you?*

- You can also have your own Shape Portrait in case there is an odd number of children, and include other adults (the principal or other teachers if necessary).

- As children are assembling the Friendship Quilt, the other children will be given new 5 × 5 sheets of paper and tangrams or shape stencils to create their own new quilt square(s). You can have a slide deck of quilt patterns with interesting geometric designs that children can use as an inspiration or a resource. For additional inspiration, children can refer to the designs included in *The All-Together Quilt* book. Children can create several squares until all children have their portrait in the Friendship Quilt. The 5 × 5 quilt squares can then be added to the border of the Friendship Quilt.

Source: Parker Felton-Koestler

Summarize (10 minutes)

- Once everyone has placed their Shape Portrait, and the Friendship Quilt is taped/secured so you can display it on the wall, ask the children to sit together to observe and analyze it. Ask questions such as these:

    + *What do you notice?*

    + *What is the same?*

    + *What is different?*

    + *How does our quilt show friendship?*

- You can highlight the importance of including everyone in the class, with everyone's unique identity, and highlight notions of similarities and differences.

- You should discuss with children that it's okay to be different, but it is also important to include others and not exclude anyone (and remind them how that makes one feel when they are left out). You may say:

    + *We all have similarities and things we have in common. We all have differences that make us unique. Differences make the world more interesting. We can learn from someone who is different from us. We can also share our differences with others.*

- If, by chance, many children design similar portraits, acknowledge the similarities, and yet recognize the unique features each portrait has (placement of shapes, color, shading, etc.). It is important that children are able to attend to their unique features and, guided by the teacher to proudly do so, that the portraits will reflect the diversity of the class.

- Before concluding the lesson, highlight the idea of diversity. Say something like this (and have children share their thoughts):

  + *Our Friendship Quilt is an example of how beautiful we are together and of how diverse we are as a class.*

  + *Let's invite the school to see our Friendship Quilt. Perhaps we will inspire and teach people to be kind to others, to be good to and proud of themselves, and to include others who might be different from themselves.*

  + *This Friendship Quilt is a celebration of diversity. What do you think diversity means?*

TAKING ACTION

- Host a Community/Family Diversity Night. Have children discuss their Friendship Quilt, and share the books and/or topics explored in class. Invite family members and community members to contribute to the Friendship Quilt.

- Ask a local art gallery to display the Friendship Quilt. Again, host an afternoon with teachers, parents/caregivers, and community members. Read some of the books read in class, and ask children to talk about the construction and elements of the Friendship Quilt. Again, ask community members to contribute to the Friendship Quilt.

- Similarly, a local library can display your Friendship Quilt and host a family/community discussion about your project.

- You could approach your district office to also display your Friendship Quilt and host a family/community discussion about your project.

- Write letters and send photographs of the Friendship Quilt to UNICEF, and ask for ways that the children can engage in conversations of diversity with international children in support of international efforts to meet the needs (education, health, housing) of children around the world.

- Similarly, write letters and send images of the Friendship Quilt to local and state government officials, if diversity is under threat in your area.

- Establish pen pals (e.g., videos, drawings, dictation and/or writing) through online communication with other schools in the United States and/or internationally, and engage in conversations about diversity, identity, similarities, and differences in a cross-cultural and/or international context.

- You may also choose to use this exploration as a springboard into better understanding the importance of voting. If it is an election year or close to an election cycle, a suggestion can be made to parents/caregivers and community members to vote. No particular candidate will be supported, but the children may ask family members and community members to consider candidates who express support for policies that are supportive of immigrants, refugees, and underserved populations.

COMMUNICATING WITH STAKEHOLDERS

- Communicate with the principal and other administrators regarding this social justice geometry lesson. Extend an invitation for them to participate and/or observe the children exploring mathematics as well as social justice discussion.

- Communicate with colleagues at your school. Extend the invitation to teach the lesson to their respective classrooms or at least extend an invitation to contribute to the quilt that is the culminating activity. Perhaps this can be an opportunity to engage them in discussing geometry as well as issues of identity and diversity.

- Communicate with parents/caregivers and family members. Invite them to participate during the lesson or, at least, to help construct the quilt so that they may contribute and engage in the discussion of the geometry concepts as well as the topics of identity and diversity.

ONLINE RESOURCES

 Available for download at **resources.corwin.com/TMSJ-EarlyElementary**

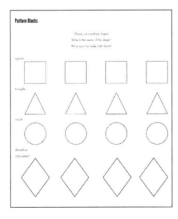

▲ Teacher Resource 1: Pattern Blocks (in English and Spanish)

▲ Teacher Resource 2: Shape Portrait Templates (in English and Spanish)

(Continued)

Online Resources (*Continued*)

▲
Teacher Resource 3: Shape
Portrait Examples

▲
Teacher Resource 4: Example
Letters to Stakeholders

BACKGROUND OF THE LESSON

Heather and Juan Manuel had presented at a conference and even developed and taught a review geometry lesson where they connected the concepts of geometric shapes to the experiences of immigrant students. They integrated Juan's commitment to social justice and mathematics education as well as Heather's passion for valuing the identity of her kindergarten students and being responsive to their educational needs.

While teaching the lesson, Juan Manuel experienced challenges maintaining the students' attention and was recommended by the mathematics coach to probe student thinking more often, and he witnessed Heather's expertise for transitions and engaging students. They felt satisfied with the lesson but realized that they could have probed students' thinking, as was recommended, as well as discussed concepts of diversity and social justice more explicitly. The current lesson was an opportunity to build on that lesson and address what they felt were its limitations. This lesson also increases the rigor of the geometry concepts as well as deepens the connection of the lesson to issues of identity and diversity. For Juan Manuel, developing this lesson was a good reminder to not underestimate young students and their mathematics understanding as well as to acknowledge their stances regarding social justice. Heather believes that it is essential for young children to develop a sense of identity and connection to and understanding of others in authentic, meaningful ways. She firmly believes that young children are the foundation for a healthy, inclusive society.

We want to express our heartfelt gratitude and appreciation to the kindergarten teachers at Barkstall Elementary in Champaign, Illinois, who helped pilot this lesson and provided valuable feedback. Thank you to Amanda Bila, Jami Spencer-Tanner, and Susan Thompson and your students.

ABOUT THE AUTHORS

Heather Winters is a white cisgender woman and a veteran elementary school teacher. She has over 20 years of teaching experience, most of those years as a kindergarten teacher at an ethnically and linguistically diverse school. She is currently a multilingual teacher supporting multilingual learners at Barkstall Elementary School in Champaign, Illinois. Early in her teaching career, Heather observed that a significant number of Black kindergarten girls drew themselves as blond, white girls. She decided to strive to help these girls and all her students see themselves as they truly are and to be proud of themselves. This endeavor included using art, music, and building a classroom library that reflects her students. Her students engage in self-awareness activities such as the one presented here.

Juan Manuel Gerardo, PhD, is a Chicanx cisgender man and currently a visiting assistant professor at the University of Cincinnati Department of Middle Childhood Education. Juan Manuel was undocumented and is from a working class immigrant family from México. His research focus is on understanding how mathematics educators reject the traditional teacher–student dynamic and engage in mathematical sensemaking with students in formal and informal settings. As a mathematics teacher educator, he engages preservice teachers to develop a political stance and sensibilities to advocate for minoritized students, particularly bilingual, immigrant (possibly undocumented) students.

- I see that the way my family and I do things is both the same as and different from how other people do things, and I am interested in both. (Identity 3)

- I know that life is easier for some people and harder for others and the reasons for that are not always fair (Justice 14)

MATHEMATICS DOMAINS AND PRACTICES

- Number and Operations

- Measurement

- Data Collection and Analysis

- Make sense of problems and persevere in solving them. (MP1)

- Construct viable arguments and critique the reasoning of others. (MP3)

- Model with mathematics. (MP4)

CROSS-CURRICULAR CONNECTIONS

- Language Arts

- Science

- Social Studies

LESSON 5.4 EXAMINING AIR QUALITY

Maria del Rosario Zavala

AIR QUALITY

In November of 2019, schools all over California were learning to deal with a new and dangerous season: smoke season. While California is no stranger to wildfires, the amount and size of the fires that arose in the 2019 fall season, when California is at its driest, created the new phenomenon of air so unhealthy that health experts started issuing guidelines for children to stay inside. "Spare the air" days, which are days where the air quality is so unhealthy that it's recommended to not engage in strenuous exercise, gave way to "stay inside" days. Most San Francisco Bay Area schools were built for the mild climate that was the norm in the mid-20th century: large outdoor play areas, classrooms that are connected by exterior hallways, and, perhaps most problematic, no central air systems and many older or portable buildings with no air conditioning.

When the first unhealthy air day was announced, children suddenly were inside during recess. Teachers were asked to keep windows and doors closed to limit poor-quality air coming inside, which only led to further issues. Understandably, kids were looking at the window and seeing no rain, and wondering why they needed to stay inside for recess on sunny days. This lesson is designed to help children explore what air quality measurements systems are, and how they relate to whether air is safe to breathe or not. While this lesson does not go extensively into the science of measuring air quality, it could be a springboard into those kinds of questions.

DEEP AND RICH MATHEMATICS

The mathematics in this lesson are meant to support number concepts central to kindergarten. Many children in kindergarten are learning numerals, number names, and rote counting by ones. They are making sense of quantities and how our number system is ordered, exploring ideas like how the more digits a whole number has, the bigger it is. Alongside this, they are reasoning about the meaning of amounts and are learning concepts to compare numbers such as "more than" and "fewer than."

More than the particular concepts of number, a central goal of the lesson is to help the children connect numbers to the world outside. The very idea that we can and *do* measure things like particles in the air through some kind of scale is a mathematical goal in this lesson. This lesson is intended to help plant a seed to continue talking about air quality at home, to have some sense of why it's measured, and to show how the number that is measured impacts how we choose to act.

ABOUT THE LESSON

The lesson is introduced in 1 day, but ideas can be revisited in subsequent days. The lesson intentionally has variation in structures for participation: whole group, small group, and then whole group again. Depending on what kinds of resources you have (e.g., a projector), you may need to gather printed-out materials the day prior to the lesson, including large-format images of different regions of the world with varying air quality. You should make the materials easily accessible for all children at their table groups. (Examples of maps are listed in the *Resources and Materials*.)

This lesson can be done in 1 day, over an approximately 45-minute chunk of time. While this lesson highlights specific locations near the school, teachers could modify these locations to include those relevant to the children in their particular context.

Although this lesson was designed for and taught in a kindergarten classroom, it would be appropriate for preschool and primary classrooms. Additional adaptions could be made for other grades, including higher education methods coursework. One suggested extension for older children is included after the lesson flow.

Resources and Materials

For the lesson, you need the following:

- Maps of relevant locations with varying air quality. One good source is PurpleAir (https://www2.purpleair.com), especially on days when local areas have poor air quality. Therefore, you may need to plan ahead and collect images of maps from days that are of interest because of the range of air quality. Otherwise, you can search AirNow's archival data and see if you can find relevant map data (https://www.airnow.gov/).

- Teacher Resource 1: *Maps for Exploring Air Quality*. This resource provides an example of the different ways two sites show data and the maps described in the lesson.

    + The images utilized when this lesson was initially designed, and therefore recommended as a starting point, are as follows:

        - Lake Tahoe, California, because many children go there with families in summer and winter, with really good air (green dots);

        - New Delhi, India, which is the city with the distinction of the worst air quality on average (dark purple dots);

        - The entire state of California, which has a variety of dot colors, given the fires; and

        - The school with a two-block radius to include a few sensors, with a variety of dots ranging from green to dark orange.

The following may be helpful too:

- A large image of an air quality table (see Teacher Resource 2: *Three Ways to Display How Air Quality Is Measured*)

- Air quality "number line" meter

- Small stickers for children to predict air quality on the meter

- Teacher Resource 3: *Sample Family Letter on Supporting Children to Keep Exploring Air Quality*

Prior to teaching the lesson, here are suggested resources to develop background knowledge on air quality for yourself.

- Article: "Study finds wildfire smoke more harmful to humans than pollution from cars," NPR (https://n.pr/3d6Gr5c)

- Article: "Long wildfire seasons also mean extended periods of dangerous air quality," NPR (https://n.pr/3rqxax0)

- Radio story: "Smoky air from wildfires impacting parts of California differently," KQED (https://bit.ly/3pdt7S6) [Smoke story starts at 5 minutes]

- Website: California Air Resource Board, "Children's Environmental Health Protection Program" (https://bit.ly/3odWpAX)

LESSON FACILITATION

Launch (5 minutes)

Introduction to the Maps

Call children over to sit on the rug in spots or in rows. Show a map of California (or the state in which the class is located). The goal of the launch is to establish that the class is looking at maps that show them air quality readings.

- Show the map of the whole state of California, and ask children if they know what this is. Give children some time to observe the map and point out what they notice about it. Ask questions to facilitate exploration, and ask children to listen and respond to what other children say. Support them in making connections to the numbers and colors on the map.

    + Ask questions such as these:

    + *What does the map show?*

    + *What colors do you see?*

    + *What numbers do you see?*

    + *What do you think different numbers and colors mean?*

    + *Is this a big number?*

    + *And it means what?*

    + *Why are we reading this map?*

    + *What does it help us see?*

    + *Could we just go by the color, or does knowing the number help too?*

- Elicit connections between the map and air quality through a brief discussion about air quality, and why we would measure it.

    + Ask: *What does air quality tell us? How have we been affected by air quality lately?*

- Next, have children transition to their seats to explore the maps in small groups.

Explore (approximately 10 minutes)

Children Explore the Maps in Small Groups at Their Tables

Let students know that each table group is going to get a map, and one table group will get the map you have all just been looking at. Directions can be given while children are still in the whole group.

- One group should get the map being viewed in the launch, another group should receive a map from their local neighborhood, one of New Delhi, and other locations as determined by the local school context. Some of these maps should include locations children are familiar with (in this case, Lake Tahoe).

- At their table groups, children will repeat what they did in the introduction: look at the map, and take turns noticing and wondering.

  + *I see . . .*

  + *I know that . . .*

  + *I wonder if . . .*

Tell them you will circulate and listen to what they are noticing and wondering. It's important to let go here and listen to what children are noticing. That is the priority right now, to privilege students' observations and validate their contributions.

- You can circulate and help make connections to their maps. For example, say: *This is a map of Lake Tahoe. Have any of you been to Lake Tahoe? What do you go there to do? I see green dots with numbers around the lake. What do you think that means?*

- Ask follow-up questions to what students are noticing. Help students read aloud large numbers, if students are not sure how to say them. For example, ask: *What do you think different numbers and colors mean? Is this a big number? What is it counting? I'll read this number for us just in case: three hundred twenty-four. Does that sound like a high or a low number?*

- Prompt students to share different ideas when you return to the rug. It might sound like this: *Can I ask you to share that idea, Simone? You just said, "There's only small numbers like 5 and 6 on our map." Will you share that when we get back to the rug?*

Connect (15 minutes)

Children Make Comparisons Across Maps

Have children come back to the rug, this time in a circle. Put all maps in the middle of the circle, along with an air quality table.

- This time should be carefully structured so children are listening to each other. You might also prompt children to look at and speak to each other, not just you as the teacher. This helps facilitate how the conversation is happening between all of us, not just individual child to teacher.

- Prompt a representative from each group to share a key thing their group noticed, one by one. After each group shares, contrast the two maps with the most extreme measures (in this case, Lake Tahoe and New Delhi; the Lake Tahoe example may change based on the location of context of the lesson).

- Ask children if they think these two places have very different air qualities. For example, ask: *Which place would have been safer to be outside without a special mask for breathing? How do we know?*

From here, support children to make sense of the map of their neighborhood. Hold up the map of the neighborhood around the school and revoice the observations of the group that had this map.

- Facilitate a discussion about how different families are managing with changing air quality. Ask: *Did you go outside yesterday? Did you take precautions?* Students can share their experiences, listen to each other's activities, and notice similarities and differences in how families adjust for changing air quality.

Summarize (5–10 minutes)

Students Take a Position and Support It With Evidence

Tell children that they can use all of this new information to make a decision about whether they can go outside. The teacher holds up the air quality map of the area surrounding the school. In this case, the monitors are giving us different readings, but the principal of the school has to make a decision. The goal of this time is to connect it to the local context. If the decision were up to children, using the information we have, would they declare this an indoor or outdoor recess day?

- Ask children to think, *Do you think the air is mostly good, mostly moderate, or mostly unhealthy? Should we stay inside for recess? Why or why not?*

    + Children may not use the data presented to draw their conclusions. Be ready to prompt them to think about the color of the dots on the map and the size of the numbers.

- Ask for several volunteers to place stickers on the "air quality number line" where they think today is best represented. Ask them to share why they placed it there and why.

    + Once a few children have shared ideas, you can close the lesson by reminding them to listen over the next few days for when people are talking about air quality on the news and with their families, and think about the numbers behind the colors.

    + Alternatively, you can ask pairs of students to discuss and decide. The goal here is not for children to decide whether they are right or wrong, but rather to use ideas of air quality in how they decide. You should be ready to listen carefully and prompt children to make connections back to what the map around our school tells us about air quality.

- Share with children: *When you are outside and smell smoke, or see a lot of gray haze, you can ask the adults in your lives to help you look up the air quality to make decisions about going outside.*

You can play the 5-minute KQED radio story on the different impacts of smoke across California (https://bit.ly/3pdt7S6; the smoke story starts at 5 minutes). Ask the children to write down any numbers they hear, noting the following:

+ *What number did you hear?*

+ *What did it mean?* (for example, *I heard 1 month. She said that's the amount of smoke days people experience in a year now.*)

+ *Why would they include that number in the news story?*

This activity is another way to help students connect mathematics to the world around them and to see how numbers and quantities are utilized to communicate information, such as information about the air we breathe.

TAKING ACTION

Suggestions

Individual and Class
The suggested action would be for students to talk about air quality with their parents, to listen at home for when air quality was being talked about on the news, and to have more context for when recess is indoors. The lesson can also serve as part of ongoing conversations about air quality in relation to environmental justice, which could be a thematic unit the children study as some part of the school year.

Local Community, Organizers, and Organizations
Work with local agencies to explore what community/local efforts are happening to study and improve air quality. Share these ideas with school and home communities. Support the school, children, and families in partnering with these agencies.

COMMUNICATING WITH STAKEHOLDERS

Families
Send home a note to parents/caregivers on what the class had talked about and encourage their conversations with their children about the impacts of air quality on our health and why it's important to pay attention to air quality. See the suggested text in the *Resources and Materials* for this lesson.

- Either before or after the lesson, you can reach out to classroom parents and request that they ask their children what they did with air quality maps at school that day. Parents can ask children what they noticed on the maps, what other people said, and then if they have any questions. In this way, parents are supporting the students to notice, wonder, and ask and answer questions. They are cultivating their students' curiosity as well as supporting key mathematics and science practices about asking questions and engaging in problem solving. An example letter is provided in the online resources (Teacher Resource 3).

Other School/District Personnel

- Create posters to put around the school about why recess is sometimes indoors. Younger children might pair with older children to make them.

- Create an air quality monitor and incorporate it into daily calendar routine for a month or so following the lesson. Teachers can make a bar graph and retrieve the measurement from nearby monitors on PurpleAir (https://www2.purpleair.com), either on a laptop or their phones, and children could fill in the bar graph for the right range. It may be sufficient for the teacher to include just the first four categories and make the fourth one a catch-all for any reading over 151. It should also be anticipated that we have all good or mostly good days, with some moderate days, which would still have mathematical value.

ONLINE RESOURCES

 Available for download at **resources.corwin.com/TMSJ-EarlyElementary**

▼ Teacher Resource 1: Maps for Exploring Air Quality

▼ Teacher Resource 2: Three Ways to Display How Air Quality Is Measured

▼ Teacher Resource 3: Sample Family Letter on Supporting Children to Keep Exploring Air Quality

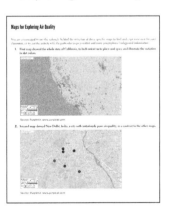

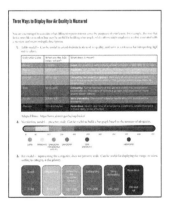

BACKGROUND OF THE LESSON

As residents of California will tell you, we have had "spare the air" days as long as we can remember—days when the state's air quality board would send out announcements to our radio stations to tell people not to exercise too strenuously or burn unnecessary fires if they weren't needed for heat or cooking. Spare the air days are a result of taking a scientific approach to the smog and smoke that are part of living in our state. However, even as clean-air vehicle initiatives have been successful and industrial pollution has declined in California, we have seen a rise in wildfires. This rise has led to an increase in poor air quality days, and fears for children's health should they breathe the cancerous particulates released during wildfires, especially fires that burn toxic materials used in housing. This is also to say nothing of the families who lose their homes to wildfires, and the trauma left in the wake. In my community in Oakland, California, a community that remembers a devastating fire in the Oakland hills in 1991, children are growing up with multiple days out of the year in which they are kept inside or kept home from school due to poor air quality. This is exacerbated by the COVID-19 pandemic, as protocols require children to eat lunch outside because there is less possibility of COVID transmission, but there is still the possibility of poor air quality.

When this lesson was developed, it was prior to the start of COVID, but not much. My son was a kindergartener and I was volunteering in his class. There were 2 days in a row that children were not allowed outside for recess, and it was frustrating for both the adults and kids. I asked the teacher if I might do a lesson on air quality to help children understand that even if they couldn't *see* why they couldn't go outside, there was a reason. The air quality lesson was developed as a result of me virtually spanning the globe through the PurpleAir.com map and looking for places where we could contrast the air quality. With the visual anchors of the maps, the rest of the lesson fell into place.

When I did this lesson with the kindergarteners, it was November of the school year. The lesson was launched in a whole-group setting with noticing and wondering about the map of California. After a few minutes of sharing what they noticed and wondered and establishing that this was a map of the state of California and that it had different-colored dots, the children were dismissed to their table groups to pore over one of the maps and prepare to report back on what they saw on their map. What color dots were there? What numbers? What do they think the dots and numbers mean? Most students thought the numbers were street addresses.

After a few minutes in small groups, they returned to the rug. A representative from each group shared their noticings. The table for air quality and concept of air quality was explicitly introduced at that point. We focused on the contrast between the Lake Tahoe map (great air quality, low number also indicated by green) and our school map (not great air quality, in the low hundreds, indicating harmful for sensitive groups). We spent the last few minutes trying to decide if the map of our area meant we should or should not go out for recess. Finally, students were reminded to talk with their parents about air quality, listen to the news for when air quality was talked about, and know that there are numbers behind how we decide that air is good or bad to breathe.

ABOUT THE AUTHOR

 **Maria del Rosario Zavala, PhD,** is an associate professor of elementary education at San Francisco State University, with a focus on culturally responsive mathematics teaching, mathematics identity development, and bilingual education. She had various roles in education spanning K–12 schooling prior to her role at SFSU, and she continues to work in classrooms whenever she has the chance. In terms of social justice, she gives credit to her college professor at the University of California, Santa Cruz, Dr. Julia Aguirre, whose class she took as an undergraduate mathematics major. This course helped her to call out and start to really wonder about inequities in mathematics education and to make sense of her own experiences as a bilingual Latina woman. She views the teaching of mathematics as open to creativity, with limitless opportunity to connect to issues that impact children's communities and lives.

SOCIAL JUSTICE OUTCOMES

- I like being around people who are like me and different from me, and I can be friendly to everyone. (Diversity 6)

- I can describe some ways that I am similar to and different from people who share my identities and those who have other identities. (Diversity 7)

- I want to know about other people and how our lives and experiences are the same and different. (Diversity 8)

MATHEMATICS DOMAINS AND PRACTICES

- Number and Operations

- Measurement

- Data Collection and Analysis

- Make sense of problems and persevere in solving them. (MP1)

- Reason abstractly and quantitatively. (MP2)

CROSS-CURRICULAR CONNECTIONS

- Language Arts

- Art

LESSON 5.5 FAMILY COUNTS! MATHEMATICS, FAMILY, AND THE DIVERSITY ACROSS OUR HOMES

JaNay Brown-Wood

FAMILY DIVERSITY

This multiday classroom activity focuses on building a classroom community, ensuring that everyone feels as if their voice matters, that their family members matter, and that they matter. The goal is to cultivate a community of caring individuals, modeling how to build relationships with those who are similar and different, with the hope that children will continue these practices outside of the classroom. Further, since children have family members or people who are integral within their lives, this classroom activity intends to give children a common ground to start from. They can consider who their family members and loved ones are that live at home, and then begin comparing their experiences with the other children in their classroom. Subsequently, you can use these activities to draw parallels between what children share regarding families and utilize this to set the stage for highlighting that each child is a part of a classroom family, cultivating care and community within the four walls of the classroom. Building connections across children with differing backgrounds can then help to tear down walls that might exist due to differences, ultimately nurturing caring relationships, connection, empathy, and respect.

This lesson gives children the opportunity to consider who makes up families, who are the important people in our lives and homes, and how much variation (and similarity) can exist. This activity then segues seamlessly into a discussion about how the classroom is also like a family, ultimately setting the grounds for a caring classroom community and respectful connections with those who are both similar to and different from each other—as well as emphasizing how beautiful diversity really is! Although we list kindergarten standards, this lesson would be appropriate in any early childhood or elementary classroom.

DEEP AND RICH MATHEMATICS

This lesson engages children with data concepts and statistical thinking. Specifically, children reflect on their own homes and families to consider who is a part of their families and how many people live with them. Doing so gives them opportunities to count (family members in their homes, family members based on classmate experiences, family members in a text) and make comparisons about family size (big, medium, small) and across classmates (number of family members at home). This activity also covers graphical representations as you and the children in your classroom work together to capture data concepts graphically (pictures, bar graph, etc.) and consider ideas about the data. Furthermore, this lesson integrates mathematical concepts with literature and provides opportunities for children to engage in speaking and listening tasks with classmates and as a whole class—thus empowering them mathematically and in other disciplines as well.

ABOUT THE LESSON

Family Counts! is a multiday activity that can span 3–4 days and be separated into four parts. Each part will take about 40–45 minutes. Day 1 will introduce a discussion of families and individual household sizes. On Day 2, you will review household sizes, then read a family-centered counting book, followed by counting and classifying family members and friends from the book. Day 3 will provide children an opportunity to work in groups to practice counting, categorizing, and comparing. Finally, Day 4 will give children a chance to analyze their own families, compare with a partner, and work with you to represent data graphically and then consider the diversity in their own "Our Big Class Family" representation.

Resources and Materials

- Book: *Grandma's Tiny House: A Counting Story!* by JaNay Brown-Wood

- Worksheet 1: *Family Member Cutouts* (1 per child, several for teacher)

- Worksheet 2: *How Many Family Members and Friends in Grandma's Tiny House?* (1 per group)

- Worksheet 3: *Family at Home* (1 per child)

- Large poster paper titled "How Many Family Members and Friends in Grandma's Tiny House?" with boxes labeled based on family members and friends

- Large piece of butcher block paper to create "Our Big Class Family" poster

- Plastic sandwich bag labeled with each child's name or paperclip and label (1 per child)

- Pair of scissors for each child

- Markers, color pencils, or crayons to color

- Pencils for worksheets

Optional

- Weeks prior to the lesson series, you might solicit a family photo or drawing from parents and caregivers, to hang on the wall while you explore family structure. This visual anchor can help children start to see the various ways family is defined across their classroom community.

LESSON FACILITATION

Day 1: What Is a Family?

Launch (10 minutes)

- Sitting together, begin by saying that this week we will talk about family.

- Prompt children with questions such as these:

  + *What is a family?*

  + *Who is a part of our families?*

- Allow children to discuss, making sure they have broad and open conceptions of families to be inclusive of all kinds of families, especially of children's families in your classroom and beyond. Be sure to include loved ones who are close to be included as family.

- Discuss sizes that families can come in, including big, small, and medium, and how these might be relative depending on what you are used to. If you took the option to invite families to bring in photos, you can reference the photos for this part as well.

- Explain how for today's activity, we will consider sizes based on who lives in our home. It is important to note that children may have more than one home (e.g., those who have divorced parents, those who sometimes live with their grandparents, those who live with foster parents). It is very important to be supportive and inclusive to children especially, but for all children to know that all kinds of families and all kinds of homes are valid and valuable. For the activity today, you will need to come up with working definitions of different sized families. Together with children, come up with class definitions. You can write these categories on the board or on a poster to refer to later and throughout the lesson. Here is an example:

+ Small Family: 2–3 family members at home

+ Medium Family: 3–6 family members at home

+ Big Family: 7+ family members at home

Explore (25 minutes)

- Begin by having children return to their seats.

- Next, let them know that we are going to think about who is in our family and which family members live in our homes. (Again, be mindful of those children who may have more than one home. For this next part, if they want to focus on more than one of their homes, that's fine; or they can choose to focus on one.) Be sure to use the word "home" to be inclusive of those who may not live in actual houses.

- In pairs, have children discuss:

  + *Who is in your family?*

  + *What are their names and who are they (Mama, Abuela, Pop, etc.)?*

  + *Which of those family members live in your home?*

- Next, give each child Worksheet 1 (*Family Member Cutouts*) or a sheet of blank paper. Each child will color pictures of their family members who live in their homes. Children should also include themselves. After coloring, children will use the scissors to cut out the members of their family.

- Have them put each cutout in a bag or paperclip them together, labeling them with the children's names.

- Collect each child's work and save them for Day 4.

Summarize (5 minutes)

- Ask a few children to raise their hands and share someone from their home that they colored today.

- Let the children know we will continue thinking about families again tomorrow.

- **Note:** In preparation for Day 2, you should color people from Worksheet 1 to match each family member from the *Grandma's Tiny House* book. These family cutouts will be used as a model for the children.

Day 2: Counting Grandma's Family and Friends

Launch (5 minutes)

- Sitting together, begin by having the children reflect on what they talked about yesterday (families and different sizes) and what they did yesterday (colored family members who live at home with them).

- Remind them of the sizes we discussed (big, medium, small). Have them share with a partner which size they think their family is (big, medium, small) and how they know (they counted, etc.).

- Now have children turn to another partner and do the same thing.

- Ask the children questions such as these:

  + *Did you notice any differences between your family size and your partners' families?*

  + *Did you notice any similarities?*

  + *Who has a small family? Big? Medium?*

- Discuss again how families can come in all sizes and kinds.

Explore (30 minutes)

- Pull out *Grandma's Tiny House* and introduce children to the author, illustrator, and the cover. Ask the children what they think the book is about, who will be in it, and how they know this.

- Bring attention to the A *Counting Book!* part of the title, discussing how this lets the reader know that there will be counting in the book.

- Have the children make other predictions about what they think the book will be about.

- Read the book.

- After reading the book, ask: *Which family members were a part of the story?*

- Next, create a large poster titled "How Many Family Members and Friends in Grandma's Tiny House?" (similar to Worksheet 2) and ask children, *Do you remember how many of each family member there was?*

- Next, write the family members' titles at the bottom of each box on the large poster. For example, "Grandma" will be written out in the first box, followed by "Neighbors" in the next box.

- At this point, you will need to pull out your own completed colored *Grandma's Tiny House* family members from Worksheet 1 (*Family Member Cutouts*, which will need to be completed before the activity) that match the characters from the book. This will include family members (colored in and cut out). These family cutouts will be used as a model for children.

- Pull out Grandma from your completed *Family Member Cutouts*.

- Have children count with you: "One Grandma." You can open the book and show the children as you and the children collectively count Grandma in the book corresponding to the page that says "One Grandma . . ."

- Tape Grandma in the box labeled "Grandma," write the numeral "1" and the word "one," and discuss the fact that the book had one grandma.

- Repeat this step with the rest of the family members.

- In order to increase participation from the children, you can hand the completed family member cutouts to different children, so they can come up and tape the family members to the large poster. For example, for "three neighbors," you can hand three children one neighbor (colored in and cut out) each, and those three children will come up and tape their "neighbor" in the "Neighbors" box.

- Then, everyone can collectively count "one, two, three," as you point to each of the neighbors taped to the poster.

- Write the numeral and number word in each relevant box.

Summarize (5 minutes)

- Summarize each family member and the number, starting with "One Grandma." Be sure to point to each as you do this.

- Finally, add and/or count the total number of family members and friends that joined Grandma's house. Encourage a variety of child-centered strategies, such as counting the figures, using blocks, and/or using a calculator. Next, write that number and write "Total Number of Family Members." If appropriate and children are interested, you can write equations to represent the sum.

- You can ask if this family is a small, medium, or big family based on the criteria that were initially decided on yesterday.

- Allow for any other discussion, and tell children you will continue working on families tomorrow.

Day 3: Grandma's Family and Friends (*Continued*)

Launch (5 minutes)

- Let the children know that today they are going to do their own counting to see if they each get the same number of visitors to Grandma's tiny house.

Explore (30 minutes)

- Give each group a *Grandma's Tiny House* copy to share if possible. If not, be ready to read the book aloud.

- Give each group a copy of Worksheet 2 (*How Many Family Members and Friends in Grandma's Tiny House?*).

- Have children work in their groups to count each of the family members and write them on their sheet. They will be counting each family member only once, based on the page where that family member is introduced with a number. Facilitate each step. For example, say:

  + *First, count Grandma in the book with your group. Once you do this, write the number on the sheet.*

  + Continue to guide them through the completion of the sheet.

  + Encourage them to use various strategies to find the sum of people who visited Grandma. They could use Unifix cubes, base-10 blocks, calculators, and so on.

- After they have a chance to do this, bring the group back together.

- Have them share what they got and compare it to your large poster.

- Next, begin asking children, *Which group of family members or friends had more or less?*

  + *For example, let's start with Neighbors and Uncles. Which are there more of: Neighbors or Uncles?*

  + Have them share with their groups and pick groups to share with the whole group. Be sure to ask: *How do you know?*

  + Continue with different configuration comparisons of family members and friends, switching the wording of "more" and "less" and occasionally "the same number"

Summarize (5 minutes)
- Ask children to share what they discussed and learned about today (e.g., checking work, more or less).

Day 4: Our Big Class Family

Launch (5 minutes)
- While children are in their seats, begin by reviewing what they did the previous day.

  + Pull out the large poster titled "How Many Family Members and Friends in Grandma's Tiny House?"

  + Ask for a few comparisons. For example, you could ask: *Which are there more of, Grandmas or Aunties? How do you know?*

- Remind children of the work they already started doing with their own families and how they are going to continue this work.

- Hand back the children's work from Day 1 that represents their own families. You may need to give them a few moments to become reacquainted with what they did.

Explore (10 minutes)

- Have each child discuss their work with a partner. They can share the number of people they made, who they are, and so on.

- Give each child Worksheet 3 (*Family at Home*).

  + Have them label their *Family at Home* sheet by putting their name at the top.

  + Have them glue their cutouts onto their sheets so the family members are inside the house.

  + Have them write their total number of family members in their home someplace on their sheet.

- Have them share with their partner what they notice. Here are some examples:

  + Have them compare similarities and differences with their families (e.g., who is in their home).

  + Have them compare the number of people in their home.

- Have all the children come back together. Now you can lead them through some counting.

  + Have each student share how many people live in their home by holding up their fingers.

  + Mention that if we add all our family members together, that makes for a BIG family. Tally up how many are on the board and then count up the total. Write the total tallied number on the board.

  + You can also have children get Unifix cubes to represent their own families and then put them all together to represent all of the family members from the class. You can find the sum of these by counting by ones or by putting them in groups of 10.

- Continue mathematizing the data you have. For example, you can ask children to use Worksheet 3 to create class pictographs to show the number of people in each family.

  + Begin by asking children to raise their hands regarding how many family members are in their families (e.g., *Raise your hand if you have only two family members*). Continue to do this until everyone has had a chance to respond.

+ Using the pictograph, ask children questions about the data, such as how many families are in each category, and ask them to make comparisons. You can also ask children about how many small, medium, and big families there are in the class.

Summarize (10 minutes)

- Summarize what the children have learned. Observations might include these:

    + Families come in different sizes.

    + Some families have more members, some have less.

    + Some of us have the same number of family members in our homes.

    + Some of us have the same types of family members in our homes, some of us don't (moms, grandmas, etc.).

    + People have similarities and differences, but is that a bad thing? No.

    + Similarities and differences makes us interesting and beautiful. Even though we are different, we can work together.

    + We can make a pictograph that represents us.

    + We have family members who don't live with us too.

- Have each child bring up their completed Worksheet 3 and tape it on the large piece of butcher block paper titled "Our Big Class Family."

- Finish by saying that even though we may have different experiences, come from different families, and look different, we can come together and make up one big class family that loves each other, helps each other, and works together.

TAKING ACTION

You will have an opportunity to discuss the beauty and importance of diversity at the end of the lesson to ensure children understand that while we are diverse, we are still one big family. Children can create posters to share around the school about family diversity.

COMMUNICATING WITH STAKEHOLDERS

In this lesson, you provide many opportunities to talk about differences and similarities in a positive way. Be sure to highlight the importance of diversity as well as redirect teasing or harmful comments that might arise. Additionally, you will end the entire lesson by creating a visual of each child's "home" together making up the classroom family and emphasizing that they all work together as one. The "Our Big Class Family" poster can stay up for many weeks along with class-generated "community rules," which you can refer back to often to remind children that we are all a class family. This can help you with conflict resolution and establishing a caring classroom community as well.

You can document each step of the activity, taking pictures to include in a newsletter or email for parents/caregivers, administrators, and stakeholders. The artifacts produced from this activity provide you with ample chances to communicate this important work with stakeholders—especially during school events. For example, the large poster can be showcased in a public space such as the school cafeteria or auditorium (and if similar activities are carried out across other classrooms within the school, this could allow for the "One Big Family" idea to apply to the entire school community). You can give children a chance to write and share their thoughts about what they learned regarding social justice and mathematics at school events through letters and speeches, and the poster would supplement the public sharing of child-produced work. Finally, since so many schools acknowledge the importance of embracing, valuing, and encouraging diversity, this class activity can support this work within the classroom and set the stage for branching out to influence the entire school community.

ONLINE RESOURCES

 Available for download at **resources.corwin.com/TMSJ-EarlyElementary**

▼ Worksheet 1: Family Member Cutouts

▼ Worksheet 2: How Many Family Members and Friends in Grandma's Tiny House?

▼ Worksheet 3: Family at Home

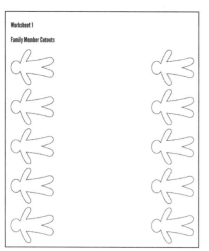

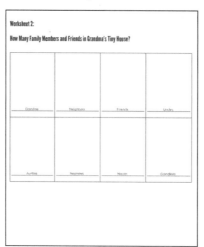

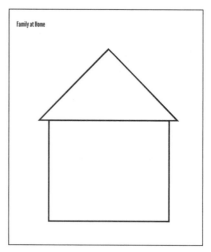

BACKGROUND OF THE LESSON

California State University, Sacramento is a diverse university that is committed to social justice. Many of the students I work with in my classes become teachers and practitioners within the field of early childhood education as well as the K–12 educational system. This lesson evolved from core commitments to diversity: working with others who are different than you helps build camaraderie and care, and helps individuals to value the beauty diversity brings. Combining my commitment to diversity with the warmth and familial love of *Grandma's Tiny House* set the foundation for the creation of this lesson. When it comes to my classroom, I believe that learning happens best when it is a part of an active process of knowledge building. Thus, I believe that an optimal classroom includes the following core components: (1) a learning environment that activates a student's current understanding and personal experience as a starting point to integrate new knowledge; (2) curriculum content presented in ways that engage different types of learners, giving them a variety of avenues to learn and master the material; and (3) a student-centered classroom that affords students an opportunity to learn from and with the professor as well as fellow learners within the classroom. These are integral parts of my philosophy of teaching, ultimately establishing a classroom environment where students can participate in the understanding of content and construction of knowledge in a meaningful way. This lesson series brings these ideas to life.

ABOUT THE AUTHOR

 **JaNay Brown-Wood** is an award-winning children's author, educator, and scholar who lives in California with her husband, Catrayel, and daughter, Vivian. Currently, she is an assistant professor at California State University, Sacramento in the Child and Adolescent Development Department. Her research interests include investigating how the lack of diversity in children's literature affects young learners, their academic outcomes, and their biases. Additionally, she has written several poems and picture books for publication, and her children's books have received a number of accolades and awards. Dr. JaNay Brown-Wood believes that if children are given the opportunity to build strong and positive connections with individuals who have different backgrounds than them, this will help build empathy, compassion, and community—decreasing prejudices and biases. She wants children and adults to not just state that diversity is important, but to value it and act in ways that promote and highlight diversity within their daily lives as a way to dismantle injustices that persist within our society.

SOCIAL JUSTICE OUTCOMES

- I want to know about other people and how our lives and experiences are the same and different. (Diversity 8)

MATHEMATICS DOMAINS AND PRACTICES

- Number and Operations

- Data Collection and Analysis

- Reason abstractly and quantitatively. (MP2)

- Construct viable arguments and critique the reasoning of others. (MP3)

- Attend to precision. (MP6)

CROSS-CURRICULAR CONNECTIONS

- Art

LESSON 5.6 LEARNING FROM OUR ANIMAL FRIENDS: MATHEMATIZING WITH THE ARTWORK OF RICARDO LEVINS MORALES

Courtney Koestler and Anita Wager

TAKING CARE OF OURSELVES AND OTHERS

This multiday lesson draws on students' empathy and sensitivity to others to explore how to support each other during a crisis such as the COVID-19 pandemic. It currently is envisioned as a 3-day exploration, but may be longer or shorter depending on the children involved. We present a vision of how this might play out; and, depending on how the lessons are structured, this lesson series could be utilized across PreK–2.

This lesson is designed to support early childhood teachers with a tangible, child-appropriate entrée into critical conversations about "what to do in a pandemic" and centers on the gorgeous, affirming artwork of Ricardo Levins Morales called *What To Do In a Pandemic (Animals)*.

It is important to note that while this lesson does center on content related to a pandemic, the lessons can be used at any time, as they are related to taking care of oneself, one's friends and family, and one's community, which are timeless themes related to peace and justice. You may choose to implement this lesson during times when illness is more prevalent (e.g., "flu season" or during an outbreak of a childhood illness at your site) or simply adapt to broader themes of taking care of oneself and others.

DEEP AND RICH MATHEMATICS

The mathematical portion of the lesson has two features: (1) data collection and representation and (2) recognizing common features or patterns and sorting. During this part of the lesson, the children make sense of the data they collect from the class, make a bar graph, and ask and answer questions about the data. The extension consists of identifying a rule in the collection and sorting the artwork based on that theme.

ABOUT THE LESSON

This 3-day lesson explores the artwork of Ricardo Levins Morales and discusses children's experiences with the pandemic and ways of being good citizens to themselves and to others. The lesson could be extended beyond 1 day to a multiday lesson when taking action to distribute knowledge beyond the classroom community.

Resources and Materials

- Art: *What To Do In a Pandemic (Animals)*, a 10-piece collection of 8 × 10 mini-posters by artist Ricardo Levins Morales (for purchase and/or download at the artist's website, https://bit.ly/3dajUUZ) (sets for groups of children if possible)

- Poster paper, sticky notes, markers, and other coloring supplies

- Butcher paper for class murals

- Paint and paint brushes

LESSON FACILITATION

Day 1

Launch (15 minutes)

Display the 10 posters of *What To Do In a Pandemic (Animals)* so that students can see them all. Depending on the children with whom you work (i.e., their age, the number in your class), you may choose to work with a smaller number of images than all 10.

Source: Images courtesy of Ricardo Levins Morales Art Studio. To view and download these images, visit rlmartstudio.com. Used with permission.

- Review the images one by one, reading the captions on each or asking for children to do so. Depending on the amount of time, pose questions such as these:

    + *What do you notice?*

    + *What do you wonder?*

    + *How do these make you feel?*

    + *Can you describe the animal(s) and what they are doing in the images?*

    + *What messages do each of these pieces of art tell us?*

- You can collect these observations in a variety of ways, depending on the children. For example, you can have them write sticky notes and post them near the posters or you can draw pictures on poster paper. Children may want to act out different scenes together.

Explore (10 minutes)

- Provide each small group with their own set of the images. (Images can be downloaded from https://bit.ly/3dajUUZ.) Ask them what they notice that is similar or different about each image (referring to the earlier discussion).

- Have groups sort the images in different ways that make sense to them, telling them that they should be ready to share their sorting sets with the whole group.

Summarize (20 minutes)

- After groups have had a chance to sort (and re-sort if wanted), have children share how they sorted the images and why they chose to sort them that way. For example, they might choose to sort by number of animals in the image, what animals they consider the "cutest," the kinds of habitat shown, how many legs the animals have, and so on.

- You may want to discuss other ways and encourage specifically mathematical ways of sorting the images as well.

Day 2

Launch (10 minutes)

- Briefly review the images and the observations the children made the prior day. Discuss the different ways that groups chose to sort the images. You may say:

    + *What are some other ways we could have sorted these?*

    + *I've been thinking about how I might sort these. We are going to play "guess my rule."*

- Use the groups identified here and begin by placing the images one by one in the groups to see if children can identify the rule you are using to sort.

Group 1	Group 2
• Stay aware (#1) • Limit exposure (#3) • Wash frequently (#4) • Rest (#8) • Accept your feelings (#9)	• Support those most vulnerable (#2) • Spread calm (#5) • Check in with each other (#6) • Offer healing support (#7) • Organize for a better future (#10)

- Have children identify the rule and label the groups. Although children should use their own language, you may frame them as *Ways to Help Ourselves* (Group 1) and *Ways to Help Others* (Group 2).

Explore (45 minutes)

- Explain to children that they will be choosing one of the images from each group (Group 1 and Group 2) to inspire the creation of new artwork for the school community.

- Have children write their names on a sticky note and "vote" for the piece they like the most and wish to focus on, one from each group. Before they vote, you may ask them to brainstorm ideas of what to base their vote on, such as the message expressed in the image, the feeling the image evokes, the imagery of the animal(s) and habitat, and so forth.

- Encourage children to represent the data in different ways. For example, does a bar chart make sense to represent the data, or do other representations make sense? Depending on your context, you may collect children's votes informally (e.g., simply leaving the sticky notes on the images) or formally (e.g., in a bar graph).

- Once every child has a chance to vote and the children have had a chance to organize and analyze the data, prompt them by asking:

  + *Which image has the most votes? Do you think all of you who voted for this image did so for the same reasons? Does anyone want to share why they voted for it?*

  + *I noticed that this image had few votes. Even though there weren't many votes, it is a very powerful image. Does anyone want to share why they chose it?*

Summarize (10 minutes)

- Once the children have had a chance to analyze the data and understand the class's agreed-upon favorite images from Group 1 and Group 2, tell children they will be designing murals inspired by these two pieces to hang in the school to communicate to others the importance of taking care of oneself and taking care of others. Here are possible questions to ask:

+ *What is a mural?*

+ *Where have you seen murals?* (You might have images available of murals in your community.)

+ *What are murals used for?*

- Depending on children's experience, you can also include your own ideas such as to use as decoration, to advertise something, or to make a statement.

Day 3

Launch (15 minutes)

- Review the conversation from Day 2 about what murals are and how they are used.

- Remind children about the images they selected and brainstorm the message they want to share and incorporate in their mural for the center/school community.

Explore (45 minutes)

- Have the children brainstorm about what they might draw in their mural and begin working on sketches or different parts of the actual mural. There are multiple options for creating the mural depending on your class. Some children may choose to do their own drawing to be included in the class mural or not; the children might all draw on the same large sheet or create a collage with the message on the sheet and individual drawing added.

- They can also begin making their own posters based on the same or similar themes. (If needed, have additional reference books about the featured animals and habitats to support children.)

Summarize (5 minutes)

- Because it might take longer than this class session, you can wrap up today's work with some culminating prompts, such as these:

+ *Do you think our mural about taking care of oneself is going to help our school community? In what ways?*

+ *Do you think our mural about taking care of others is going to help our school community? In what ways?*

+ *Where should we hang our mural?*

+ *How should we let the community know about our mural?*

TAKING ACTION

- Once the murals (and individual posters if children make them) are done, the children can take action in various ways. Very simply, their artwork can be hung up around the center/school or sent to other places around their community to spread important messages of care about oneself, others, and community. You can invite local media to interview children about these messages and the artwork to share their stories.

- Children can share their knowledge through Public Service Announcement videos, newsletters, or announcements about the artwork they created to broadcast more widely about the messages they learned about and the artwork they created.

COMMUNICATING WITH STAKEHOLDERS

Here are some suggestions organized by stakeholder, progressing in various levels.

- Before teaching the lesson, it may be important to discuss the activities in this lesson with school directors/principals because it deals with a potentially sensitive topic (and one which has affected millions of people worldwide). It is likely that the pandemic has immediate and lasting effects on the local and regional community. While it is important that you address real-world issues like the pandemic, the messages about the importance of taking care of oneself and one's community in the artwork are enduring and extend well beyond the pandemic.

- As you gear up to teach the lesson, communication to families can be sent regarding the goals related to the social justice topic and other curricular goals. Any classroom artifacts that are created through the activities can be shared with families as they are typically done through email or classroom newsletters.

- As a way to introduce the topic with children in your classroom, you can begin by simply posting the artwork in the classroom. Because children are naturally curious, discussions may begin before starting any formal lessons. You should be aware of any children who are particularly sensitive to the topic of illness, just as you would be about any real-world topic that connects to children's lives.

ONLINE RESOURCES

To download or purchase these posters, visit **rlmartstudio.com**

Source: Images courtesy of Ricardo Levins Morales Art Studio. To view and download these images, visit rlmartstudio.com. Used with permission.

BACKGROUND OF THE LESSON

In March of 2020, the United States was hit hard by the coronavirus pandemic, just as other countries around the world were or would be. Teachers went into crisis mode after schools closed and they attempted to reach their students via online efforts or by providing physical instructional materials using drop-off/pick-up methods.

> A *few weeks after schools closed [this past spring], the Yale Center for Emotional Intelligence (YCEI) invited educators to describe the emotions they were experiencing. More than 5,000 educators responded. Over and over, the same words bubbled to the top. Stressed. Anxious. Worried. Overwhelmed. Confused. (Walker, 2020)*

In the fall of 2020, when schools reopened again for the new school year (many of them remotely/online), many teachers still felt unprepared or underprepared to address the pandemic explicitly in their classrooms, despite the importance of acknowledging the reality of students and their communities. Ricardo Levins Morales developed a series of artwork called *What To Do In a Pandemic (Animals)*. His work provides guidance to children to make sense of how to help each other in a pandemic, through the playful imagery of animals doing their best to follow safety guidelines (like "wash hands") and take care of themselves and others (such as "check in with others" and "rest"). The authors wanted to see how they could develop a lesson that had empathy and care at the center, as well as mathematics, while supporting children to make sense of and express feelings about the pandemic.

At the center of this project is developing and supporting child-centered and humane classrooms that take seriously the needs of students during this horrific pandemic that suddenly shut down schools all over the United States in March 2020. In many anecdotal conversations with local teachers, they were at a loss of how to discuss COVID-19 with their students in productive and safe ways. We believe that engaging children in talking about their feelings is an important part of social-emotional learning and creating welcoming classrooms.

ABOUT THE AUTHORS

Courtney Koestler has been working in their current position at Ohio University since 2014, where they have had the opportunity to spend time in schools working alongside elementary school teacher-colleagues in their classrooms. They have been an educator since 1998, when they started their career as a middle school teacher, going on to work as a second-, fourth-, and finally fifth-grade classroom teacher before becoming a K–5 mathematics coach. It was in this role that they met administrators and colleagues who believed in child-centered and critical pedagogies, centered on taking an assets-based approach to teaching where students' (and families') interests, practices, and "funds of knowledge" were important resources on which to build and connect. Exposure to critical literacy and critical pedagogy made them question their teaching and realize they could be more intentional and purposeful about the kinds of lessons and pedagogical approaches they taught. Now, as a university-based teacher educator, they center equity and justice in teacher education and professional development work. Courtney recognizes that teaching is non-neutral; it is a political act.

Anita Wager has been in her current position at Vanderbilt University since 2017, where she works with prospective teachers in both the undergraduate and professional programs to engage in socially just and humane mathematics teaching. From 1999 to 2004, she taught fifth grade in a linguistically, ethnically, racially, and economically diverse elementary school where she centered her mathematics instruction on the strengths that children brought from their homes and communities, revising lessons from the district to adapt to children's lived experiences. Anita loved integrating the arts into her classroom where children used mathematics to analyze poetry, build sets for performances, and create cities for their geometry unit. At that time, her district was tracking children in mathematics starting in the second grade. Anita's concern over this inequity ultimately led her to graduate school and the work she does now.

- I know when people are treated unfairly. (Justice 12)

- I know some true stories about how people have been treated badly because of their group identities, and I don't like it. (Justice 13)

- I can and will do something when I see unfairness. (Action 17)

- I will speak up or do something if people are being unfair. (Action 19)

MATHEMATICS DOMAINS AND PRACTICES

- Geometry

- Model with mathematics. (MP4)

- Use appropriate tools strategically. (MP5)

CROSS-CURRICULAR CONNECTIONS

- Art

- Social Studies

LESSON 5.7 ACTIVISM THROUGH ART

Lauren Murray

ACTIVISM THROUGH ART

This multiday lesson series is rooted in the ideas of social movements and activism, with the Black Lives Matter movement at the core of children's learning. In order to effectively teach this lesson, teachers need to have a strong understanding of systemic racism in the United States as well as the Black Lives Matter movement and its goals. You can read about the history, goals, and current work of the Black Lives Matter movement on their website (https://blacklivesmatter.com/about/). For educator-specific information, the National Education Association has resources (https://bit.ly/31r5Wf2) for teachers to help them facilitate conversations, inspire action, and incorporate the Black Lives Matter message in their classrooms. Additionally, Learning for Justice (formerly Teaching Tolerance) featured a two-part article written by Jamilah Pitts in 2017 titled, "Why Teaching Black Lives Matter Matters" (https://bit.ly/3DfKRRV) and "Bringing Black Lives Matter Into the Classroom" (https://bit.ly/3rqmcI3). Prior to teaching this lesson, you can read these articles to learn more about why anti-racist teaching is necessary and why teaching children about activism movements is essential.

The lesson series can be applied to any classroom grades K–2 in any school or school community. In this lesson, children engage with topics of nationwide inequity facing our country today, such as the Black Lives Matter movement, and social causes that children identify as important to them. All children, regardless of identity or age, have the capacity to care about inequity, social causes, and activist movements; therefore, this lesson can be applied universally to any school or community context. You are encouraged to adjust these lessons around a social movement of significance to your local communities.

DEEP AND RICH MATHEMATICS

The primary mathematics domain embedded in this lesson is geometry. Through this activity, children practice identifying and describing shapes as well as composing and creating shapes on their own. Depending on the learning goals for the class, you might talk about shapes with lines of symmetry, other types of symmetry (such as rotational), and properties of specific polygons.

While each child will be required to use a certain number of shapes in their mural, they have the autonomy in this lesson to decide which shapes they want to use and how they will incorporate these shapes into their mural. Making room for children's choice supports the development of empowering mathematics identities, and leaves room for children to choose shapes that they think will best illustrate the cause they care about.

ABOUT THE LESSON

This is a multiday lesson. Day 1 elicits what children understand using videos, K-W-L charts, and a media study presentation. On Day 2, children explore shapes and other features in artwork and plan to create their own art pieces. On subsequent days, children make their own art and prepare to share it. Day 3 also closes with reflections and connections to the *Taking Action* section. Optional extension activities are provided.

Resources and Materials

Day 1

- Black Lives Matter K-W-L chart pre-prepared, or large chart paper to make it

- Suggested Media Resources for Day 1

    + Video: "Black Lives Matter Protests," from BrainPOP (https://bit.ly/3ocijEs)

    + Article: "The 'Black Lives Matter' street art that contains multitudes," by Julia Jacobs, *New York Times*, August 4, 2020 (https://nyti.ms/3oagfNk)

    + Video: "Artists Have 2 Days to Paint Cincinnati's 'Black Lives Matter' Mural," from (https://bit.ly/3lr55ly)

    + Website: The Verge Photo Essay, "33 Powerful Black Lives Matter Murals" (https://bit.ly/32GTmbU) (many have identifiable shapes)

- Current events articles and pictures, pre-prepared by teacher (1 set for each table)

- Brainstorming note catcher or mathematics journals ready for notes

You may use your discretion to assign the required shapes if time or resources do not allow for the children to choose the shapes themselves. Even if you decide the shape requirements, children are still given the autonomy in this lesson to decide how their shapes are going to be used in their own mural design, which supports the development of empowering mathematics identities.

Day 2

- Teacher Resource 1: *Day 2 Mural Examples*

- Resealable bag (1 per child)

- Pattern blocks/tiles or paper shape cutouts (1 set per child)

- 1-inch grid paper (1 sheet per child)

- Writing utensils (pencils, crayons, markers, etc.; 1 set per child or enough to share)

- Exit ticket

Day 3

- Sticky note pad (1 per child)

- Camera/smartphone to capture mural presentations and artist reflections

- Notecard for artist statement (1 per child)

Optional Extension Activity Materials

- Sidewalk chalk (larger class sets or 1 pack per child)

LESSON FACILITATION

Day 1

Launch (15 minutes)

- Begin by gauging children's level of background knowledge regarding the Black Lives Matter movement. Ask children if they have heard of Black Lives Matter before, or if they have any ideas about what it is or what it means. For more on how to support children through conversations about race, see the *Resources and Materials*.

- Facilitate this conversation through a classroom K-W-L chart ("What I Know," "What I Want to Know," and "What I Learned"). Through this initial discussion, fill out the "Know" and "Want to Know" columns to represent children's initial knowledge and wonders, leaving the "Learned" column blank to be filled out later at the end of the lesson.

Explore (35 minutes)

- Using children's initial knowledge as the foundation for further learning, study different media sources that explain the Black Lives Matter movement, specifically in the context of the June 2020 protests (media resources as listed in the *Resources and Materials*).

- During the media study, engage children in conversations about racism (including structural racism), activism, and protests. Questions to pose can include these:

  + *Why was the Black Lives Matter movement started?*

  + *What does structural racism mean? What does it look like in our community? In our country?*

  + *Why do people protest?*

  + *In what ways do people protest? Are the artists painting the murals protesters? Why are they protesters?*

  + *How did the murals help the protesters' cause?*

  + *What do you think the murals made people think about?*

  + *What does it mean to treat everyone equitably? Does everyone need the same things to live happy, healthy lives? What if some people, or groups of people, already start out with more than other people, or other groups of people?*

  + *What does injustice look like?*

  + *What does it mean to be an activist?*

- After the Black Lives Matter media study, give each table group a collection of current event articles and pictures to study. Tell children that they are going to get to be activists and create art to protest a cause that they care about.

- Ask them to think about something that is not fair or something that needs to change in the world. Remind them it should be an issue about fairness, and it could be to create more opportunities for people to be treated more fairly and for people to have access to the resources they need.

- Using the Black Lives Matter study, articles, and pictures as inspiration, children can fill out a brainstorming note catcher and list/draw pictures of causes that they care about on their note sheet. Near the end of the work time, tell children to look over their list and pick the one cause that they want to keep working with over the next few days in class.

Summarize (10 minutes)

- Begin by asking table groups to briefly share their final idea with one another. Once children have had an opportunity to share, return to the

K-W-L chart from the lesson launch. As a class, fill out the last column ("What I Learned") based on today's lesson. Collect all children's brainstorming note catchers with their brainstorm list and final idea selected at the end of the class period.

Day 2

Launch (15 minutes)

- Begin by pulling up the Black Lives Matter street murals examples from Day 1 and look at additional examples of murals found in Teacher Resource 1 (*Day 2 Mural Examples*).

- As you go through the mural examples, have a discussion with the class about what shapes can be found in the murals. Some questions to guide this discussion could be:

  + *What shapes do you see in the mural? What characteristics or attributes of the shape make you say that?*

  + *How many sides does the shape have?*

  + *Are all of the sides the same length?*

  + *Could we divide this shape into equal pieces?* (for children who have started partitioning)

  + *Could we use any other shapes to build up to this shape that we're seeing?*

  + *Do you see any 2D shapes in this mural? Do you see any 3D shapes in the mural? How can you tell the difference?*

Explore (35 minutes)

- Begin by telling children that over the next few days, they are going to be activists and protest injustice by creating their own murals about the cause they chose yesterday. Tell children that when their murals are complete, they will be shared with a public official in the local community (mayor, county commission, city council, school board, etc.) in the hope that their murals will create real change within the community.

- Give each child a sheet of 1-inch grid paper to design their mural. Tell them that today they are planning their mural on their grid paper.

- Hand out a resealable bag to each child. At each table, put a tub of pattern blocks or tiles (paper shapes can be cut out if pattern blocks or tiles are not available), and have each child pick a designated number of shapes to put in their bag. Tell children that the shapes they choose to put in their bag are the shapes that they need to include in their mural.

+ The number of shapes children choose can vary based on your discretion.

+ Emphasize to children that additional shapes that are not in their bag may also be used in their mural design if they choose; however, the shapes in the bag are required shapes.

+ Depending on grade level and children's experience, some children may trace their shapes, while others may want to make their shapes bigger or smaller than the tiles or cutouts. You should use discretion when giving children guidelines and supporting them through their design process.

+ Depending on children's experience, the shapes offered may vary; you may want to offer 2D shapes, 3D shapes, or both. The shapes should be ones that children have learned about in class and/or can recognize and name based on their attributes. You should use discretion when deciding how extensively to review these shapes before beginning this unit. This unit could serve as a culminating project at the end of a unit about shapes in the classroom where children get a chance to work with shapes in a real-world application design.

• Hand back children's brainstorming note catchers from Day 1. Children should have listed issues they care about the previous day and selected one that they wanted to pursue for their mural design.

• Allow children time to complete their mural designs. Remind children as they work to make sure they are including all of their shapes from their bags in the mural. As children are working, you can circulate and engage children in conversation about their designs. Questions to engage children with may include these:

+ *Why did you decide to use those shapes?*

+ *How do you plan to use this shape in your mural?*

+ *How many times are you going to use that shape in your design?*

+ *What attributes will you need to think about when drawing that shape in your mural?*

+ *What would it look like if your shape was [bigger or smaller] than the pattern tile or cutout?*

Summarize (10 minutes)
• Hand each child an exit ticket. At the top of the exit ticket, children can record the name or draw each shape they used in their murals and how many times that shape was used in their design. At the bottom of the exit ticket, there is a sentence starter for children to complete. It says: *My mural is important because* . . . Children may use words and/or pictures to explain their mural's significance and connect it to activism.

Day 3
LAUNCH (8 MINUTES)

- Begin by telling children that they will be sharing their murals with their classmates today as they do a gallery review.

- Children will have their bag of required shapes with them at their table, and children will display their shapes in front of their mural. At each mural, children should look at the pattern tiles the child used and see if they can find all of the shapes in their mural design. The artist can assist classmates if they are unable to find any of the shapes used.

- Children can have sticky notes and a pencil with them. While they are observing murals during the gallery review, they can use the sticky notes to write and/or draw a compliment, connection, or reaction and give them to their classmates.

- Finally, assign each child a number from 1 to 4. Tell children that if they are a 1, they will start at their mural first while the rest of the class circulates between them and looks at each mural in a gallery review. Tell children that while they are stationed at their murals, they should share a bit about their mural design and mural purpose with their classmates.

Explore (40 minutes)
- Begin by instructing the children assigned 1 to stand by their murals. Remind all children of gallery review procedures, and then begin the first 10-minute round of sharing.

- While children are observing each other's murals, go to each child sharing during that round and take a picture of their mural (ask the child to be in the photo with their mural, assuming photo consent forms are on file). After 10 minutes, end the first round and announce that it is time for all of the children assigned 2 to stand by their mural and share with the class, while the other three groups participate in the gallery review.

- Continue this process for 40 minutes total, allowing each child a chance to represent their mural for a 10-minute round and observe their classmates' murals for three 10-minute rounds.

- By the end of the 40 minutes, you should have a photo of each child and their mural, and children should have gotten to see all of their classmates' activist art.

Summarize (12 minutes)
- After the gallery review is complete, tell children that it is important as activists for them to share their message with others. Remind children that activists want to make sure that their protest efforts are used to create change, so they are going to be shared with a local public official (mayor,

county commission, city council, school board members, etc.). Show them who the public official is and explain their job and role in the community. This can also be collaboratively decided on with the class. (**Note:** If the community member is going to attend the gallery review during class, this would need to happen earlier.)

- Ask children to each write one sentence on a notecard about their mural and how their mural design advocates for their chosen topic, especially related to fairness and other important issues related to justice, supporting them with the dictation when necessary. Provide a sentence stem for children to support them in completing this step. These sentences will serve as artist statements that will go with the children's mural photos when they are sent to the public official.

- In addition to sharing the murals, print out all mural photos after this lesson and display them in the classroom or more publicly in the school with the children's artists' statements attached. Keep children up to date on any correspondence with local officials regarding their murals.

Extension Activity Options

Option 1
- All children could create their murals outside using sidewalk chalk. Using their mural blueprint designs from class, children could iterate their designs to the best of their abilities outside. This activity could be done at any time after the lesson sequence was finished.

Option 2
- After the gallery review, the class could vote on which mural they want to take outside to create on a large scale with sidewalk chalk. You could outline the basic shape of the mural and divide the mural into quadrants. Each table could be assigned a quadrant to complete outside as a group.

- Depending on grade level, once the mural was complete, you could lead the class through a partitioning activity. Each group could be assigned a required shape to find in the mural and partition equally into smaller pieces.

Option 3
- After the gallery review, the class could vote on which mural they want to take outside to create on a large scale with chalk. With the school's permission, the vote could be opened to the entire school, and the mural to receive the most votes could be created outside with sidewalk chalk on the school playground, parking lot, or pavement area in the local community close to the school.

- School staff (such as the art teacher, school administrators, support staff, etc.) as well as parents/caregivers could volunteer to outline the mural on a large scale, and each class could then be assigned a quadrant of the mural to complete in full. You could divide a copy of the original mural design into the correct number of quadrants, and each classroom participating would then receive a copy of the original design, as well as a copy of their assigned quadrant specifically. Each class could take turns completing their assigned quadrant outside on the large-scale mural with sidewalk chalk.

TAKING ACTION

These suggestions are organized by varying levels and articulate long- and short-term goals.

- **Local Community/Organizers/Organizations:** Children's murals and artist statements will be shared with a public official in the local community (see more about this process in the Day 3 "Summarize" section).

- **School:** You may invite the children's families or other classes in the school to attend the gallery review or to a second gallery review after the initial class one. Involving families and the broader school community would extend the children's messages beyond the walls of their classroom and could help to incite change within their school community by bringing awareness to a local social movement.

- **Social Media:** If you use social media in the classroom (Instagram, classroom blog/website, Twitter, etc.), you could share children's murals and artist statements on their social media account if permission grants. This would allow other teachers, children, and community leaders across the country and around the world to see the children's activism work and engage in conversations inspired by the murals.

COMMUNICATING WITH STAKEHOLDERS

Before conducting this lesson, you should communicate the nature of this lesson to parents/caregivers and school administration. It is important for you to share the Black Lives Matter media resources with these stakeholders and to provide them with a list of discussion topics and questions. Ask for family input on the lesson, and adjust accordingly to adhere to feedback when relevant, feasible, and appropriate. Here are some suggested prompts to ask family members:

- Do you think social movements, specifically the Black Lives Matter movement, are framed appropriately in this lesson? If not, what changes could be made to represent these movements in the most authentic and accurate way?

- Is the wording in this lesson sequence developmentally appropriate? Do you have any suggestions for how discussion questions could be worded differently to make more sense to your child?

- Have you talked about activism, social issues, or protests at home before? If so, which ones? How did these conversations go?

- Does it feel like anything is missing from this lesson sequence? If so, what information or activities should be included to make this lesson more beneficial?

Additionally, you might provide both families and administrators with an overview of the lesson, including an invitation to the mural gallery review to encourage attendance. In addition to inviting parents/caregivers to the class gallery review, an additional afterschool event could be planned to accommodate as many schedules as possible. During the gallery review, children get the opportunity to share their social justice learning and mathematics learning with their families, classmates, and school staff. By explaining the messaging behind their mural, children are demonstrating their social justice understanding; by explaining their creation process, children are demonstrating their mathematical understanding.

For involvement with community stakeholders that may not be families of the children in your classroom, you can invite families and community members to attend the gallery review and/or the afterschool event with everyone invited.

Lastly, if you choose to do Extension Activity Option 1, then this invites the school community and families to not only see the finished murals but also to be involved in the creation process.

ONLINE RESOURCES

 Available for download at **resources.corwin.com/TMSJ-EarlyElementary**

◀
Teacher Resource 1: Day 2 Mural Examples

BACKGROUND OF THE LESSON

As a teacher, one of my primary goals is to make sure that my children's lives in the classroom feel deeply connected to their lives outside of the classroom. I believe that proceeding with this intent in mind creates more meaningful and impactful learning experiences for children. I have found that children of all ages crave relevancy and seek to understand the *why* behind the material that they are learning. I also believe that it is necessary to talk about current event topics with children of all ages, being mindful in making sure these conversations are done in a developmentally appropriate way. As educators, we are in a unique position of being able to combine both real-world relevancy and critical conversations through our teaching in the classroom, and in doing so, we are better preparing children to be informed citizens in an ever-changing world. In thinking about important critical conversations that deserve a place in the classroom, issues of race and systemic racism are among the most important. Systemic racism permeates all facets of society today, and having conversations with children early on about issues of race within their communities and country is absolutely necessary. I created this lesson with the intent that it can be used to start these critical conversations in early childhood classrooms in a way that is informative and inspires children to action, while still being developmentally appropriate. Some children may be learning about the Black Lives Matter movement and systemic racism for the first time, while other children may already be familiar with these topics. Regardless of children's current understanding, this lesson provides more contextual understanding of systemic injustice and an opportunity for action and empowerment, advocating either for a cause that directly affects them or for the fair treatment of other groups.

ABOUT THE AUTHOR

 **Lauren Murray** is a kindergarten teacher in Lansing, New York. She completed her master's degree in elementary education at Vanderbilt's Peabody College. She completed her undergraduate education at the University of Michigan, where she earned a bachelor's degree in environmental science with a concentration in education. After serving a year with AmeriCorps in Seattle Public Schools, she realized she wanted to stay in the public education sector and dedicate her career to being an educator that brings socially and culturally relevant content into the classroom. Through her experiences in AmeriCorps in Seattle and since then in public schools across the country, Lauren has seen the need to aid children in understanding the power of social movements to advocate for change, and yet social movements are not always taught, especially not in connection to mathematics. She thought that children—the smallest people who need the biggest processing space—are often overlooked in conversations about social movements. She became and is committed to being a social justice educator from a desire to make space for children, even young children, to have conversations about societal inequities, movement building, and social justice.

- I can feel good about myself without being mean or making other people feel bad. (Identity 4)

- I like being around people who are like me and different from me, and I can be friendly to everyone. (Diversity 6)

- I know everyone has feelings, and I want to get along with people who are similar to and different from me. (Diversity 9)

MATHEMATICS DOMAINS AND PRACTICES

- Patterns and Algebraic Thinking

- Data Collection and Analysis

- Number and Operations

- Make sense of problems and persevere in solving them. (MP1)

- Reason abstractly and quantitatively. (MP2)

CROSS-CURRICULAR CONNECTIONS

- Language Arts

LESSON 5.8 SEEING THE COLORS OF OURSELVES AND OTHERS

Sam Prough and Eric Cordero-Siy

SKIN TONE REPRESENTATION IN PICTURE BOOKS

This lesson is geared toward the representation and empowerment of diverse people in our world. Many of the most popular children's books feature mostly or only white people. While this may not appear as an issue for children who are white in predominantly white classrooms, it does not represent the diverse population of the world and does not work to empower children of Color by seeing themselves represented in the books read to them. As teachers, we can help children recognize that such diversity exists within the rest of the world, whether or not that is immediately reflected in their current classroom. Being able to see oneself and more diverse people in the stories that are read at school and at home can have a significant impact on children and their connection to other people.

Children will see how they can empower themselves with the access to reading material that better represents who they are and others in the world around them. According to the Cooperative Children's Book Center (https://ccbc.education.wisc.edu/), out of the thousands of children's books published in 2021, they counted that around 30% of the books were about characters who were Black, Indigenous, or other people of Color. There is harm when children and families are consuming literature where they do not see a diversity of characters. First, if the majority of the images we present to children are white, they could come away thinking that white is the norm, which harms children of Color in judging their identity and worth against whiteness. Second, not all children come in contact with individuals of other races and ethnicities, especially in predominantly white areas; thus, their conceptions and beliefs about Black, Indigenous, or other people of Color are heavily influenced by media representation. According to Welch (2016),

> If characters of Color are missing or distorted in children's literature, then children of Color do not have an opportunity to see themselves reflected in a variety of contexts, and white children do not have an opportunity to imagine and emotionally invest in the subjective experiences of persons of Color. (p. 373) (Color has been capitalized here to emphasize this perspective.)

By looking at the books available in the classroom, library, and/or at home, children will investigate what that representation looks like and study a sense of "fairness" in who and/or what is represented. Further, through exploring variations in skin tone, children uncover new meaning and depth usually subsumed under monolithic categories of Black, Brown, and white. To make a connection to why these nuances matter, the activity will conclude with a book on empathy and answers to why it is important for diverse people to be represented in books.

The goal of this discussion is to introduce characters from the book that will support children to later respond to questions during the lesson. *If a previous activity was done with children using self-portraits, connections can be made to what colors people used to color themselves in.* Children will realize that people come in all different skin colors, grappling with the nuance of skin tone that is traditionally expressed only in monolithic categories. Prompt children to pay attention to the different characters who may have the same or similar skin color to themselves. You may also prompt children to express their curiosity about how colors of skin are described in the book they read.

DEEP AND RICH MATHEMATICS

Children will use data from categorizing books to determine the disparity in representation of people of Color. They will use categorization to place books into groups of those with only white people and books with people of Color. Individuals will work on counting (or adding) and comparing the number of books in each category, and the class as a whole will create a chart to represent the number comparison.

ABOUT THE LESSON

This activity is framed as a 1-day lesson. However, each section of the lesson is designed so that it could be done one after the other or across multiple days. Also, depending on the age and experience of the children, you can extend the lesson to support their thinking.

Resources and Materials
- Book: *The Colors of Us* by Karen Katz (multiple copies if possible)
- Book: *I Am Human: A Book of Empathy* by Susan Verde

- A big selection of picture books from the library to explore skin tone representation

- Tasksheets 1 and 2: *Who Is In My Books?* (1 per child)

- Teacher Resource 1: *List of Characters and Skin Tones From The Colors of Us*

- Teacher Resource 2: *Template Letter to Families* (1 per child)

- Website: Social Justice Books (https://socialjusticebooks.org) is a good resource for more information, including a list of books that more closely fit the learning needs of the children in your classroom

LESSON FACILITATION

Launch (10 minutes)

- Gather children to read *The Colors of Us* by Karen Katz. As with any read-aloud, be sure to read the book ahead of time and note any vocabulary that may be new for children.

- As you are reading or after you have finished the book, you may ask questions such as these:

    + *What did Lena learn about in the book?*

    + *How did Lena feel about her friends?*

    + *What do you notice?*

    + *What do you wonder?*

    + *How do you feel?*

- After a brief conversation, discuss all of the different skin tones in the book. Remind children that in real life there are a lot of people of different skin tones, but not all books show this in their illustrations. You may also ask children to think of recent picture books that they have read and think about the skin tones of those characters.

Explore (30 minutes)

- Next, you will ask children to analyze the skin tones of the characters in a selection of books from the library or using books currently in your classroom. The goal of this task is for children to recognize if their libraries (or classrooms) carry books that have characters of Color or only white characters.

- **Note:** If you are implementing this activity with older children, you may want to do this activity in the library to have a much wider selection of books for children to choose from.

- You can say something like this:

  + *Today we will be looking at the books in our classroom [or library] and the kinds of characters in them, and we will collect data on the kinds of characters in them, specifically their skin tones.*

  + *Here's what you are going to do. You will select five books that look like they will have human characters (and not animal characters).*

- **Note:** You may choose to have children analyze more books depending on availability and their age/experience. Each child should pick out the same number of books but should be given input into what books they'd like to pick out.

  + *You will then review the books to find what kinds of skin tones the characters have. We want to note whether the characters in a book look like Lena (who has skin the color of cinnamon), her mom (who has skin the color of French toast), Isabella (with chocolate brown skin), or Lucy (with peachy tan skin), or like the other characters in the book.*

  + *You will group books into two categories: whether all the characters look only like Lucy (with peachy tan skin) or whether the characters have people with many different skin tones.*

  + *How do you think we should go about this process?*

  + *How do we check a book to find all the characters?*

  + *What does it mean when you find a character in a book that looks like Lena?*

  + *How can we keep track of what's in each book?* (Facilitate physical organization and record keeping on the worksheet.)

  + *You can use a copy of The Colors of Us to help you determine the different skin tones that you find.*

- Consider supporting children with strategies of how they can find characters in the book (looking at every page) and how to keep track of who is in these books (people that only look like Lucy or people that look like many of the characters from the book). If children are ready for the connection, you can describe the categories as looking for characters who are only white or characters with many different skin tones. The chart in the *Resources and Materials* section can be projected for the entire class to offer examples of characters and their skin color.

- Ask children to arrange books where they see characters that look like the characters in *The Colors of Us*. Children can choose how to arrange books, perhaps by physically separating them into piles. Using Tasksheet 1 (*Who*

Is In My Books?), have children record in some way the number of books they are finding in each category. The worksheet suggests using tally marks to keep track, but use of the symbolic number or picture representation of each book may be more appropriate for your class.

- You may use the following prompts as children begin collecting data:

  + *I see you have your books organized into groups. How are you keeping track of the number in each group?*

  + *What will you write down for how many of your books have characters that only look like Lucy?*

  + *How can you check to make sure your numbers are right?*

- Once children have had a chance to sort and record their books, put them into groups to combine the data about their books and numbers in each category.

- Ask children to use Tasksheet 2 and combine what they found with their books. By combining their data, children may engage in adding numbers of different magnitudes. Support their work by facilitating conversations around their strategies for addition. You may ask questions like these:

  + *How did you know?*

  + *Did you add in a different way than a groupmate?*

- When they have added, encourage children to use different representations to identify their findings—this could range from self-made representations or more standard representations such as bar graphs.

- Manipulatives may be beneficial to support children's addition strategies when placed in groups. Given that children are working with single-digit addition, the use of base-10 blocks (or Unifix cubes in sets of 5 or 10) would be helpful.

Summarize (20 minutes)

- In the whole group, have children report on their findings. To support children's understandings about elements of effective data representations, you can ask the following questions if they created self-made representations:

  + *What does the representation tell us?*

  + *What do you like about this group's representation?*

  + *What questions do you have about this representation?*

  + *How was this group's representation similar to what you did?*

- You should also promote connections between the different representations, and encourage children to ask questions and compare and contrast their findings.

- End the show-and-tell by asking children if they notice anything about the number of books depicting different skin tones. Encourage children to use the language of "more" and "less."

- Shift the discussion to addressing how Lena might feel to see how many books have people that look like her vs. books with people that do not look like her. Grounding the conversation through Lena's eyes (rather than children's eyes) ensures that if you have children of Color in your classroom, they are not put on the spot. This also supports children who do not see themselves reflected in the books to still engage in conversations where children use the data to think about empathy.

- Note that few books in most libraries have characters that look like Lena and the characters of Color. Explain that we know there are a lot of people in the world who have different shades of skin, but that many of the books in libraries do not show all of those different people. Talk about how the books in your classroom or library represent the people in your community, our country, and our world.

- Finally, decide on a discussion of "fairness" from the text and their activity. Talk with children about how we can share what they learned with others. Ask children what they would like to do to share their thinking with others, which can include other people at the school, people at home, or people in the community. Children may come up with their own suggestions first, which can be encouraged. However, if children are unsure of who to talk to or how, provide a set of options from the *Taking Action* section. Actions taken for communication within the school can be coordinated for the whole class, a small group, or even an individual child.

EXTENSION

- **Note:** This reading may be beneficial for your class to further recognize why it matters that other people are also represented in books.

- To address empathy and caring for others who look different from oneself, read *I Am Human: A Book of Empathy* by Susan Verde. Although you should preread the book, some new vocabulary for young children may include *timid, compassion, equality*, and *thoughtfulness*.

- Some prompts for facilitating discussion with children are as follows:

    + *Have you ever felt the same things as the character in the book?*

    + *In what ways are you curious? Playful? Fearful?*

    + *What are some choices that the character made that show thoughtfulness to others?*

    + *What are some other ways you can show thoughtfulness to others?*

    + *Why do you think it's important to be thoughtful and kind to others?*

- Revisit the work from *The Color of Us* activity. Have children look at the work from the library and ask them about how we can be thoughtful to Lena when she looks at the charts. Broaden the conversation by saying that there are a lot of things that aren't fair aside from the books we looked at. Ask children how they might feel if they know someone else is upset because they are being treated unfairly. How do they feel if they see friends or other people not treated fairly in books?

TAKING ACTION

Action at Home

Children can share a summary of what they learned from their worksheet on who/what is represented in books and what this means. This may support changes in at-home children's books to be more diverse, where children may advocate for themselves to have more diversity in the people of their stories. A template letter to families (Teacher Resource 2) can provide more context into the lesson and possible extensions at home, adapted based on your classroom needs.

Action at School

You and the children may express the results (through display of the consolidated side of the worksheet in Tasksheet 2) to the school board. Along with you, children present what they learned and how it makes them feel to the school librarian and principal. The librarian and principal may already desire new and inclusive texts; after children talk with these school stakeholders, they may also speak to the school board. The children, along with the stakeholders that they have already spoken to, can then present their case to the school board as a call for more books within the school and the district that represent more diverse people, that children can both learn from and see themselves represented in literature.

Action in the Community

With assistance from you, children can invite a local children's book author (either from the community or the state) who features characters of Color in their book to come and do a read-aloud with other children within their grade using their findings and discussions from class. Children can invite their school community, family, and others in their local community to this event. At the read-aloud event, children can do a read-aloud of *The Colors of Us* and share these findings and discussions with those invited, such as the number of characters who "look like them" and who "look like Lena" and what they learned about empathy. After the author reads their book, they can talk about why it's important for them to write and tell stories about underrepresented characters.

ONLINE RESOURCES

 Available for download at **resources.corwin.com/TMSJ-EarlyElementary**

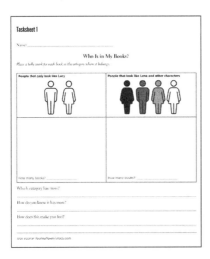

▲ Tasksheets 1 and 2: *Who Is In My Books?*

▲ Teacher Resource 1: *List of Characters and Skin Tones From The Colors of Us*

▲ Teacher Resource 2: *Template Letter to Families*

BACKGROUND OF THE LESSON

We are currently early education practitioners who work with elementary teachers on their practices around discussion in mathematics. One of us, Sam, has specifically explored the impact of the role of families in early childhood mathematics learning. In doing research with families of young children, several expressions about reading and representation came up in conversations of mathematics. When parents/caregivers returned to books that were childhood favorites, they were dismayed to find a lack of diversity in the people of the stories. These families wanted stories that showed their children the diversity that existed in the world and empowered their children of Color to recognize that they could be seen in stories too. In looking at lists of the most popular children's books, we were shocked to find most of them contained no people of Color at all.

Seeing the overwhelming whiteness in many popular children's books and how often teachers may not be aware of the limited representations drove us to create this lesson. We wanted children and their teachers to investigate this issue and explore what literature is available at their school, make mathematical arguments about fair representation, and, if needed, advocate for better representation.

ABOUT THE AUTHORS

 **Sam Prough** is a postdoctoral fellow at the University of Delaware. They taught high school mathematics and currently work with preservice and in-service elementary teachers. They are particularly interested in supporting parents in making meaningful connections to mathematics with young children. Sam became a social justice educator after seeing students enter their classroom who believed they could never be "good at math." Sam's work with students and reflections on readings showed that these student perspectives were embedded in a system that did not value all students as mathematically capable.

 **Eric Cordero-Siy** taught high school mathematics both in the United States and abroad. He currently supports elementary school teachers to incorporate rich discussions in their classrooms. He has worked to create spaces for LGBTQ+ people. As a cis Asian American Pacific Islander man, he intends to support teachers to create equitable mathematics spaces. Eric became interested in social justice after working with Dr. Dorothy White at the University of Georgia. While working with her, he read work on critical issues in mathematics and became more aware of the inequities built into the system of mathematics education and privileged mathematical practices.

LESSON 5.9 HUMAN DIVERSITY AND DISABILITY: DO WE ALL HAVE 10 FINGERS?

Jennifer R. Newton, Courtney Koestler, and Jan McGarry

BODY DIVERSITY AND DISABILITY

This lesson explores human diversity (i.e., different kinds of bodies), disability, and ableism. It is meant to be launched during or after a typical lesson found in many textbooks that assumes children all have "typical" bodies, such as having 10 fingers, and are able to participate in "typical" ways. Children can use critical literacy skills to examine the mathematics lesson as presented as usual (in many textbooks) as well as resources in their classroom to see how bodies, disability, and ableism are presented. Oftentimes the topic of disability in mainstream classrooms is invisible or explicitly not talked about unless absolutely necessary, and it is important for children to see others (both children and adults) with disabilities represented in their classrooms through empowering ways. Disabilities should be portrayed in ways that avoid deficits and stereotypes and instead accurately describe the disability and/or portray people with disabilities living their lives (whether or not disability is the focus).

DEEP AND RICH MATHEMATICS

This lesson engages children in using their bodies (i.e., their fingers) as a physical representation to support skip-counting groups of 10 and multiples of 10. Depending on the age and experience of the children, you may bring in concepts of doubling and halving.

ABOUT THE LESSON

This 1-day lesson includes ideas for continuing the work throughout the year, since talking about disability should not happen in just 1 day.

Resources and Materials
- Chalkboard/whiteboard, chalk/markers, or another way to record children's thinking

SOCIAL JUSTICE OUTCOMES
- I like being around people who are like me and different from me, and I can be friendly to everyone. (Diversity 6)
- I can describe some ways that I am similar to and different from people who share my identities and those who have other identities. (Diversity 7)
- I know everyone has feelings, and I want to get along with people who are similar to and different from me. (Diversity 9)

MATHEMATICS DOMAINS AND PRACTICES
- Number and Operations
- Patterns and Algebraic Thinking
- Make sense of problems and persevere in solving them. (MP1)
- Reason abstractly and quantitatively. (MP2)
- Construct viable arguments and critique the reasoning of others. (MP3)
- Look for and make use of structure. (MP7)

CROSS-CURRICULAR CONNECTIONS
- Language Arts (including Critical Literacy)
- Social Studies

- Book: *What Happened to You?* by James Catchpole and Karen George

- Book: *Intersectional Allies: We Make Room for All* by Chelsea Johnson, LaToya Council, and Carolyn Choi

- Book: *Critical Literacy Across the K–6 Curriculum* by Vivian Vasquez (for background knowledge about critical literacy)

- Also choose some of these books to include in your classroom library:

  Picture Books

  + *The Bug Girl* by Sophia Spencer

  + *Emmanuel's Dream: The True Story of Emmanuel Ofosu Yeboah* by Laurie Ann Thompson and Sean Qualls

  + *Hello Goodbye Dog* by Maria Gianferrari

  + *I Am Not a Label* by Cerrie Burnell

  + *A Kids Book About Disabilities* by Kristine Napper

  + *Mama Zooms* by Jane Cowen-Fletcher

  + *Rescue and Jessica: A Life-Changing Friendship* by Jessica Kensky and Patrick Downes

  + *Terry Fox and Me* by Mary Beth Leatherdale

  + *All Are Welcome* by Alexandra Penfold

  Chapter Books

  These may be more appropriate for older grades:

  + *Braced* by Alyson Gerber

  + *Roll With It* by Jamie Sumner

Additional Resources

- Article: "How to talk to your kid about disabilities," by Caroline Bologna, *Huffington Post*, March 1, 2021 (https://bit.ly/32Svi68)

- Lesson: "Picturing Accessibility: Art, Activism and Physical Disabilities," from Learning for Justice (https://bit.ly/3oeLVkC)

- Lesson: "What Is Ableism?" from Learning for Justice (https://bit.ly/3oe0kh9)

- Lesson: "What Is a Disability?" from Learning for Justice (https://bit.ly/3lrFFUG)

LESSON FACILITATION

Launch (10 minutes)

- A common elementary mathematics activity is to count by tens by counting all the fingers in the classroom. This implicitly makes an ableist assumption that all people have 10 fingers. This unit engages children in questioning those assumptions and thinking about different mathematical contexts we can use for making tens. Prior to implementing this unit, we recommend you consider your classroom and how you want to frame the topic. This is important for all classes, but it is especially critical if you have any children who do not have 10 fingers. The *Resources and Materials* section has several links that can be helpful in thinking about how to discuss these topics with children in your classroom. If you have a child in your class who does not have 10 fingers, we suggest you discuss the unit with the family and child to make sure you are approaching it in a way that feels inclusive and supportive to them. While we provide suggestions for some possible approaches to navigating this space, you should adjust based on your context.

- Begin the lesson by saying something like this to the children:

  + *I have been thinking a lot about today's activity and wanted to talk to you about it. It is an activity that is in a lot of math books because it is usually really good at getting kids to think about important math tools attached to our bodies (our fingers!) and patterns and numbers, but I also am wondering about some assumptions it makes about kids and bodies.*

  + *Let's talk about the task and think about some of the ideas in it before we start.*

- You may have to adjust what you would say depending on your context. For example, if you have already done work on critical literacy with the children in your classroom, the children may be familiar with the idea of how textbook authors' assumptions and biases can be analyzed. If not, you may have to discuss it a bit more, perhaps by asking if they know what an assumption is and if they can give any examples. For more information, see Vivian Vasquez's (2016) *Critical Literacy Across the K–6 Curriculum.* Also, you will want to be responsive to any needs the children have as well. For example, if you have a child in your class with a physical disability, you would want to exercise extreme sensitivity.

- Continue by using prompts and asking questions such as these:

  + *The activity that is usually in math books is to figure out the total number of fingers in our class counting by tens.*

  + *What does this problem assume about people's bodies? About their fingers?*

+ *How do you know the problem assumes this?*

+ *Do you know anyone who has a body that is different?*

- If children do not have experience with regard to different kinds of bodies, you can offer the following:

    + *Some people may lose fingers in an accident, and some people are born with less fingers—or even no fingers—or more fingers on their hands.*

- Allow children to respond, ensuring that they are not expected to speak as a "representative" for those who are different or disabled.

Explore (30 minutes)

- At this point, move forward with the lesson if you feel like children are comfortable counting by tens with their fingers as mathematics tools as commonly stated. Otherwise, you may ask the class to brainstorm other things that come in tens that you can use for the problem (e.g., markers, donut holes, bowling pins). You may choose this second approach if anyone in the class does not have 10 fingers.

- Begin the count by having children show their two hands in front of them and raise their hands as they say their "10" as you go around the circle counting by tens. You can also keep track of the count by listing the numbers on the board (10, 20, 30 . . .), drawing a number line representation, using a hundreds chart, or asking children for other ways to keep track.

- Try it more than once, starting with a different child. Ask them to describe what they notice.

- Ask children questions about what would happen in different scenarios. For example, if there are any children absent from class, what would be the number of fingers if they were present? What if the art, music, and physical education teachers all joined the class? Be sure to entertain multiple strategies for solving the tasks (e.g., counting on by tens, adding on by the multiple of 10 [or 30 in the given example]).

- Continue to extend and challenge children's thinking by changing the context in slight ways. For example, you could ask:

    + *What if we counted our toes too?*

    + *What if we all invited a friend (to double the total number)?*

    + *What if we only counted the fingers on one of our hands?*

    + *What if we counted only our hands (and not fingers)?*

- Next, ask children to consider the assumptions that were embedded in the task. In other words, this task assumed that everyone in the class had 10 fingers.

- Begin a conversation about body diversity, disability, and ableism. Some suggested prompts might be as follows:

  + *Does everyone in our world have 10 fingers? Why or why not?*

- You may want to explain again that some people are born with more or less than five fingers on their hands or some people lose fingers during their lifetime due to injury or disease.

- It is often good to start with a story of your own or, like in the earlier example, explain that people can be born differently or have events in their life that change their bodies. You may continue to prompt children with the following:

  + *Ask: Do you know anyone in your life that has a different kind of body or a disability?*

  + If children think they would feel okay with the task, how would that change the solutions to the task [if the assumptions are taken for granted]?

  + Ask children if they have questions about disabilities.

  + *Ask: Who gets to decide what counts as a disability?*

- Oftentimes, upon reflection, children think this task might make a person feel uncomfortable. Challenge the children to change/think of a new context for the task to still be about counting by tens but that doesn't focus on counting fingers.

Summarize (30-plus minutes/days)

- To end the lesson, read *What Happened to You?* by James Catchpole and Karen George.

- While you are reading or once you finish, have children share questions they have about body differences and disabilities.

- At the end of *What Happened to You?* there are excellent suggestions for adults on how to respond if children have questions about disabled people. You should answer children's questions directly and matter-of-factly, and do not make them feel awkward for asking their questions. Tell them that disability is a normal feature of humanity.

- From Catchpole and George's book, remind children of the following.

  + *When you meet someone with a physical disability or a different body like Joe in the book, it's good to be curious BUT . . . you don't know this person specifically and it has to be okay not to know. It's not polite to ask people you don't know personal questions.*

- Introduce children to the other books in your classroom library that are specifically about disability or that include characters with disabilities. We highly suggest that you continue to have books like those suggested in the *Resources and Materials* in your classroom throughout the school year so children see that these are part of the classroom library and not just as part of a lesson on disability.

TAKING ACTION

Idea 1

- Read the book *Intersectional Allies: We Make Room for All* by Chelsea Johnson, LaToya Council, and Carolyn Choi. As with any book, you should preread this one because there is text in languages other than English that you should learn how to pronounce.

- Discuss generally what it means to be an ally to others, asking children what they think the word means and asking for examples of allyship. For example, you may ask:

    + *What are ways that the children in the book acted as allies for their friends?*

    + *What are ways families supported other families?*

- Next, discuss how allyship was framed in the book(s) you used in the lesson. Were there friends who offered supports and accommodations that provided access for the people in the book(s)? In what ways?

- Ask children if they know of examples of supports and accommodations that provide access for people with disabilities at their school or in public buildings. If children are unaware, you can tour the building and look for different kinds of resources (e.g., automatic door openers, braille lettering on signs, accessible parking, accessible restrooms).

- Ask children to analyze the ways in which the school building is welcoming and safe for different kinds of people, especially for those with different kinds of disabilities.

- If possible, invite a guest speaker, such as a local disability advocate, to collaborate. If or when the children in your classroom find issues with accessibility, support them in taking action by communicating via letters or a presentation with building and district administration, school board members, and community members.

Idea 2

- As an ongoing investigation, have children examine ways in which people are portrayed in the books in your classroom, including in your mathematics curricular materials and the assumptions made about people in those core textbooks:

+ For example, you may compare how people with disabilities are represented in *All Are Welcome* by Alexandra Penfold (i.e., where the children just happen to be using a wheelchair or a white cane, but not specifically discussed as having disabilities) vs. in *Emmanuel's Dream: The True Story of Emmanuel Ofosu Yeboah* by Laurie Ann Thompson and Sean Qualls (i.e., where his true life story is illuminated about what it was like growing up with a disability). You can create a data collection unit about books that do not include characters with disabilities and books that do (and how they do so). If children find that there are not a lot of books that feature characters with disabilities (which is often the case), support children in writing letters to school administrators and school board members to ask for funding to purchase books for classroom and school libraries.

+ Begin a critical literacy investigation with children for other tasks (like counting by tens with our hands) that make assumptions about people (especially in terms of being able-bodied). They may choose to take action by writing letters to different audiences, such as the textbook publishers or district administrators (curriculum coordinators), to describe their findings, let them know how this is not an accurate depiction of people in their community, and give suggestions of ways to make the task or lesson more inclusive. While this activity ideally is child-led, children may need some assistance in developing more inclusive tasks.

COMMUNICATING WITH STAKEHOLDERS

It may be useful to share with families how this lesson has gone when we have done it in the past. Certainly, the way this lesson is implemented will depend on the children (and families) in your classroom community. For example, if all of the children in your classroom are typically able-bodied, this may go differently than if, for example, you have a child (or someone in a child's family) who does not have 10 fingers. Every time we have taught this lesson, children seemed to feel comfortable sharing stories about loved ones or acquaintances who were different. However, this may be sensitive for some children (and/or their families). You will have to be sensitive and responsive in the moment, and try to sense any discomfort when a child is sharing any information that may be personal to them. For this reason, you may communicate in advance with families about the lesson you plan to do, or send a follow-up letter home encouraging families to keep exploring human diversity.

In addition, some of the links in the *Resources and Materials* could be shared with families to continue the conversations at home about the diversity of human bodies and experiences.

BACKGROUND OF THE LESSON

Courtney created a version of this lesson in the moment when collaborating in a colleague's second-grade class. Courtney was asked to teach a lesson about counting by tens using hands to keep track, and they were worried about the implications and messages sent if the class didn't have an opportunity to discuss the assumptions embedded in this task. So, along with the collaborating teacher, Courtney had a quick discussion with the second graders.

Shortly after that, Courtney realized there was a need to learn more about how to more fully develop the lesson to incorporate more of a purposeful discussion on and about disability. So they reached out to Jen and Jan to collaborate on the lesson in this book.

ABOUT THE AUTHORS

Jennifer (Jen) R. Newton began her career as an inclusive early childhood educator in 2000, and has worked across states and settings to promote inclusive practices for students with disabilities. She has worked with children with disabilities and inclusive classrooms in North Carolina, Virginia, and Missouri, before making a home at Ohio University. She credits the opportunity to collaborate with Courtney, her co-author, for helping advance anti-racist and anti-ableist work within teacher education. Her work has focused on addressing bias about disability as well as misunderstandings and misapplications of special education in an effort to diminish the barriers to access for so many students. She credits working with people with disabilities for providing her with a lens on the civil rights and social justice angles of her work. Over the years, she has come to see that teaching is a political act and that in order to be an inclusive educator, her role must be to dismantle the systems of oppression for all learners.

Courtney Koestler has been working in their current position at Ohio University since 2014, where they have had the opportunity to spend time in schools working alongside elementary school teacher-colleagues in their classrooms. They have been an educator since 1998, when they started their career as a middle school teacher, going on to work as a second-, fourth-, and finally fifth-grade classroom teacher before becoming a K–5 mathematics coach. It was in this role that they met administrators and colleagues who believed in child-centered and critical pedagogies, centered on taking an assets-based approach to teaching where children's (and families') interests, practices, and "funds of knowledge" were important resources on which to build and connect. Exposure to critical literacy and critical pedagogy made them question their teaching and realize they could be more intentional and purposeful about the kinds of lessons and pedagogical approaches they taught. Now, as a university-based teacher educator, they center equity and justice in teacher education and professional development work. Courtney recognizes that teaching is non-neutral; it is a political act.

 **Jan McGarry** is an elementary teacher in Athens, Ohio. She has had the privilege of working with first and second graders in Appalachia for 20 years. Jan has a passion for fostering inclusive classroom families that center students' voices and encourage connections with the community and current events through the lens of social justice education.

- I know everyone has feelings, and I want to get along with people who are similar to and different from me. (Diversity 9)

- I can and will do something when I see unfairness—this includes telling an adult. (Action 17)

MATHEMATICS DOMAINS AND PRACTICES

- Number and Operations

- Patterns and Algebraic Thinking

- Make sense of problems and persevere in solving them. (MP1)

- Model with mathematics. (MP4)

CROSS-CURRICULAR CONNECTIONS

- Language Arts

- Social Studies

LESSON 5.10 FEEDING OURSELVES AND OTHERS

Elizabeth Barnes, Jordan Barnes, Natalie Uhle, and Sandra M. Linder

POVERTY AND HOMELESSNESS

The social justice topic we are choosing to focus on is poverty and homelessness, with an emphasis on soup kitchens. This topic relates to children's lives because some children may have had to go to a food pantry or soup kitchen for food at some point or there may be people who live in poverty in their communities. This lesson also informs children who have never been exposed to poverty about this part of our society. It may also allow children who have had to rely on a soup kitchen for their meals to feel heard, and it could open up discussions that allow them to appreciate others' understanding of their situation.

We have found that teachers may need to know about some of the deficit-oriented and incorrect stigmas that some families may have about poverty and homeless people, so they can address and correct these misconceptions through instructional experiences grounded in inquiry practices. This particular lesson may allow children to develop a better understanding of what poverty is and how they can do their part to help, with an emphasis on community soup kitchens.

This experience focuses on addition, pricing, number sense, and self-checking through collaboration in pairs. This lesson will take approximately 45 minutes and can be completed in 1 day with extensions through multiple days following as needed. In addition to academic standards, this social justice lesson explores concepts such as poverty, community service, volunteering, compassion, and respect for others. The mathematics lesson also integrates other areas of academic standards such as Social Studies, ELA, health, and economics. While the standards we list are for first grade, they could be modified for a variety of grade levels.

DEEP AND RICH MATHEMATICS

The mathematics content in this lesson focuses on addition, subtraction, economics, budgeting, and number sense. This inquiry-based lesson empowers children by allowing them to create their own money-focused addition strategies to engage in problem solving that directly relates to helping their community. It provides children an opportunity to see how mathematics is used throughout our communities on a daily basis and empowers them to apply their strategies and knowledge to other aspects of their lives.

ABOUT THE LESSON

In this 1-day lesson, children will work collaboratively in pairs to explore a real-world issue.

Resources and Materials

- Book: *Uncle Willie and the Soup Kitchen* by DyAnne DiSalvo-Ryan

- Real or pretend grocery items (e.g., chicken, carrots, tomatoes, peas, potatoes, broth, onions, parsley, string beans) *or* printed pictures of items (at least five items per pair)

- Price tags for each item (prices can be "friendly numbers," such as whole numbers)

- A blank sheet of paper and pencil or a whiteboard with a dry-erase marker (1 set per pair)

- A set of thirty $1 manipulatives in a paper clip for each pair of children

LESSON FACILITATION

Preparation

- Organize a "grocery store" and supply all items labeled with price tags needed beforehand. Ensure that the store is set up in the back of the classroom to minimize distractions for children working throughout the classroom.

Launch (20 minutes)

- Display on an interactive whiteboard (or document camera or projector) a premade list of all the groceries that are available at the store and their prices.

- Engage children in whole-group discussion by asking them questions about how it might feel to not have enough to eat:

  + *Have you or someone you know experienced being hungry before? What would happen if you or someone you knew did not have enough money to buy food when they are hungry?*

+ *What are some ways that you have seen people help others who might be hungry?*

+ *Have you ever been to a soup kitchen before?*

+ *What can you tell the group about soup kitchens?*

+ *Why do you think someone might go to a soup kitchen? What makes you think that?*

- Read the story *Uncle Willie and the Soup Kitchen* by DyAnne DiSalvo-Ryan and ask questions throughout to ensure children's engagement and comprehension.

- During the reading, you may ask questions such as these:

+ *Why do you think the little boy wanted to turn in the other direction when he saw the can man?*

+ *Why is the little boy being so quiet when all the people are coming in?*

+ *I noticed when the little boy sees a person who is homeless, he wants to turn the other way. But Uncle Willie stops and talks to the man. Why did Uncle Willie do this and how do you think this made the man feel? Why do you think the boy reacted that way?*

+ *Let's make a prediction. Do you think he will talk to any of the people? Why or why not?*

- After the reading, ask questions such as these:

+ *What did the little boy learn about giving back to the community?*

+ *Was he scared of the people without homes in the end? Why not?*

+ *Why is it important to respect all people even if they are different from you?*

+ *How does this story relate to other stories we have read?*

+ *Has anyone ever felt like the little boy in the story?*

Note: Be prepared to listen to children's responses with an open mind and with acceptance and curiosity in relation to their own experiences. Use support from the read-aloud to guide your responses. Children should be comfortable asking uncomfortable questions, and you should set the stage for acceptance and open-mindedness in the learning environment. This should be established at the beginning of the year, but can be worked into the classroom through a use of different strategies beginning with talking less and listening more. It is important to understand how children are reacting to the topic while relating any misconceptions and inappropriate comments back to the central idea of humanity and becoming more aware of aspects of the community that may not directly affect them.

- Following the read-aloud discussion, explain to the class that they will be making their own soup just like Uncle Willie did, as if they were helping their local food pantry or soup kitchen.

- Explain that, while soup is a delicious meal that can be enjoyed by anyone, it is particularly great for people who may not be able to afford a lot of food to still have a warm meal with lots of vegetables and nutritious ingredients. Soup is typically inexpensive and easy to make, and you can use a wide variety of ingredients.

Explore (20 minutes)

- Go over the items that you have selected to be available at the store, depending on your children's experience with the items. The following list is an example, but feel free to shorten or lengthen the list based on the relevance of your class. This shared list can be created using interactive writing strategies and could be developed based on the foods that are common to your community.

Groceries Available at the Store

	$5	Chicken
	$2	Potatoes
	$2	Vegetable Broth
	$1	Carrots
	$1	Peas
	$1	Green Beans
	$1	Tomatoes
	$1	Parsley
	$__	(extra ingredient)

Source: chicken icon by egudinKa/iStock.com; beets, cabbage, carrots, and peas icons by uiliaaa/iStock.com; potatoes, tomato, and meat icons by Thomas Lydell/iStock.com; rice icon by matsuriri/iStock.com; green beans icon by Satsuki Ioku/iStock.com

- Let children know that they will be working with a partner (predetermined based on mixed experiences as well as relationships and compatibility between children) to come up with a recipe for the soup and tell them that these are the items available for it. Remind children that a soup made from these items can be made with or without meat, and it will be relatively inexpensive, healthy, filling, and delicious. There might be items that you include that are necessary (such as the broth), others that you come up with as a class, and additional items that you allow pairs to decide to include.

- Send each predetermined pair back to their table or an area of the room where they can discuss their list of soup ingredients.

- Allow each pair to add one extra ingredient to their soup that they establish themselves after appropriate communication and agreement. They must be able to explain why they chose this item and how much they estimate it will cost.

- As they are working, ask questions such as these:

  + *What ingredients are you putting in your soup?*

  + *How are you going to make sure you have enough ingredients to feed everyone?*

  + *Why did you choose the ingredients?*

  + *How do you think these ingredients might be good for someone who hasn't eaten in a while?*

  + *What other ingredients can you use to add nutrition to your soup?*

  + *Do you think that it is possible to add too much of one ingredient? Why?*

  + *What was your "extra ingredient" that you decided to add? Why did you choose this ingredient? How do you think it will make your soup even better? How did you estimate the price? How did the other items listed affect the price you decided on?*

- After the pairs have developed their lists, allow them to visit the "grocery store" and pick out the ingredients they chose. Then have the children figure out how much money they will need to buy their items (the sum based on the prices of the items).

- Encourage them to show their strategies for figuring out how much money it will cost on their whiteboard or paper. Once they have represented their strategies, they can bring you their items along with the correct amount of money.

- As you are checking to see that they have the right amount of money, discuss with each pair their strategies for deciding on ingredients and finding out the total sum. Remind children that they had $30 to spend and encourage them to think through the amount of each ingredient they chose and whether or not they should make any changes to their shopping list.

- Ask questions such as the following:

  + *What strategies are you using to find the sum of your ingredients?*

  + *How do you know you have enough money?*

  + *Explain to me how you all are coming up with your total price.*

  + *Why did you add these numbers first and then these?*

  + *How might you use the rest of your money?*

  + *How many people do you think your soup will feed? How do you know?*

  + *Have you ever had a meal that simply was not enough for your whole family?*

  + *So if your soup can feed 5 people, how can you make it feed 10 people?*

- As you facilitate these small group discussions about what ingredients they used and how much money they ended up spending, focus on comparing and contrasting different sums and ingredient lists (similarities and differences) and explaining the effect of ingredient price differences on the overall sum.

- You can extend and challenge children by asking questions such as these:

  + *What if you had a donation of broth and didn't need to purchase that for your soup. Then what would be the cost?*

  + *What if you had free, fresh tomatoes from the community garden and didn't have to pay for them. Then what would be the cost of your grocery bill?*

  + *How would it make you feel if you didn't have to spend money on that item for your soup? Could you use that money to go toward another ingredient to make your soup even better or for something else?*

Summarize (10 minutes)
- Bring the class back together as a whole group and facilitate discussion by asking children to share what ingredients they chose and how much money they spent.

- Consider these prompts:

  + *Is your soup healthy? Why or why not?*

  + *What kind of protein does your soup have?* [chicken or beans]

  + *Is your soup vegetarian? What would you change to make it vegetarian or vice versa?*

  + *Why do you think your soup would be tasty?*

  + *Is your soup expensive compared to others?*

  + *How could you change your soup to make it cheaper?*

- Decide beforehand as you are speaking with children who you will choose to share during this discussion. Look for children who chose different recipes, as well as different strategies for finding the sum, to discuss how the strategies were different.

- Also look for children who chose strategies that are successful but may require more communication in order for other children to understand, as this will facilitate child-to-child discussion and justification of the process they used to find the sum. Other possibilities for ways to facilitate this discussion include identifying those who communicated well with one another, children who chose different grocery list items, or children who made a mistake but then corrected themselves to frame the reflective discussion.

- Following this discussion of addition strategies, brainstorm with the children what it might be like to bring their soup to a soup kitchen or food pantry. Ask questions connecting both to the read-aloud and to real-world contexts:

  + *How might making your soup help people?*

  + *How many people do you think it could feed? Explain how you know.*

  + *In the story, how did making all the food for the people who are homeless make the little boy feel?*

  + *Why is it important to give back to people in our community?*

  + *How should we treat people that may be different from us or come from different backgrounds?*

  + *What are some ways that we could help out in our own community?*

  + *How do you think that making soup for a soup kitchen would make the people who need it feel?*

  + *How does helping people make you feel?*

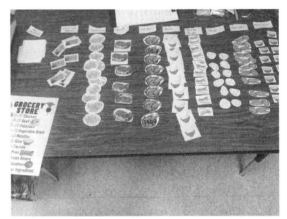

TAKING ACTION

Individual, Class, or School

- Visit a soup kitchen.

    + The class or grade level could organize a field trip to a local soup kitchen or food pantry.

    + Classes would get an in-person understanding of what they had learned about previously. They may be inspired to take their families to a soup kitchen in the future or consider a soup kitchen as a volunteer opportunity as they get older.

    + The class would be able to interact with the people they are helping and hopefully be inspired to do more for those around them.

Local Community Organizers or Organizations

- Write letters to homeless shelters or other community organizations focused on supporting those in need.

    + This is a good alternative if a soup kitchen field trip is not feasible.

    + Have children draw pictures or write letters of hope for those who may need it.

- Hold a canned food drive for or collect money to donate to a local food pantry.

    + Food is still donated to those who need it.

    + Children can discover how to help others for the rest of their lives in an easy and inexpensive way.

COMMUNICATING WITH STAKEHOLDERS

Families

This lesson can be communicated to the families through the weekly newsletter or virtual communication tool (e.g., text-based app, email, learning management system) and presented in a way that introduces the goals of the lesson, both the social justice topic as well as academic goals. Ideally, families would be deeply engaged in the Taking Action tasks following the lesson. If there is a family in the class that utilizes a food pantry regularly, you could approach them to let them know about the work the class has been doing in mathematics and tell them that you are hoping their child's class can work to understand how important these concepts (community-mindedness, empathy, and support for others) are for all families to benefit from and, ultimately, for children in your class to understand the importance of helping others.

(Continued)

(Continued)

Explain that you hope to inspire the children and their families to get involved within local soup kitchens or food pantries. You could also ask families if there is anything they would like you to highlight to the class in particular about supporting their community and helping local families. You might ask if they are willing to share their story if you feel it appropriate and respectful. Further, it is important for teachers to continuously communicate strategies for families to engage in discussions at home around inequities that are present in the community and to make plans for how they might combat these inequities as a family. These strategies might take the form of weekly discussion topics that the teacher proposes to families, weekly read-alouds to share, or tasks that families can embed into their everyday living (finding the ingredients they used in their soup at the grocery store when shopping with their families).

Community

If the lesson is extended and the children participate in any of the Taking Action suggestions, the children in your classroom will be able to display their contributions to society in a variety of ways. The children in your classroom will be able to communicate directly with stakeholders if a trip is organized to visit a community soup kitchen or if they are able to write letters to people affected by homelessness or who are in need of the local soup kitchen.

BACKGROUND OF THE LESSON

The schools where these lesson experiences were developed are located in the upstate region of South Carolina. The schools were identified because of their diverse populations and commitment to meeting the needs of children while also supporting the needs of the community. These Title I settings also place emphasis on the development of 21st century skills with a specific focus on the Learning for Justice domains of Identity, Diversity, and Action by implementing instruction grounded in the processes of inquiry and connected to real-world contexts.

This lesson focuses on a first-grade classroom but could be modified for PreK to second grade easily by adapting the cost of items, the number of ingredients, and the depth of discussion emerging out of an experience in which children create a plan for making soup that might be distributed in a food pantry or soup kitchen.

ABOUT THE AUTHORS

Elizabeth Barnes graduated with a Masters degree in Early Childhood Education from Clemson University through the Teacher Residency program in spring of 2022. She is a member of the Clemson's honors fraternity Alpha Lambda Delta as well as Clemson's Council for Exceptional Children. Elizabeth feels she was shaped to be an advocate for social justice education because of her experiences in a year-long Head Start placement. After seeing so many children with adverse experiences within her community, it allowed her to truly understand how important it is to advocate for those around her.

Jordan Barnes graduated from Clemson University in the Spring of 2021 with a degree in early childhood education. She is now a first-grade teacher at Beaufort Elementary. While at Clemson, she was a member of Alpha Delta Pi Sorority where she served as vice president of panhellenic relations. She was also a member of the Diversity, Equity, and Inclusion Committee for the Undergraduate Student Advisory Board for the College of Education. She switched her major to education her sophomore year and saw how local school districts did not have many people of Color in leadership roles. Jordan once heard a little girl who happened to be the only Black student in her class say that she wished she was white, and she realized how much students need positive role models who looked like them in the education system. She joined the Diversity, Equity, and Inclusion Committee at the university, started talking to peers who looked different from her, and really saw the need to push for more people of different racial, cultural, gendered, and other identities in our education system. In order to make that happen, schools must be a place where we can listen to people who have experienced injustice and work together with them to make a difference. Jordan's goal is to be a voice for every one of her students and help them to understand that differences should be embraced because that is what makes us special.

Natalie Uhle graduated from Clemson University in May 2021 with a degree in early childhood education. During her time as an undergraduate student, she was a member of Kappa Delta Sorority, where she served on the Diversity, Equity, and Inclusion Committee and was a member of Clemson's Council for Exceptional Children. She is now attending the Medical University of South Carolina, pursuing a master's degree in speech language pathology. She is on track to graduate in the summer of 2023. Having an older brother with a disability is what first ignited Natalie's passion for social justice. She believes that he is capable of anything, and she has always been an advocate for people with disabilities in the same way. After having field placements at Clemson University and being exposed to children of all races and ethnicities, abilities, and socioeconomic backgrounds, her passion for equity and social justice only grew. She had loved working with so many students and believes that, just like her brother, each one of them deserves the opportunity to accomplish anything.

Sandra M. Linder is a professor of early childhood mathematics education at Clemson University. Her research focuses on increasing parent and child interactions around mathematical play and supporting teacher practices around early mathematics. She started engaging in teaching through a social justice lens after realizing that while her teacher preparation included a focus on culturally responsive practice, it did so in a passive way. While part of teaching through social justice is certainly focused on teaching children to respect and honor other cultures, there is also a more active lens grounded in preparing children to become advocates for themselves and for those around them as they grow. It is with this lens that she strives to support both preservice and in-service teachers as they implement instruction.

LESSON 5.11 REPRESENTATION MATTERS IN MATHEMATICS CLASS

Amber Beisly and Brandy McCombs

MATHEMATICAL ACCESS AND IDENTITY

The social justice outcome we are working toward is mathematical access and identity for all children in the classroom—that all young children in the classroom see themselves reflected in the class materials and as capable and confident mathematicians. Mathematics education organizations like NCSM and TODOS (2016) have highlighted the need for educators to take asset-based perspectives toward the diversity of learners in mathematics classrooms, yet children who do not get the chance to see themselves reflected in curriculum may continue to languish in mathematics if they are not connected to the subject. The lesson presented here is designed for children to critically analyze representation in mathematics curricula, address the lack of representation through making their classroom a space where they feel connected to the work of mathematics, and see themselves as valuable mathematical people.

These lessons support children to engage with anchor standards from two Learning for Justice domains: Identity and Diversity. From the Identity 1 standard, children will "develop positive social identities based on their membership in multiple groups in society" (2016, p. 3). We chose this standard because we want children to see themselves as mathematicians capable of engaging in mathematicians' work—developing ideas, collaborating with others, and sharing ideas. Indeed, when children begin to see themselves as capable mathematicians, it can nurture other parts of their identity. Without seeing themselves in the curriculum, children may feel that they have different parts of themselves—a school self and a home self, or even an English-speaking self and a Spanish-speaking self. However, when teachers bring children's community knowledge into the classroom, children may feel more connected to the mathematics as well as feel whole and humanized, creating more positive social and cultural identities.

From Diversity 8, children in your classroom will "respectfully express curiosity about the history and lived experiences of others and will exchange ideas and beliefs in an open-minded way." As part of this lesson, children will bring in items from home that can be part of a counting collections activity, and they will have

- I know and like who I am and can talk about my family and myself and name some of my group identities. (Identity 1)

- I like being around people who are like me and different from me, and I can be friendly to everyone. (Diversity 6)

MATHEMATICS DOMAINS AND PRACTICES

- Number and Operations

- Make sense of problems and persevere in solving them. (MP1)

- Construct viable arguments and critique the reasoning of others. (MP3)

opportunities to talk with classmates about their different items and the significance of items to each other. They may even make connections to each other, telling stories about their lives and what these items mean to them. For children who do not see their realities reflected in mathematics curriculum, we want them to see themselves in the mathematics they are learning.

We connect the goals of lessons like these to larger issues of how children see themselves as complex beings in the world. We hope that when children can affirm their membership in multiple groups and are willing to exchange ideas and beliefs in an open-minded way, they will be more inclined to recognize and respond to others. Children can understand how they can be at once a multilingual person, a first grader, a Latinx student, and a member of a given neighborhood, for example, and how these identities help shape their ideas and beliefs. Children can then recognize how others with similar or different identities have been mistreated or excluded and learn to critically examine mathematics curriculum for representation.

DEEP AND RICH MATHEMATICS

In this session, children will work toward understanding the concept of unitizing through collections. They will get multiple opportunities to hone their counting skills (number name, number order, one-to-one tagging, organization, etc.) as they engage in counting collection-type activities. Children will have multiple opportunities to talk about how items can be grouped as part of efficient counting strategies for large sets of objects and to bring items from home to share and count. Throughout the lesson, children will have opportunities to develop proficiency in counting in home and school languages (e.g., Spanish and English, or whichever home and school languages are part of your context).

ABOUT THE LESSON

This lesson's main idea is to use children's objects from home to practice mathematical skills; children use their own objects to count or use their own pictures as inspiration for solving number stories. To launch the lesson, present examples from the curriculum for the children to examine. As children notice a lack of representation in these items and number stories, they are encouraged to bring items from home and pictures to create their own curriculum. As part of these lessons, children tell number stories about the items they bring to count from home. When the children bring in items from home, they share the items and why they were chosen. The items become part of the classroom manipulatives library—part of the classroom tools for learning mathematics.

This set of lessons could be presented as a unit or a classroom routine. As a standalone unit, it may occur over 1 or 2 weeks, with children given daily opportunities to practice counting over consecutive lessons. This lesson works well at the beginning of the year for second graders to work on their unitizing and counting skills. It also works early in the year for first-grade children to gain sophisticated counting techniques. The lesson works for kindergarteners in spring to challenge them to count up and into decades and hundreds. With small collections and an explicit focus on developing counting skills, this lesson could work for PreK children.

As a routine, this lesson can take place once per week or once every few weeks as needed. Children could engage in "counting collections Monday" to build on their counting skills. The story-problem strategy can also be utilized to connect the taught concept to the real-world application at the end of a daily lesson. For 1 week, the same picture can be used as you apply the concept in different ways.

Resources and Materials

- Counting baskets (large containers to hold items). Select the size of the containers carefully, as you will challenge children at one point to fill them. Smaller baskets for small items might make sense for younger children, whereas older children may be challenged to fill the same-sized containers with smaller objects like beads, coins, and so on.

- Counters

- Worksheet 1: *Counting Collections Recording Sheet*

- Ten-frames, hundreds charts, or other materials children may use to organize and make sense of their collections

- Images of children's native countries and cultures

- Teacher Resource 1: *Math Game Directions*

- Teacher Resource 2: *Sample Family Letter*

- Coins and items for buying/selling (for an extension activity)

LESSON FACILITATION

Day 1

Launch (15 minutes)

- Ask children to sit in a circle, next to partners. Partners should be set up to support and scaffold language as necessary (i.e., an intermediate-level Emergent Bilingual child may be paired with a multilingual child).

- Post images taken from your first-grade mathematics textbook (or other publicly available mathematics worksheet or curricula) for the children to see. The pictures may include a set of base-10 blocks (tens and ones), a sample number story, or images from the textbook (see the following sample pictures).

- Begin the discussion by telling children you have some pictures from a mathematics textbook to show them. Ask that they look at the pictures and simply think about these questions:

  + *What do you see in these pictures?* (Ask children to name the items in the pictures if they are familiar with them)

  + *Who is represented in these pictures?*

  + *What do these pictures mean? Do the pictures mean anything to you?*

  These questions are adapted from the say-mean-matter framework found in Yeh and Otis (2019).

Source: cake and milk icon by R-DESGIN/ iStock.com; popcorn icon by Barkarola/ iStock.com; cupcake icon by Designer29/ iStock.com

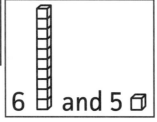

Source: Irina_Strelnikova/ iStock.com

- Children can discuss with a partner first before discussing with the whole group.

  Note: Some children may not have experience with base-10 blocks yet. If so, you may respond that they are a mathematics tool that some mathematics thinkers use to help them count.

- For *What do these pictures mean?* you can encourage children to think about if the objects have meaning to them: their lives, their classroom, how they do mathematics, and so on. For example, encourage children to think about if the children look like people they know; if the objects you show are things they are familiar with; etc. Some children may have this knowledge, some may not. The children know that these pictures came from a mathematics book and may try to make sense of the pictures mathematically by creating a story around the pictures—for example, purchasing items from the prices given. However, children may also struggle to make sense of the pictures mathematically, and we can name that too.

- After a brief discussion, pose a prompt such as this:

  + *Why does this matter?*

- Children may not be able to precisely answer this question, so you can ask a follow-up question:

  + *Do you see people or items like this in your home or community?*

  + *Do these pictures represent the math calculations that you need in your life?*

  + *Do you think your math textbooks and math problems should be about real problems in your life?*

- The picture of the children, in particular, is not representative of many classrooms. This would encourage children to connect that what counts as "math" is not reflected in children's images of themselves or their communities in this mathematics curriculum.

- You can then read or show another example of a mathematics problem found in the textbook. We provide one next for planning purposes; but we encourage you to find one that is from your text, as the farm context may not be relevant to children in your classroom.

  + *The problem: On Mr. Smith's farm, there are some pigs. Seven are eating corn, and 8 are drinking water. How many pigs are there all together?*

- Ask questions such as these:

  + *What does this problem say?*

  + *What does it mean? What is the math involved?*

  + *Why does it matter?*

  + *Do you do these kinds of calculations at home?*

- To ensure that children begin to take a critical look at the curriculum, you can use a think-aloud sharing where they model some of the thinking (*This kind of problem isn't the kind of math thinking that I would have to do at home.*) You can also respond by asking follow-up questions.

- You can connect to this lesson's content by saying:

  + *We are going to use our own pictures and items as the curriculum for this lesson.*

Explore (20 minutes)

Note: The following is an example.

- Introduce pictures that children have brought in. Support children to notice what can be counted in their images.

    + *Today we are going to look at an image that one of you brought in of a building.* (Have the child describe the picture.)

    + *I'm noticing the building in this picture has 7 columns, or very large posts, right here. I wonder how many more columns would we have to add to make a total of 10?* (Point to the columns so children understand the feature to attend to.)

- Select an authentic mathematics question that came up from your mathematizing, and ask children to share how they would solve it with partners and then with the whole group.

- Using the same image, encourage children to create their own questions (e.g., number stories, "how many" questions) with their partners (this can be using the same picture or partners, each using a different picture).

- As children are developing mathematics problems based on the pictures, encourage use of home languages and sharing of traditions at home.

- Ask children to share their stories, and have them discuss their answers to the stories. When children are sharing their strategies, be sure to ask questions about both the images and the mathematics:

    + *Where is this picture from? Who is in it? What are you doing?*

    + *Show us how you solved that. How did you know what to do? How else could you have solved that? Is this what you were thinking [as you represent their thinking]? Have I summarized it correctly?*

Day 2

Launch (15 minutes)

- Review with children what was discussed the previous day.

- Ask a child to develop their own number story (or mathematics problem) to solve related to something that they have recently experienced at home or in the classroom.

- Connect to the lesson's mathematical content (unitizing) by talking about how mathematicians work to develop strategies for solving problems, communicate those strategies to others, and compare their strategies with each other.

Explore (20 minutes)

- Provide children with counting baskets (small containers to hold items) by saying:

  + *These baskets hold manipulatives, but I am unsure of exactly how many manipulatives they can hold.*

  + *How many of your favorite manipulatives do you think this basket can hold?*

- Let children work in purposefully paired small groups of two (or three) to fill their baskets, come up with a strategy to count out the manipulatives, and complete Worksheet 1 (*Counting Collections Recording Sheet*). Be thoughtful in putting together children with different experiences and language backgrounds so that children can learn from one another.

- As children write and record their answers, circulate and ask children to explain their grouping/counting. Encourage them to use words, pictures/drawings, or other representations.

- Take notes about which strategies children are using and invite several children to share their strategy with the whole group when you reconvene (so that they are prepared).

Summarize

- After children have counted their collection of items, call the group back together.

- Together with the class, create an anchor chart to record how groups of objects can be counted. The chart will become an ongoing list of children's strategies and should reflect the variety of children's thinking. You may want to have a child share their thinking while another child records that thinking on the anchor chart, as appropriate to your class.

- Children should have opportunities to listen to different counting strategies. Throughout the lesson, you should emphasize that there is more than one correct way to group and count items. As children demonstrate a counting strategy, others may practice the strategy to make sure they understand. Encourage children to ask questions about how they record strategies (e.g., *Why did you choose to circle groups of 3? What does this 5 mean?*).

- You may want to use sentence starters and prompts, such as these:

  + *Can you show us what you did?*

  + *I disagree because_____. I think instead that the answer is _____.*

  + *Who can say that in their own words?*

- When children are finished sharing, review the anchor chart with them to summarize the strategies developed throughout the lesson. Reinforce the idea that multiple strategies exist, and that mathematicians use and share multiple strategies.

Day 3

Day 3 is a time for you to choose what the children in your classroom are ready for.

Option 1: More Collection Counting

Repeat the Explore counting activity from Day 2 with new collections. Encourage children to take up new counting strategies or to try things out they are not as familiar with. Encourage them to bring in new collections to count. With increased counting opportunities, children get to work with different, larger, and more complex problems. Also, many days of counting collections gives more opportunities for children to bring in collections of objects from home to count.

For more on supporting multilingual children in the mathematics classroom, see *Teaching Math to Multilingual Students, Grades K–8* by Chval et al. (2021).

As the opportunities for counting large sets of objects continue, the number of items collected gets larger and larger, requiring children to focus their energy on more efficient ways of grouping items. By working in groups and using whatever language is comfortable, children have the cognitive energy to focus on the task at hand—keeping track of all those items. You can also utilize other strategies to ensure that multilingual children can access the content without relying on English-only language. Strategies include allowing children to respond in their home language or translating content from English to their home language using student or computer-assisted translators. You can also support *translanguaging* by attending to how children use multiple languages, gestures, and expressions to communicate their understanding.

Option 2: Setting Up a Store

This activity encourages children to continue to tell mathematics stories and apply their counting strategies to money. In our classrooms, we set up a panadería (bakery). Ideally, the store would be a replica of a store seen in the children's neighborhood or community. Bring in as many authentic items (menus, pictures of the store, decorations) as possible and let children create the items and price tags. Children can use any combination of coins (dimes and pennies, nickels and pennies), including coins that are not U.S. currency, or children can even create their own currency. Give children time to practice buying items and being the panadera (baker). Because of the use of money, we recommend you decide if this activity is appropriate for your age group.

Option 3: Math Games!

Maybe children in your classroom are ready for a different kind of counting challenge. In Teacher Resource 1, we provide the instructions and materials sheet for a mathematics game to keep the counting going.

TAKING ACTION

Our lesson's social justice components involve first graders seeing themselves as mathematicians and as part of a community of mathematicians. There are several ways children, teachers, administrators, and the community can follow through on this lesson to support children's identity development. The ideas in this section represent separate lessons that could occur before the counting lessons, alongside the counting lessons, or after children have completed the entire lesson.

You and the children in your classroom can work to define what mathematics is, what mathematics looks like, and how to do mathematics. Children can use multiple resources to build on this knowledge. First, they can look at their mathematics curriculum/textbook. By completing a picture review, children can examine how mathematics is pictured in the textbook. You and the children in your classroom can ask questions like these:

- *Are the pictures in the textbook familiar to the children?*

- *Are they similar to the pictures that the children brought in to represent their families and culture?*

- *Do the number stories use familiar words and names?*

Children can then report the results to the administration. If children find that they are not represented in the mathematics curriculum, they can set up a meeting with the principal to explain why. From this meeting, the principal may be able to offer children and you more flexibility in incorporating activities and images into the mathematics curriculum that are more representative.

Children, teachers, and the community can also look for ways to bring mathematics into the classroom. For example, you and the children in your classroom can go on a mathematics review around the neighborhood. If that's not possible, you or the children can take pictures of buildings and stores in the children's community to examine what sort of mathematics is present or to look for ways to connect family practices to mathematics. For example, in our community, children may visit a panadería (bakery) or a pastelerías (pastry shop) to look at ways in which the bakers use counting.

By utilizing pictures from different cultures and regions of the world, all children's perspectives are expanded. Comparisons and similarities can be drawn between the various images. Appreciation for differences can be made, and connections can be made through the similarities. An additional benefit of this approach is the opportunity for communication. Teachers can intentionally create a welcoming atmosphere that supports rich conversations about differences and similarities. Using the universal thread of mathematics, differences that were once viewed as vast can now be seen as connected.

COMMUNICATING WITH STAKEHOLDERS

- During this lesson, you are in regular contact with parents/caregivers about the lesson's progress. At the beginning of the lesson, send home a letter (see Teacher Resource 2) asking for pictures and items for counting. You can then send home weekly reflections on how the lesson is going, including pictures of how children are counting. In the letter, highlight the importance of bringing in elements of the home into the classroom. If you anticipate doing a mathematics review, you will need to inform parents/caregivers about the review's purpose and details.

- You will also need to communicate to the principal before engaging in this kind of lesson, especially if you are expected to closely follow a specific curriculum. You will need to communicate the lesson's goals and let the administration know that children are engaging in identity work and critically examining the mathematics curriculum.

- Children have opportunities at the end of each lesson to summarize and synthesize their learning on a topic. They can then communicate with their parents/caregivers about their learning. Children choose their own images and pictures to create connected story problems that utilize mastered mathematics concepts. By selecting the backdrop of the mathematical story problem, the children are empowered to express their mathematical comprehension and application and personal cultural connections.

ONLINE RESOURCES

 Available for download at **resources.corwin.com/TMSJ-EarlyElementary**

▼ Worksheet 1: *Counting Collections Recording Sheet*

▼ Teacher Resource 1: *Math Game Directions*

▼ Teacher Resource 2: *Sample Family Letter*

BACKGROUND OF THE LESSON

The school district in which this lesson was developed is in Tulsa, Oklahoma, and has approximately 16,000 children in PreK through Grade 12. Over the past 10 years, the district and the city of Tulsa have seen increasing population growth, including among Latinx families, Burmese refugees, and other communities of Color. In addition to bringing cultural and linguistic diversity into Tulsa's classrooms, these families bring a wealth of experiences and academic knowledge. Many district schools utilize a "community school model," which means that the school has a health clinic and services from many community agencies. This community-mindedness does not necessarily trickle down into the mathematics classroom; however, we think there are ways it could. We want the lesson series presented here to cultivate community in the mathematics classroom and to help highlight how each individual child brings brilliance to the classroom, so they can feel their cultures represented within the mathematics classroom.

We are well aware of the research on what happens to children through schooling. When many children first begin school, they feel confident in their mathematics abilities and are eager to learn more (Fisher et al., 2012). In schools with many multilingual children, our student population is even more vulnerable to deficit-based labeling if they are not able to participate in mathematics lessons. Multilingual children are learning English while at the same time learning mathematics content in that unfamiliar language. This dual challenge makes it especially difficult for children to feel successful and see themselves as mathematicians (Galindo et al., 2019). Teachers can support children's mathematical identity by tapping into the knowledge sources children bring from their homes and communities. Gustein proposes a framework to help us understand mathematics as composed of three essential sources of knowledge—classical, community, and critical (for more information, see Gustein, 2006).

We have focused this lesson on making mathematics relevant to children by bridging home and school connections. One way to do this is to create mathematical experiences where children can examine mathematics alongside issues of fairness and where children can make a personal connection to what they are learning (Wang & Degol, 2014). Simultaneously, teachers must utilize strategies that scaffold multilingual children's understanding of language while providing rigorous academic instruction. Children will create an identity as a mathematician when provided with instruction that incorporates their background and gives them multiple opportunities to actively construct their own knowledge while examining how mathematics and those who do mathematics have been portrayed in the curriculum. When children can do this in collaboration with their classmates, the classroom becomes a community of mathematicians. The lesson series we developed highlights these principles and more, supporting children who are not traditionally positioned as mathematically brilliant children to apply their talents to critical analysis and action taking.

ABOUT THE AUTHORS

 **Amber Beisly** has worked as a classroom teacher for over 10 years with the same school in Tulsa, Oklahoma. Over her tenure, the population of the school shifted to include classrooms of majority Emergent Bilingual children. Yet the district's curriculum and teaching methods remained the same, and she found that she could not reach all students effectively. As she began to research other ways to teach mathematics, she realized it would become critical to include her students' rich backgrounds as much as possible to involve them in learning and help scaffold their learning. It provided a familiar anchor for them to guide their mathematics development. Attending to the whole child, not just focusing on their mathematics achievement, created more competent students who could do mathematics.

 **Brandy McCombs** teaches first grade in a suburban elementary school serving approximately 550 students in a highly impoverished and highly diverse area of Tulsa, Oklahoma (the same school as her co-author Amber). Forty-six percent of the students are categorized as Emergent Bilingual learners utilizing 16 different home languages. During Brandy's college years, she studied in another country. While attending a university and living with a host family, she gained a deep appreciation for learners who walk on different soil. As she became an elementary teacher, her appreciation changed to respect. Witnessing young learners who have experienced their entire worlds change before their eyes and continue to grow and hunger for knowledge has given her a passion for supporting them along the way.

LESSON 5.12 RESPECTING OUR HOUSE: PROTECTING OUR SALMON NEIGHBORS

Julia Maria Aguirre and Melissa Adams Corral

PROTECTING THE WATERSHED

This early childhood mathematics lesson centers on protecting the homes of the sacred salmon in the Pacific Northwest. It was adapted from two early learning units from Since Time Immemorial (https://bit.ly/3damXfT), which is a Washington State–mandated Indigenous-centered curriculum designed to help school districts "incorporate curricula about the history, culture, and government of the nearest federally recognized tribe or tribes so that children learn about the unique heritage and experience of their closest neighbors" (Revised Code of Washington, Curricula—Tribal history and culture, 2015).

The social justice focus is on collaborating with local tribal communities to be natural helpers and protect the watershed (home of salmon) from pollution. The Coast Salish peoples of the Pacific Northwest have been stewards of the land since time immemorial. Salmon are sacred. However, their growth and survival have been threatened over generations by pollution, dam construction, and overfishing by non-native people. Many of the local tribes run fish hatcheries to help strengthen the salmon population. This lesson also tries to address the erasure of local tribes from traditional school curriculum. The salmon cycle and recycling are common topics studied in pre-school and primary classrooms. However, many times, local tribes' contributions to these topics are not part of the traditional science, social studies, and language arts curriculum. We urge readers to visit their local tribes' websites and community centers to make sure more local Indigenous connections to social justice topics in traditional school curriculum are made. For example, in this lesson, we connect to the Northwest Indian Fisheries Commission (https://nwifc.org/). We all have a responsibility to collaborate with our Native American communities to make sure the land, air, and water remain clean and healthy for us and for our animal neighbors.

DEEP AND RICH MATHEMATICS

The mathematics embedded in this lesson focuses on early numeracy including practice with cardinality, one-to-one correspondence, subitizing, finding patterns, and sorting by characteristics.

SOCIAL JUSTICE OUTCOMES

- I find it interesting that groups of people believe different things and live their daily lives in different ways. (Diversity 10)

- I will speak up or do something if people are being unfair, even if my friends do not. (Action 19)

- I will join with classmates to make our classroom fair for everyone. (Action 20)

MATHEMATICS STANDARDS

- Number and Operations

- Measurement

- Data Collection and Analysis

- Make sense of problems and persevere in solving them. (MP1)

- Reason abstractly and quantitatively. (MP2)

- Construct viable arguments and critique the reasoning of others. (MP3)

- Model with mathematics. (MP4)

CROSS-CURRICULAR CONNECTIONS

- Science

- Language Arts

- Social Studies

This involves engaging with multistep problems using basic operations. This lesson also uses a mathematical modeling problem in which children are engaged in quantitative reasoning and problem solving about real-world phenomena.

ABOUT THE LESSON

This multiday lesson builds on children's understanding of respecting ourselves and others by being natural helpers to our salmon neighbors. It is adapted from the Since Time Immemorial Early Learning Curriculum offered in Washington State's Department of Children, Youth and Families (https://bit.ly/2ZKXLJP).

Resources and Materials

In-Person Learning
- Water/sensory table with the following materials:
    + Water
    + Rocks
    + Twigs/wood
    + Moss
    + Salmon rocks
    + Items collected on a nature walk
    + Plastic sandwich bags
    + Animal figurines
    + People figurines
    + Sand
    + Cornstarch
    + Pollution materials such as recyclable plastics, paper, wrappers, rubber, oil (please make sure they are nontoxic and nonhazardous)
- Vimeo Video: "Through Salmon Eyes," from Northwest Treaty Tribes (https://bit.ly/3G0s0fg)

Hybrid/Virtual Learning
- Adapted slides with images of a river bed; icons representing pollution materials

Additional Background
- Website: Washington State's Department of Children, Youth and Families, "Since Time Immemorial Early Learning Curriculum Lessons 2 and 3" (https://bit.ly/2ZKXLJP)

LESSON FACILITATION

Launch (20 minutes)

- Gather children in the whole group and pose the following question:

  + *How do we respect the place we live in?*

- Allow children to respond in a variety of ways and continue the discussion by saying something such as this:

  + *The place we live or **our home** can be many things—it can be our room, our house, or our apartment; it can be our neighborhood or community, it can be the land we walk on, the water we drink, and the air we breathe.*

  + *We are going to learn more about respecting our home, the land, and water that is so important to our lives.*

  + *We are going to learn this by taking the point of view of our animal neighbors, the salmon of the Pacific Northwest. The Coast Salish people in the region (Muckleshoot, Nisqually, Puyallup, Duwamish) work to protect the salmon, as they are important resources for the health of people and the health of the earth and water.*

- Watch the 12-minute Vimeo video produced by Northwest Treaty Tribes, "Through Salmon Eyes" (https://bit.ly/3G0s0fg).

- Prompt children with possible questions such as these:

  + *What were some things you learned about respecting the salmon's home?*

  + *How did Salmon Woman help bring the salmon back home?*

  + *What will keep the salmon healthy?*

- Next, tell children:

  + *From **August through November in our community** [some communities if you don't live there], our salmon friends come back home to lay their eggs to make baby salmon. It is a long and often dangerous journey because many things block their path home.* (Optional: Show the life cycle of salmon.)

- Show a picture or video of pollutants in the watershed (salmon home) and ask:

    + *What do you notice?*

    + *What do you want to know about this picture?*

    + *What do you wonder?*

    + *How do you feel?*

    + *How can we be helpers to our salmon friends?*

Explore (30 minutes per day)

- Introduce the water table (or your online slides if teaching remotely; see the *Resources and Materials* for suggestions). Say something like

    + *Your job, as natural helpers, is to clean this part of the salmon's home. What do you need to know to do this job?*

    + *How can we come up with a plan to clean up the water?*

    + *How do you know it is clean?*

- Let children come up with strategies to clean the river.

- Try/test out plans to clean the watershed. If you are teaching online, you can take direction from children about their plans (and families can participate and help too).

- Over the course of a few days, try to test out and discuss the advantages and disadvantages of various plans.

Note: Here are some examples of anticipated ideas and possible teacher responses.

Anticipated Ideas for Cleanup Strategies (Different Helping Strategies)	Possible Teacher Responses

All go at once and grab everything you can	• Discuss what worked and did not work about that strategy.
	• Analyze what the children were able to pick up, by counting or sorting. When sorting, consider what to do with the trash now:
	  • *Should we sort based on our ability to recycle or reuse? How can we do this?*
	  • *Did any trash remain in the watershed or fall elsewhere? How much?*
	• Attend to time phrasing: *This was really quick* or *We could clean this up very fast if everyone did it.*

Anticipated Ideas for Cleanup Strategies (Different Helping Strategies)	Possible Teacher Responses
One person and one thing at a time	• Discuss what worked and did not work about this strategy. • Use tally marks or another mechanism to keep track of the total number of items picked up as each child returns with their item. • Talk through the time that one-at-a-time strategies took.
Teams (decide on number of people) take out a category (color/shape) of objects. Use a different category per person	• Before enacting their plan, have children settle on decisions such as the number of people in a team and the categories they will use (trash type, plan for trash after pick-up, etc.). • After enacting their plan, talk through the advantages/disadvantages of the strategy. • Compare the number of items for each category. Ask: *How did that affect the plan?* • Talk through the time it took to sort while picking up objects.

Small groups (decide on number) go at a time and grab a designated number of objects (decide on a number)	• Before enacting their plan, have children settle on decisions such as the number of people going at one time and the number of objects to be picked up at a time.
	• After enacting their plan, talk through the advantages/disadvantages of the strategy.
	• Ask:
	  • *What strategies can we use to count the total number of objects?*
	  • *Can we skip count to a total number of objects removed?*
	  • *After counting, how can we sort our trash and plan next steps?*

Sort/classify: extend lesson
 	
Assign roles for the cleanup: certain children are picking up items, others are holding a container to put them in
	• Have teams/pairs count and sort what they picked up. When sorting, consider what to do with the trash now. Ask:
	  • *Should we sort based on our ability to recycle or reuse?*
	  • *How can we do this?*
	  • *Discuss and compare.*
	• Discuss ways of counting and tracking that teams were able to do. Ask:
	  • *How did the teams work together to make decisions about what to do with the trash?*

(Continued)

Anticipated Ideas for Cleanup Strategies (Different Helping Strategies)	Possible Teacher Responses
STEM connection: using tools to facilitate the cleanup process	• Encourage children to think about what properties would make for useful tools and to design, create, and test out tools for collecting trash on the riverbank or in the water. • Compare tools' relative effectiveness. Ask: 　• *Do certain tools work better for certain kinds of trash? Why?* 　• *How can we tell if we have a good tool?* 　• *Can numerical data help us to evaluate a tool's effectiveness?*

Summarize (20 minutes)

- As a class, compare and analyze each plan.

- Revisit the important qualities that the plans have in common and how the plans are different. Discuss the benefits and drawbacks for each plan. Decide which plan(s) they, as a class, agree that they liked the best.

TAKING ACTION

- **Share Learning With Local Tribal Communities.** Share and write the steps of the plans as part of a letter to the Northwest Indian Fisheries Commission (https://nwifc.org/) to explain how we are being natural helpers. This letter can include video recordings or pictures of the children's work.

- **Share Knowledge With Family and Community:** Independently/asynchronously, have children make a visual/picture to help salmon homes be safe. Invite children to share their knowledge with others by using their pictures on a sign that they can place in a window, in the school hallways, or elsewhere in their communities.

COMMUNICATING WITH STAKEHOLDERS

- Before teaching the lesson, you can let children's families know that you will be mathematizing with the Since Time Immemorial curriculum to investigate the preservation of the salmon's home.

- As the investigation is implemented in the classroom, you can encourage families to work together to do the following:

  + Learn what it means to live in "the house of the salmon" through a reading of the children's book *A River Lost* by Lynn

Bragg (2019), or by watching the video "Through Salmon Eyes" (https://bit.ly/3G0s0fg). Have discussions, participate in the investigation, and even create a river habitat or "home."

+ Through local trips, explore some of the many components of a healthy river habitat and the impact of pollution on this habitat and the living things connected to it.

+ Have a better understanding of why the salmon's home is important to humans, nature, and other living beings.

+ Begin to develop a sense of place, in relation to where and how children and their families live today.

+ Become aware that there were and are Native families since time immemorial, living where children and their families live today.

+ Learn the importance of stewardship and about the stewardship of natural resources that Native families have practiced since time immemorial.

• Following the activity, you can encourage parents/caregivers to ask children about their plans. Invite tribal community members to share with the class how they work to preserve our lands.

BACKGROUND OF THE LESSON

This resource was adapted from original materials provided by the Office of Superintendent of Public Instruction in partnership with the Federally Recognized Tribes in Washington State. Original materials may be accessed on the Since Time Immemorial (STI): Tribal Sovereignty in Washington State website. It was shared among early childhood educators as part of a year-long professional development focused on culturally responsive mathematics teaching with a content focus of mathematical modeling. It was also shared as part of our university mathematics methods courses. The goal of our adaptation was to explicitly connect to the STI curriculum and show how lessons with science, social studies, and literacy content could be modified in ways that incorporate mathematical modeling practices. STI is an example of a state-mandated curriculum that seeks to center Indigenous cultures, histories, and ways of life in the public school curriculum. The curriculum was mandated in 2015. Yet in our conversations with pre- and in-service teachers in Washington, we learned that this curriculum and the state mandate were not common knowledge. We designed this lesson to challenge the historical erasure of Indigenous knowledge and community contributions by bringing attention to the high-quality materials that were developed as part of this curriculum, while also demonstrating how educators can modify the curriculum in ways that incorporate mathematics.

In the lessons prior to this focus on the salmon's habitat, the STI curriculum suggests that children engage in thinking about their families and the values they hold, while learning about a family from the Arrow Lakes Tribe that experienced a profound sense of loss when the Columbia River was dammed and their village was flooded. This lesson also introduces them to the ways that the river, and salmon, are key to this community's way of life. These ideas are extended in this lesson, where children begin to think of ways that they can directly have an impact on mitigating the harm to local rivers and salmon habitats. In subsequent lessons, the STI curriculum teaches children about watersheds, caring for watersheds, and uses cedar mat-weaving techniques to bring together the class's intentions with regard to caring for their local waterways.

By taking existing lessons and modifying them to include mathematical modeling tasks, we also hope that this lesson can help teachers think about connecting to local tribal communities as resources for lessons. We want teachers to better understand how existing social justice lessons and content can be expanded in ways that allow for children to engage in mathematical thinking that supports their developing critical consciousness.

ABOUT THE AUTHORS

Julia Maria Aguirre is a professor of education at the University of Washington Tacoma. She grew up in a home with a social justice activist father and educator mother. She identifies as a mixed-race Chicana woman of Mexican descent with a social justice agenda. As a student, she was involved in identity-affirming STEM programs in which she could bring her whole self to the learning space—the expectations were high and all young people were supported to meet them. This kind of transformative learning informed her mathematics teaching in formal and informal settings. Julia believes mathematics is a powerful analytical tool to understand and make change in the world. The work of Paolo Freire inspired her to understand mathematics education as a liberation tool. Bob Moses was the first to help her understand mathematics literacy as a civil right. And she is forever grateful for her anti-racist and culturally responsive mathematics journey with collaborators Danny Martin, Karen Mayfield-Ingram, Rochelle Gutiérrez, and Maria del Rosario Zavala. She is committed to supporting youth to experience mathematics with a sense of joy and justice, to be fully prepared to participate in our complex democracy, and to make informed decisions and take action; and she wants to prepare and collaborate with teachers who center children and their families as resources for learning and teaching mathematics. She is forever learning on this journey.

Melissa Adams Corral is an assistant professor of bilingual education at California State University-Stanislaus. She was a bilingual elementary school teacher in Austin, Texas, for 7 years, where she taught second, third, fourth, and fifth grades. During those years, she developed her practice as a social

justice educator, designing and teaching units on topics such as Afro-Latinx identity and anti-Black racism in México, street art and social change, and immigration and our community. The children she worked with encouraged her practice; their questions were what drove the curricular units and their ideas on how to shape our world are still what give her hope. Since then, she has been a co-teacher and researcher in preschool, elementary, and high school classrooms in Ohio and California, as well as a teacher-educator working with preservice and in-service teachers. Regardless of where she is teaching and learning (because she asserts these activities are inseparable), she chooses to center the people she is with—their questions, their desires, and their journeys.

- I can describe some ways that I am similar to and different from people who share my identities and those who have other identities. (Diversity 7)

- I want to know about other people and how our lives and experiences are the same and different. (Diversity 8)

- I find it interesting that groups of people believe different things and live their daily lives in different ways. (Diversity 10)

- I know that life is easier for some people and harder for others and the reasons for that are not always fair. (Justice 14)

MATHEMATICS DOMAINS AND PRACTICES

- Number and Operations

- Data Collection and Analysis

- Make sense of problems and persevere in solving them. (MP1)

- Construct viable arguments and critique the reasoning of others. (MP3)

- Model with mathematics. (MP4)

- Attend to precision. (MP6)

CROSS-CURRICULAR CONNECTIONS

- Language Arts

LESSON 5.13 EARLY ELEMENTARY MATHEMATICS TO EXPLORE PEOPLE REPRESENTED IN OUR WORLD AND COMMUNITY

Courtney Koestler, Eva Thanheiser, Mary Candace Raygoza, Jeff Craig, and Lynette Guzmán

THE DIVERSITY OF THE "GLOBAL VILLAGE"

The social justice topic that we explore in this lesson is the diversity of our world and how it is represented mathematically. Children explore a global context through a lens of critical literacy where they analyze a picture book as a non-neutral text, with the idea that "all texts are created from a particular perspective with the intention of conveying particular messages" (Vasquez, 2016, p. 3).

By shrinking the world into a village of 100 people and learning about different aspects of their lives—nationalities, languages spoken, religions practiced (or not!), access to drinking water, those living in poverty, etc.—"we can find out more about our neighbors in the real world and the problems our planet may face in the future" (Smith, 2011, p. 7). Exploring a global context through this lens can (1) encourage children's critical inquiry about all of humanity's access to basic human needs and distribution of resources, (2) recirculate stories about ourselves and our neighbors, and (3) open up conversations to learn from and with each other. Furthermore, engaging with these data can be affirming and/or challenge assumptions about who lives in our world and facets of their lives, empowering everyone to be more aware of and connected to the global community. Together, we resist U.S. individualism and U.S.-centric curriculum and stories about humanity.

DEEP AND RICH MATHEMATICS

This lesson prioritizes mathematical ways of comprehending problems. This includes starting problems using mathematics and mathematical language, making sense of mathematical relationships through decontextualizing and contextualizing problems, and utilizing mathematics to reconsider perspective. To accomplish these goals, children should be constantly reminding themselves that the World as 100 People is a lens for framing any problems they identify and analyze. Children use various representations (concrete such as Unifix cubes, pictorial representation, number lines, expressions, and graphs) and compare across them. Children also learn how to find data and then represent them.

ABOUT THE LESSON

This lesson highlights the value of visual representation as it helps to comprehend and analyze problems. Children can use many forms of representing these data, and they might see value in one representation over another through comparison and contrast. Children should be encouraged to view data visualizations as another conjugate within mathematical language, interconnected with the symbolic and numeric. Discussions should explore how certain kinds of representations make visible certain features of the given contextual situation, which might lend itself to particular inferences and meaning making.

Children can also begin to unpack the significant and nuanced discussion about objectivity and subjectivity, as it relates to mathematics and statistics. You should introduce or reintroduce the concepts of counting, sampling, and bias and demonstrate appropriate ways to question data without undermining the complexity of the task. In particular, you should assist children to approach data both without dismissive skepticism akin to these data being made up and without an undue idealism about the origins of these data. Children should discuss complex statistical concepts like precision and accuracy, alongside bias and subjectivity.

We anticipate this lesson to take between 2 and 2.5 hours in total, which could be split up across a series of days as needed. We include connections to mathematics domains that branch multiple grade levels, which could be modified based on the primary grade of focus.

Resources and Materials

- Book: *If the World Were a Village: A Book About the World's People* by David J. Smith (2011)

- Website: 100 People, "A World Portrait" (https://www.100people.org/statistics-100-people/)

- Video: "The 100 People Project: An Introduction," from 100 People (https://www.100people.org/the-100-people-project-an-introduction/)

- **Note:** On the 100 People website, "gender" is the first item discussed but it is reported as a binary using markers of male and female. This is problematic because it doesn't unpack the diversity of gender (or sex). This is a great opportunity for critical literacy. (The same issue happens in most videos related to this topic.) Thus, one suggestion is to start with the book by Smith and then follow up with the 100 People video.

- Poster paper

- Markers

- Rulers

- 10 × 10 grids

- Templates for bar graphs, pie charts cut into 100 pieces, and so forth

- Concrete materials

- Local data about race and ethnicity, languages spoken, and other topics children may be interested in (school-level, city-level, and state-level data can be appropriate)

- Teacher Resource 1: *Supplementary Video Links With Social Characteristics in Each*

LESSON FACILITATION

Day 1

Greeting (10 minutes)

- Begin the lesson with an opening circle greeting and community building activity entitled, *I love my neighbor who* . . . or *I have solidarity with people who* . . . The purpose of this activity is (1) to support children to get to know one another better and to build trust and community and (2) to challenge assumptions about one another and identify similarities and differences with one another.

- Have children circle up, seated in chairs, except for you in the middle.

- **Note:** It is suggested that you start in the middle of the circle to model the first prompt; you should participate fully as well.

- Begin by saying:

    + *I love my neighbor who* . . . and fill in the sentence with a trait or experience that is true for a child in the circle (e.g. "I love my neighbor who speaks Spanish").

- For whoever else it applies to, they must stand up and move to a new chair. The person who doesn't find a chair is the new person in the middle, and the process is repeated, similar to the game *Musical Chairs*.

- Prior to engaging in the activity, children should revisit classroom norms together (or create new norms) to ensure everyone is respectful and also knows they can choose not to participate or pass on particular prompts. In addition, children can brainstorm possible topics to include so that they are not caught off-guard thinking on the spot and so that a range of topics come up (e.g., birthday month, hair color or texture, favorite music genre, favorite hobbies). After children suggest topics, you may also offer some suggestions.

- **Note:** The activity will need to be designed around/accommodate for everyone's physical abilities.

- Close with a reflection and invite children to share what they learned, perhaps with one of the following sentence starters:

  + *I appreciated learning . . . [about one another].*

  + *We should not make assumptions about people because . . .*

Launch (15 minutes)

- Introduce the idea of shrinking the world's population down to a village of 100 people that represents it by reading the first few pages of *If the World Were a Village* by David J. Smith. Use a globe or map to provide context if necessary. (Supplementary websites or videos can also be used; see Teacher Resource 1.)

- After reading the introduction, ask:

  + *In the village of 100 people, how many people do you think would live in the United States [or North America]?*

  + *How many people do you think would speak English?*

- You may also engage children in wondering about or predicting other characteristics of the world's village discussed in the book (for example, the ages of the residents of the village, how many residents have regular access to electricity, or other aspects that you think the children would find interesting).

- Continue reading the book to explore the characteristics of the village. (We typically focus on reading the pages about Nationalities, Languages, and Religions because of the way that the data are presented, but you can also read other pages if children are interested.) You can also explore the video "100 People Project: An Introduction" (https://www.100people.org/the-100-people-project-an-introduction/).

- Next are examples of how you might support children in exploring the data, while at the same time unpacking the text using a critical lens.

- Review the Nationalities data with the children. Ask:

  + *What do you notice about the data?*

  + *What do you wonder about this data?*

  + *How do you feel about this data?*

- Children will typically notice, wonder, or ask the following. You can also bring up these ideas, making sure to provide a lot of space for children's ideas first.

  + *Five villagers are from the United States and Canada, but later on the page it says that 5 are from the United States. What do you think this means?*

  + *The author states that there are 9 villagers "from South America, Central America (including Mexico, and the Caribbean)" (Smith, 2011, p. 8). Why do you think the author decided to put Mexico with Central America when other continents are listed?*

- You might also want to explore follow-up questions:

  + *What exactly does nationality mean?*

  + *Who decides one's nationality?*

  + *How are language and culture related to nationality?*

  + *How many continents are there?*

- **Note:** Wikipedia has an interesting and informative page about continents (https://en.wikipedia.org/wiki/Continent), including a section about different ways of distinguishing the number of continents. You can discuss the socially constructed and contested nature of this information.

- Also ask:

  + *How could we represent this data?*

- Brainstorm with children multiple ways of representing data (e.g., conventional ways such as bar charts, pie charts, and pictograms) and unconventional ways such as hundreds charts (10 × 10 grids) using Unifix cubes.

- Take some time to brainstorm with children. Describe how they can use blank poster paper or templates of graphic organizers (bar charts, pie charts, 10 × 10 grids, Unifix cubes) to represent the data.

- While children are discussing representations, you should also ask them how different representations might communicate the data in different ways. For example, a pie chart shows the data in relationship to each other, whereas a bar graph more distinctly shows each piece of data.

Explore (45 minutes)

- Assign groups of four children to explore various topics. (Typically, the Nationalities and Religions data work well to begin with because of how the data are represented. The Languages data are also typically an interesting data set, but also introduce some complexity.)

- Allow for some independent think time to explore the topic and have each child sketch various representations for the topic. Then allow small groups to share their ideas and to decide on several representations to include on a shared poster. On the poster, they can freehand draw their representations or use templates to create their representations, depending on their experience with data representation. They should be encouraged to include titles, labels, and keys as well as try to show the connections between and among the different representations.

Summarize (15 minutes)

- After all posters are created, groups can display their posters and the class can do a gallery review to observe. Gallery reviews can be done in different ways; for example, children can do the gallery review silently, simply looking at the posters up close or discussing them in small groups. They could also have sticky notes where they are able to pose questions to the group, which the group members later answer during presentations. After the brief gallery review is complete, children can share in various ways about what they learned about the data and how their representations communicate these data.

> In an effort to use more inclusive language, we use the term *gallery review* for what is commonly referred to as a "gallery walk."

- Tell children they will continue the work the following day.

Day 2

Note: For Day 2, you will need to find data.

Launch (20 minutes)

- Revisit the representations children made on Day 1.

- Use prompts such as these:

    + *What do you notice about the representations you made? What do you wonder?*

    + *What is still confusing?*

    + *What is surprising about the data?*

    + *What questions do you have about the data or the issues related to the data?*

    + *What did you learn about our world from this data?*

> + *What did you appreciate working with one another here in our class-room community?*
>
> + *What do you want to know more about?*

- The two following questions are especially important to get at the critical literacy part of the lesson:

> + *How do your **different** representations communicate the data **differently**?*
>
> + *What assumptions went into the presentation of the data in the book?*

Explore (45 minutes)

- Find data about a context that you and your children are interested in—the country, their state, their city or town, and their school districts or schools. Public school and district data are also often easy to find on district or state board of education websites. (David J. Smith has also written a book called *If America Were a Village*.)

- Ask children what they notice about the data. Is the diversity (e.g., in terms of race and ethnicity, languages spoken) they see in the data represented in their own classroom? In their grade level? Why or why not?

- Repeat the process from Day 1, exploring data from children's city, town, school district, or school. (Have children create representations and discuss how different representations communicate the data in different ways.) This part could either immediately follow Day 1 or take place on another day.

- Then use these representations of the local data to make comparisons to the world data. Ask children what they notice and wonder about these comparisons.

TAKING ACTION

Individual, Class, or School

- After the lesson, children can create infographics to articulate what they have learned to their parents and caregivers about the diversity of the world to embody the Learning for Justice Standards (Diversity 8 and 10). They can use these infographics to compare their local communities to the greater world community (Diversity 7).

- Once children explore the diversity of their local context, they often are curious about resources and supports for different peoples. Teachers can engage children in using knowledge they gain to take action. For example, when children in one second- and third-grade classroom found out that there were a large number of children and families who spoke Spanish and Chinese but their school only had a Spanish Family Liaison support staff member working at the school, they wrote letters to the principal to find out why and to ask if there was any way to get funding for the Chinese-speaking families in the district.

Local Community, Organizers, or Organizations State, National, or Systems Level

- You may also support children to identify people (e.g., family members, politicians) or organizations (e.g., their own school) that may hold assumptions about who is represented in different spaces and to think about calling in or calling out those assumptions with data.

Communicating With Stakeholders

- Before teaching the lesson, you can let children's families know that you will be exploring the diversity in our world, both at the global and local levels. You can invite family members in to share their strengths, resources, and insights with the children. For example, if there are multilingual family members that would be willing to come in and share (e.g., by reading a book in a language other than English), invite them.

ONLINE RESOURCE

 Available for download at **resources.corwin.com/TMSJ-EarlyElementary**

Link	Where from	Languages	Gender	Age	Religion	Shelter	Food	Water	Toilet	Literacy	Education	Income/Wealth	Electricity	Cell Phone	Internet	Health
If the World Were a Village of 100 People: https://youtu.be/FtYjUv2x65g	X	X														
The 100 People Project: An Introduction https://www.100people.org/the-100-people-project-an-introduction/ https://www.100people.org/wp/the-100-people-project-an-introduction/	X		X		X			X		X	X		X			
If the World Were a Village of 100 People (2019 Edition): https://youtu.be/aLiFc0TJlY	X			X	X	X	X	X			X	X	X			
If The World Was 100 People (Jay Shetty): https://youtu.be/LXqOd5noN8g	X	X	X		X	X		X		X	X	X	X	X		
If The World Were 100 People (GOOD Data): https://youtu.be/QFrqTFRy-LU	X	X	X	X	X	X		X		X	X	X		X	X	X
What If Only 100 People Existed on Earth? https://youtu.be/UbffuGZHeR0	X	X	X	X	X	X	X	X	X	X	X	X		X	X	X
If the World Was Only 100 People (Knovva): https://youtu.be/A3nIB19ACg	X	X	X	X	X	X	X	X	X	X	X			X	X	X

Teacher Resource 1: *Supplementary Video Links With Social Characteristics in Each*

BACKGROUND OF THE LESSON

This lesson was developed to allow children to learn mathematics while making meaning about the world. We have all used this task in many venues, including in K–12 mathematics classrooms, in professional development settings, and with parents and caregivers. Each time we implement it, we all learn something new about our world. Eva first learned about this task from Courtney and adapted it into her own courses (and Courtney learned it from their friend and colleague, Ryan Flessner). After realizing we had each engaged in developing mathematical tasks that were similar yet distinct in focus and approach, we decided to come together to create this lesson for the book. Eva notices that children in her classroom are always impressed that they learned new things both about the world (e.g., how relatively few people of the 100 are from the United States as compared to their estimations) and about mathematics (e.g., that percent relates to per 100). She has been modifying this task over many years to then connect various things about the world (e.g., learning about the world and comparing it to a local city, country, etc.) and about mathematics (e.g., comparing fractions when comparing the world to a local city, country). Mary incorporated a version of the task in the first week of Algebra I, to offer children an opportunity to see how mathematics reveals important information about the world, sometimes challenging our previously held beliefs and telling a powerful story about people. Furthermore, it supported children to see the importance of working with fractions, decimals, and percents before launching into algebra. Lynette and Jeff helped develop parts of this lesson together, when Jeff was designing a course in quantitative literacy. Although that course was for undergraduates, we found the spirit of the lesson to be flexible, so Lynette adapted parts of it for her preservice elementary mathematics teachers to engage and unpack. We are always encouraged by the lesson, both in terms of the mathematical learning it can support and of the impactful ways children engage with questions of justice. Even as we have focused on different mathematical concepts with different groups of children, we have been consistently able to leverage this lesson in meaningful ways in our classrooms.

Here are some other places we have written about this work.

- Guzmán, L. D., & Craig, J. (2019). The world in your pocket: Digital media as invitations for transdisciplinary inquiry in mathematics classrooms. *Occasional Paper Series, 2019*(41), 6.

- Raygoza, M. C. (2016). Striving toward transformational resistance: Youth participatory action research in the mathematics classroom. *Journal of Urban Mathematics Education, 9*(2), 122–152.

- Thanheiser, E., & Koestler, C. (2021). If the world were a village: Learning mathematics while learning about the world. *Mathematics Teacher Educator, 9*(3), 202–228.

ABOUT THE AUTHORS

Courtney Koestler has been working in their current position at Ohio University since 2014, where they have had the opportunity to spend time in schools working alongside elementary school teacher-colleagues in their classrooms. They have been an educator since 1998, when they started their career as a middle school teacher, going on to work as a second-, fourth-, and finally fifth-grade classroom teacher before becoming a K–5 mathematics coach. It was in this role that they met administrators and colleagues who believed in child-centered and critical pedagogies, centered on taking an assets-based approach to teaching where students' (and families') interests, practices, and "funds of knowledge" were important resources on which to build and connect. Exposure to critical literacy and critical pedagogy made them question their teaching and realize they could be more intentional and purposeful about the kinds of lessons and pedagogical approaches they taught. Now, as a university-based teacher educator, they center equity and justice in teacher education and professional development work. Courtney recognizes that teaching is non-neutral; it is a political act.

Eva Thanheiser is a mother of three daughters and a professor of mathematics education at Portland State University. Eva has worked in elementary and middle schools regularly in a range of experiences from being a mathematics teacher for a fifth-grade class to running afterschool mathematics clubs. At the beginning of her career as a teacher educator, she focused mostly on content and motivation to learn. However, she learned at conferences about social justice, its inclusion into the mathematics classroom, and the power of that inclusion. She began trying out different activities and noticed that they allowed different kinds of participation. Over the years, she has tried more and more and kept reading up on tasks (books with tasks) and implementing them. She considers herself a lifelong learner and a contributor to improving struggles for social justice in mathematics education.

Mary Candace Raygoza is a STEMinist teacher educator at Saint Mary's College of California. Her scholarship explores teaching mathematics for social justice and critical, justice-oriented, anti-racist teacher education. Mary is a former high school mathematics teacher in East Los Angeles.

 **Jeff Craig** is committed to contemplating ethical questions in education. He also recognizes that children encounter ethical questions in their everyday life. In teaching, he reconciles ethical questioning against a backdrop of so-called Wicked Problems education, which prioritizes civic education as it relates to children as members of communities and societies. He finds the lesson presented here compelling because it engages children as both global and local thinkers who use mathematical and statistical techniques to understand their world and their positions within it.

 **Lynette Guzmán** is a mathematics education scholar who focuses on interrogating limiting discourses about people and their complexity. As a millennial who grew up with the internet, Lynette spends her time thinking about the ways digital platforms lend themselves to content creation, consumption, and remixing to promote particular kinds of discourses.

LESSON 5.14 JOURNEY FOR JUSTICE: THE FARMWORKERS' MOVEMENT

Gloria Gallardo and Emy Chen

WORKERS' RIGHTS AND THE DELANO GRAPE STRIKE

The social justice issues in this lesson series are movement building, workers' rights, and union organizing, as examined through the Delano Grape Strike. The lessons connect mathematics to English language arts and social studies to represent a comprehensive look at the farmworkers' movement and how Filipinx and Latinx farmworkers used solidarity to build a movement for social justice.

The Delano Grape Strike was a pivotal moment for unions and movement building. Filipinx and Latinx farmworkers unified to create a movement that would protect all workers, regardless of race and ethnicity. They used their collective power as laborers—understanding that without their labor, work wouldn't get done and the companies would lose profit. By withholding their labor collectively and by inspiring a national boycott of grapes, they leveraged their status as workers to make a difference in their lives and the lives of other labor unions. This lesson provides additional resources to learn more about the Delano Grape Strike and the history and contributions of the U.S. Filipinx and Chicanx farmworkers that have been untold or misrepresented in school curriculum.

This multiday lesson builds on children's natural curiosity to understand their world and develops their whole number operations. In the first lesson, children will create a timeline (i.e., a number line) to map the progression of the events that led to the strike and the formation of the United Farm Workers (UFW). The number line allows the children to visualize number sequences and strategies for counting, comparing, adding, and subtracting as they compare events from the story. Unifix cubes with alternating colors after every set of five are used to help build children's fluency with fives and tens.

In the remaining lessons, children will first be presented with the differing wages that farmworkers received in the early 1960s. As children learn about the wages labor workers earned, they will be encouraged to represent these wages in different forms using different tools and materials such as coins and place value blocks. For example, children will be asked to consider the value of what

- I know when people are treated unfairly. (Justice 12)

- I know about people who helped stop unfairness and worked to make life better for many people. (Justice 15)

- I will speak up or do something if people are being unfair, even if my friends do not. (Action 19)

MATHEMATICS DOMAINS AND PRACTICES

- Number and Operations

- Construct viable arguments and critique the reasoning of others. (MP3)

- Model with mathematics. (MP4)

CROSS-CURRICULAR CONNECTIONS

- Art

- Social Studies

Filipinx farmworkers were paid per hour ($1.25) and why it was less than Latinx farmworkers. Children will then be challenged to make sense of the value and the impact of the difference in pay compared to a day, week, or month. Then children will use these experiences to examine current labor conditions in their local area.

DEEP AND RICH MATHEMATICS

Children work on their development of number concepts and operations as they examine differential pay and utilize a number line (either drawn or with Unifix cubes as is appropriate for children in your classroom) to answer questions about events surrounding farmworkers' social movements. These lessons support children in deepening their understanding of the magnitude of numbers as they create a number line to represent Larry Itliong's life and the events that led to the formation of the UFW. The number line then serves as a visualization of number sequences and as a tool for children to count, compare, add, and subtract. Children continue development of whole number concepts and operations as they learn about the wage differences between racial and class-based groups during that pivotal time.

ABOUT THE LESSON

This 4-day lesson comprises four parts that range from 20 to 60 minutes each. The lesson launch introduces the history of the farmworkers' movement through the eyes of Filipinx labor organizer and leader Larry Itliong. Through Larry Itliong's story, children are introduced to issues faced by migrant and immigrant farmworkers using a timeline created with Unifix cubes to examine the progression of the events that led to the strike and the formation of UFW. Examining the history of the strike (the Delano Grape Strike lasted 5 years) and origins of this movement shows the power of intersectional coalitions and how common issues can unify groups of individuals.

In the explore portions of the lesson, children examine wage inequality and the exploitative working conditions of farmworkers. Children compare the magnitude of numbers and engage in number operations as they learn about the wages earned by Filipinx workers and Latinx workers and compare them to each other. Children also analyze the value of what was earned and compare it to the cost of living during the 1960s.

The lesson ends with taking action. How can children organize around an issue in their local community and take action against or for this issue? Children reflect on the farmworkers' movement and learn about farmworkers and labor unions now. Children apply their understanding of how the farmworkers' movement began, and consider the role of mathematics in building a movement. Their labor mattered, so they took collective action against the growers through protests, marches, strikes, and boycotts. Children will use the past experiences of farmworkers to examine current conditions.

An essential understanding of this lesson is knowing that there is power in community and community organizing. Throughout this lesson, children learn, explore, and realize the power of community and how they can use mathematics to build a movement that challenges injustices. This lesson helps children understand that injustices anywhere are a threat to justice everywhere. Movements are built by people who believe that there is power in communities organizing to challenge injustices. Mathematics is an essential part of this. Understanding injustices through the lens of racial and ethnic studies and mathematics presents multiple opportunities for classrooms to move beyond community to earnest solidarity.

Resources and Materials

- Book: *Journey for Justice: The Life of Larry Itliong* by Dawn B. Mabalon with Gayle Romasanta

- Mathematics manipulatives (base-10 blocks, Unifix cubes)

- Coins and dollars (or play coin and dollar manipulatives)

- Video: "The Farm Worker Movement," from PBS (https://bit.ly/2ZIjzWq)

- Website: Zinn Education Project narrative on the Delano Grape Strike (https://bit.ly/32F9r1N)

- Article for more information: "The 1965–1970 Delano Grape Strike and Boycott" by Inga Kim, *United Farm Workers*, March 7, 2017 (https://bit.ly/3xGME1a)

LESSON FACILITATION

Note: Depending on the class and school demographics, some children may possess knowledge of the farmworkers' and labor workers' movement from family members who are labor workers themselves or make connections to what they know about farmworkers or labor history and rural regions. For example, common social science standards in the early grades have children learn about their community and county as well as community workers in their community. Invite family members as well as local labor organizations to share and co-teach parts of the lesson.

Day 1

Launch (15 minutes)

- Begin with the following prompt:

    + *Draw a farmworker.*

- After children are given time to draw their own, ask them to place all drawings on display and lead the class in discussing their observations, including commonalities and differences among the drawings.

- Ask children to share what came to mind when asked to complete the task. This activity elicits children's beliefs and stereotypes about farmworkers. Children often draw a farmworker who is male and white. When a person of Color is drawn, children may refer to Cesar Chavez, depending on their experience. It may be useful to record children's initial reflections on poster paper.

- At this time, you might pause and say:

    + *We seem to have a lot of similarities in how we think of farmworkers. We have a lot of agreement. It's almost like we all tell the same story about farmworkers. Another word for a story is a "narrative." We share a narrative about who farmworkers are.*

    You could prompt children to think about whether they have heard the word *narrative* before or related words like *narrator*.

- Introduce the term *counter-narratives*. Ask:

    + *What does "counter-narrative" mean?*

    + *How can we unpack that word?*

    + *What are examples of counter-narratives?*

- For many children, this may be a new term. You can start by building from what you just discussed in their drawings. The commonalities across many drawings reveal dominant narratives (or stories) we have about farmworkers. Counter-narratives show that there is more than one story for farmers.

They do not all look the same or have the same experiences. Countering the single narrative and showing the multiple perspectives and stories are counter-narratives. Discuss collectively through additional examples that counter-narratives offer alternative perspectives on an existing story. The perspectives represented by counter-narratives are often not explored or known by many people. You might consider offering a particular working definition: counter-narratives are other stories, stories we need a chance to learn about.

- Ask children:

    + *Why is it important to hear or learn about different perspectives of the same story?*

    + *What can we learn from different perspectives?*

    + *Can anyone think of a counter-narrative that others may not know about?*

- **Note:** Counter-narratives are an important part of teaching for social justice. A white worldview often dominates curriculum to the exclusion of other racial and ethnic worldviews or, more commonly, represents diverse racial and ethnic groups within the white narrative so as to appear inclusive and universal.

- Ask further follow-up questions to deepen children's understanding about counter-narratives. Once the definition is explained, more children will realize that they know many counter-narratives and/or are part of a counter-narrative.

- Show children the UFW website (https://ufw.org/) and explore it with them.

- If children are unfamiliar, explain to them that the UFW and Cesar Chavez are widely known: they first came to prominence as the face of a strike of grape pickers in the 1960s that led to the labor union for farmworkers of America.

- Tell children that this lesson focuses on the counter-narrative of the farmworkers' movement from the 1960s from the perspective of a labor union organizer named Larry Itliong and the Filipinx migrant workers who fought alongside him.

Explore (45 minutes)

- Introduce the book *Journey for Justice: The Life of Larry Itliong* by Dawn B. Mabalon with Gayle Romasanta.

- Before beginning, introduce key terms of the lesson, such as *migrant workers, farmworkers, welga/heulga, boycott, union, wage, coins, place value, inequity,* and *inequality,* and other vocabulary words that will be new and important for the children in your classroom.

- As you read the book, have children create a timeline of Larry Itliong's life using Unifix cubes. Each Unifix cube can represent 1 year, with Larry's birth as 0 on the number line.

- Have the class map out the key events of Larry Itliong's life. For example, stop at pivotal moments where the author describes Larry's life immigrating to the United States from the Philippines and key events that led to the Filipinx and Latinx farmworkers unifying in the Delano Grape Strike. The number line provides a visual representation of how these events progressed.

- Encourage children to use the timeline created with the Unifix cubes to examine the events that led to the strike and the duration of the strike.

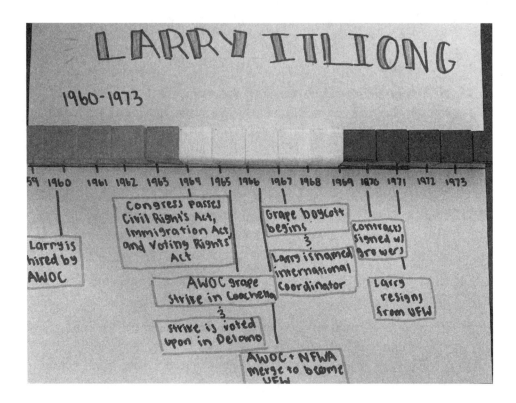

Day 2

Launch (15 minutes)

- Show the first few minutes of the PBS documentary "The Farm Worker Movement," which describes the poor pay and living conditions of farmworkers during the 1960s (https://bit.ly/2ZIjzWq).

- Next, introduce children to the Delano Grape Strike. Show children the mural of Philip Vera Cruz and Larry Itliong, and read the narrative on the Delano Grape Strike provided by the Zinn Education Project (https://bit.ly/32F9r1N).

- Remind children of the pivotal moments from *Journey for Justice: The Life of Larry Itliong*, about how much Larry and other Filipinx farmworkers were paid for their labor.

Explore (20 minutes)

- Write down the different hourly rates Larry earned. For example, when he worked as a janitor at the Frye Lettuce Farm, he was paid 12 cents an hour. Later, in 1939, he and other workers on the asparagus fields struck to protest their wages of 10 cents per hour. Lastly, by 1965, Larry was actively helping Filipinx workers organize for fair wages. Filipinx workers in Coachella Valley were paid $1.25 per hour.

- With coins (or play money manipulatives), have children represent the quantity. Allow children to find their own ways to make 10 cents, 12 cents, and $1.25 using coins. Since children are independently creating their own variations, have children share their different combinations. If necessary, have a chart available with the image of each coin and its value.

Day 3

- Revisit the activities of the prior days, including the images children created of the combinations of coins representing the wages from 10 cents in 1939 to $1.25 in 1965.

- Ask children for their observations. You may ask:

  + *What do you notice?*

  + *What do you wonder?*

  + *How do you feel?*

  + *Is the difference a lot or a little? Why?*

- Remind children that this shift in wages from the coalition building among the Filipinx farmworkers led to improved conditions. The comparison of the wages over time highlights the power of collective organizing.

- Tell children that with the formation of the UFW, the organizers asked communities to boycott the products grown and harvested by exploitative growers. This became a nationwide campaign and boycott. This became a movement. For more information, see the UFW article, "The 1965–1970 Delano Grape Strike and Boycott" (https://bit.ly/3xGME1a).

- In the 1960s and early 1970s, the UFW launched a Consumer Action Campaign to force the growers to provide them better living conditions, wages, and benefits. According to data from the period, 17 million Americans and many Canadians participated in the boycott, leading to a decrease of grape shipments in North America by one-third.

- The Delano Grape Strike was a boycott that led to a movement for labor rights. The UFW and farmworkers used mathematics to build a movement. Ask children:

    + *How did the farmworkers use mathematics to build a movement?*

Day 4

- To summarize this series of lessons, reflect with children on what they learned over the past days. Allow children to record their thinking and reflections. As a class, children should talk about the lesson's key ideas. Use prompts such as these:

    + *How is* Journey for Justice: The Life of Larry Itliong *a counter-narrative?*

    + *What did you learn about farmworkers?*

    + *What did you learn about Larry Itliong?*

- After assessing what children have learned from the reading and activities, connect back to one of the main questions of the lesson. Ask:

    + *How does looking at the past help us make sense of now?*

    + *How can people work collectively to create change?*

- As mentioned earlier, invite in caregivers or family members who belong to your local UFW and labor unions to be a part of the last segment of the lesson. The individuals can share current issues such as benefits, wages, living conditions, the effects of COVID-19, and so on.

- Work with local labor unions to develop ways for children to take action toward supporting the union's organizing efforts relevant to their community.

TAKING ACTION

Work with local labor unions to develop ways for children to take action toward supporting the union's organizing efforts relevant to their community.

COMMUNICATING WITH STAKEHOLDERS

You may want to communicate the lesson's social justice and mathematics goals to caregivers before teaching the lesson. It would be important to reach out to caregivers, grade-level colleagues, and local branches of UFW and other local labor unions to get involved in the lesson, supporting children in connecting this lesson to events in their community. You should welcome administrators to plan, observe, and join in the lesson to support and encourage schoolwide implementation.

BACKGROUND OF THE LESSON

As community workers and social justice educators, we are committed to honoring the lives and hxstories of children, our communities, and our ancestors. This lesson series is grounded in the belief that all children, including children of Color, deserve to see themselves and the hxstorical contributions of their communities in the curriculum and their capacity to challenge the injustices and inequities present in our society. Lastly, this lesson is a call for solidarity, noncompliance, protest, and mobilization. Social movements are built from multiracial groups and communities coming together for collective change. This lesson shares the untold American hxstory and our contribution, as Chicanx and Asian Americans, to labor justice and union formation!

This lesson series provides children with multiple perspectives of an important moment in California and U.S. hxstory. This story is not just about the Chicanx farmworkers or the Filipinx farmworkers; this story is one of communities coming together to build a movement. This lesson supports children to use mathematics to make sense of the injustice and the power of coalition building.

The origins of two of the earliest farmworker unions, the Agriculture Workers Organizing Committee (AWOC) and the National Farm Workers Association (NFWA), is a significant example of community organizing, coalition building, and the power of solidarity against the exploitation of farmworkers. This movement was led by Larry Itliong and Filipinx farmworkers. The AWOC was soon joined by Dolores Huerta, Cesar Chavez, and Chicanx and Latinx farmworkers. What began with a grape strike in Delano, California, soon developed into a boycott over low wages and exploitative working conditions, and ultimately resulted in an agreement to provide better wages and union benefits for all farmworkers. The hxstory and origins of this movement show the power of intersectional coalitions and how common issues can unify groups of individuals. Hxstory represents the topic as something that happened in the 1960s and was resolved by the early 1970s. However, California has nearly one-third of all farmworkers in the United States. That translates to 500,000–800,000 farmworkers. Almost 75% of farmworkers in California are undocumented. These numbers and lives matter. The injustices farmworkers faced then still exist today. Understanding the working and living conditions that farmworkers faced then and now is a social justice issue.

ABOUT THE AUTHORS

Gloria Gallardo is a social justice bilingual educator, woman of Color, proud daughter of Mexican immigrants, intersectional feminist, and aspiring writer. She is currently a graduate student in the Master of Arts in Teaching Program at Chapman University. She fell in love with learning at a young age. She was a young girl of Color with dreams so big that she felt that anything was possible. She loved learning so much because she understood from a young age that it was the only way to make something of herself.

However, her love was not reciprocated by curriculum—nothing in school honored her identity or experiences. She became a social justice educator in order to serve children in her classroom and honor the communities they come from. She knows that children of Color deserve to see their histories and communities represented and honored in the classroom. She strives to give power back to children, by empowering them to see themselves for all their possibilities and potential. She notes that she would not be the educator she is today without the support of mentors who have seen her and honored where she comes from, while believing in where she is going.

 **Emy Chen** is a student attending Los Alamitos High School. She is committed to moving ethnic studies forward in K–12 schools and is passionate about learning the hxrstories and contributions of radical womxn of Color. She shares her learnings with other youths through her blog (https://catalystforchange.edublogs.org/). Emy's path for social justice began with reading. As a nightly ritual in elementary school, she would snuggle with her mom as they pored through books about womxn of Color. Learning about hxrstory makers Dolores Huerta, Yuri Kochiyama, and Grace Lee Boggs inspired her to contribute to her community. Whether blogging, speaking for ethnic studies, or simply reading and sharing knowledge, she hopes to follow others' legacies and create her own.

PART
III

NEXT STEPS

CHAPTER 6

ADVICE FROM THE FIELD

In Part III, we conclude with guidance on how to engage in this work for yourself. In this chapter, we feature reflections and advice from the lesson authors, field testers, and reviewers of this book on teaching mathematics for social justice (TMSJ) in early elementary grades. These individuals give particular insight and meaning for implementing the lessons in Chapter 5 and as you continue to create your own social justice mathematics lessons (SJMLs) in Chapter 7.

> *When thinking about teaching explicit social justice lessons, my mind immediately jumps to reading, writing, and SEL blocks of time. I was initially intimidated in integrating social justice with math, as I haven't done it frequently. However, I found these lessons to be meaningful and impactful for students.*
>
> —Amanda Bila, Field Tester of Lesson 5.3

The voices in this chapter come from educators who have experience with TMSJ in a variety of classrooms (in PreK–2 settings, other grade levels, and teacher education contexts). All have either designed, implemented, or reviewed one or more of the lessons in this book. We asked these educators what their experiences have been in teaching SJMLs, what challenges have arisen, how they have responded, and what general words of advice they can offer fellow teachers. Fifteen experienced educators responded with their thoughts: some based on field-testing particular lessons from this book, others from their experiences being social justice mathematics educators. Next, we present their thoughts in their own words. We hope that their experiences and expertise will provide insight and wisdom as you continue and refine your journey as a social justice mathematics teacher.

ADVICE FOR GETTING STARTED WITH IMPLEMENTING SJMLS

Our lesson authors, field testers, and reviewers had much to say about preparation for and the possibility of teaching SJMLs. Here we offer words on five key areas that emerged from the responses of the participating educators.

Find Your People

"You are not alone! Find your people and work to collectively make a change!" wrote JaNay Brown-Wood, author of Lesson 5.5.

Jami Spencer-Tanner, field tester of Lesson 5.3, emphasized that it was a very positive experience to plan as a team along with their multilingual support teacher:

> [For this lesson], kindergarten teachers planned together with our multi-language learning teacher. It was very helpful to have ideas and support from the entire team to brainstorm how to do this in a kindergarten-friendly way through our math curriculum.

Finally, Anita Wager, long-time social justice educator and reviewer of all of the lessons, offers this advice:

> I look to my colleagues and community for support when faced with challenges implementing social justice math lessons. My advice would be to do your research, find allies, and know that the brilliant children in your classroom will embrace these lessons.

Build Partnerships With Families

When reflecting on her experiences as a social justice mathematics teacher, Lesson 5.12 author Melissa Adams Corral tells this story:

> I'll never forget being asked by a third grader if other classes were learning about slavery, racism, and anti-Blackness. When I said that they were not, she asked why not, adding, "Doesn't everyone deserve to learn important things?" In my experiences, teaching social justice units that incorporated mathematics engaged my students, built lasting memories and content knowledge, and brought us closer. This is a huge part of creating a vibe in my classroom that made us all want to be there.

With knowledge of her context, engagement with families, and a deep sense of place, Melissa was able to provide the learning opportunities that children in her classroom wanted and needed. Her advice: "Know your context. Have relationships with the families you work with and invite them to participate."

Lesson 5.3 author Heather Winters's advice also underscores the importance of cultivating partnerships with families:

> From day one of school, I connect to my students' families through family surveys, in-person conferences, and/or home visits. I build this relationship throughout the year. I am a partner with my students' parents/guardians. Because of these strong relationships, I believe I have fewer challenges. When challenges do arise, I can easily reach out to my students' families.

Know Your Priorities

Lauren Murray, author of Lesson 5.7, describes how when you know what you are committed to, you realize SJMLs are an integral part of mathematics instruction:

> *Social justice math lessons are just good math lessons. When you are engaging your students in math lessons that are built upon culturally responsive practices and social justice ideas, it feels authentic and engaging, for both the educator and the student. Math in elementary school classrooms is so often diluted down to black-and-white thinking, formulaic work, and learning without context. Whenever possible, we need to bring humanity into mathematics.*

Similarly, Lesson 5.1 author Jane "Sissy" Poovey reminds us that purpose and care help us realize our commitments:

> *Purposeful consideration and care are used when planning for and teaching social justice math lessons. It is extremely important to plan and implement lessons that offer diverse representations of mathematics while at the same time promoting awareness of social justice issues.*

Sometimes we may be torn between demands of the educational system and our commitments. Julia Maria Aguirre, author of Lesson 5.12, reminds us that at the end of the day, we have to reconcile with the truth about how required curriculum is part of upholding an unjust, racist system of schooling:

> *The most common challenge people share with me about implementing social justice lessons is balancing them with the pacing guides and the required math curriculum. People ask if there is a balance that can be struck. There is not a balance to be struck with a racist system. There is no balance to be struck with a violent math experience. A social justice approach to teaching mathematics is humanizing and anti-racist. It is designed to have children think critically about power relationships, fairness, and representation. It is designed to be joyful. We must teach with courage to elevate joy and justice.*

We have to decide if we will teach with courage, or maintain the status quo. But commitment alone is not going to get us where we need to be. The next few recommendations support teachers as we work with our commitments and remind us to be patient with ourselves while also seeking out support.

Take It Slow

Sonja Brandt, a reviewer of the lessons, reminds us to be patient with ourselves as we learn to teach in new ways:

> *The more teachers are willing and able to implement lessons that include social justice topics, the more natural the conversations and learning will be*

for their students. Be patient with yourself as the facilitator and leader, and be patient and willing to guide students through their learning and sharing of their thoughts and ideas centered upon the issues and topics.

On a related note, Brandy McCombs, author of Lesson 5.11, wrote: "Don't be intimidated by the implementation. Over time it becomes a part of your natural lesson organization."

Lesson 5.14 author Gloria Gallardo also reminds us that while we will be challenged, we do not need to be defeated. Of her own praxis, she writes:

I plan to be reflective and intentional. As teachers, we often know that math lessons sometimes do not work out the way we want them to. However, I will approach any challenges when teaching social justice math lessons with intention, humanity, and reflectivity. I think being open to the challenges and vulnerable with students will resolve any challenges.

Other teachers remind us to give the lessons themselves the time to land and develop. Amanda Bila, who field tested lessons for this book, notes:

Some of the lessons were a bit long and had to be modified for my class. Don't be afraid to take the lessons slow and spread out over multiple days. Use students' responses and questions to guide lessons. Provide multiple access points, and provide plenty of opportunities for discussion with peers.

Trust in Children

Much of educators' advice came from a stance of trusting that children are interested, curious, and able to engage with the mathematics and the topics. It is usually the adults in the room, we teachers, who are uncomfortable with what we feel are hard-to-broach topics. Let the children lead:

Follow your students' leads. Young children are insightful, curious, and empathetic. The discussions and learning that evolve organically from a thoughtful lesson plan are highly rewarding for the entire classroom family.

—Jan McGarry, Lesson 5.9 Author

Students are willing to do the work. When I connect math lessons to issues that matter to the students, they meet and regularly exceed my expectations. They are more willing to engage in challenging mathematics concepts because they see the math as relevant and needed for a purpose greater than a grade.

—Marni C. Peavy, Lesson 5.1 Author

When implementing social justice math lessons, I found the students are more receptive to these issues than one would imagine. Young children are often intrigued by social justice topics, which opens a door for conversations and understanding through exploration. The implementation of social justice math lessons also allows students a gateway to not only cover content standards in a meaningful way, but to provide them with confidence to talk about issues using descriptive language and use creativity to impact similar issues they identify in their communities.

—Elizabeth Barnes, Lesson 5.10 Author

CONCLUSION: PARTING WORDS TO SUSTAIN US

As we conclude this chapter, remember there are educators out there who are doing this work. Connect to those in your community and beyond, and remember these parting words.

Remember That Change Is Hard

Lesson 5.5 author JaNay Brown-Wood wrote that while change is hard, we have to keep pushing:

Change is hard. Change takes time. However, this cannot stop educators from continuing to push student thinking beyond the status quo. Thus, I meet challenges head-on with perseverance and persistence, but also with facts and information to share about the importance of this work. I understand that this is a long and arduous road, but it is worth the fight and I revel in the opportunity to keep pushing! I also remind myself that it takes all of us to make change, and I believe tapping into our communities will allow us to continue to respond to these challenges collectively, amplifying our voices, and strengthening our resolve.

Remember That the Work Is Healing.

Gloria Gallardo, author of Lesson 5.14, reminds us that the work of TMSJ is not just necessary, but healing:

Teaching math lessons with the purpose of social justice is transformative and healing. Math needs to connect to the lives, cultures, and histories of students. Social justice math lessons teach the content in a way that leads to action. Students understand that math exists beyond the classroom and that they can use it to impact lives, including their own. Remember we are called to challenge and change a racist system.

Remember to Bring the Joy

We may be personally and collectively healed through the work we do with children. In the end, we have to remember that SJMLs are part of a critical education, but also a joyful one, and one that stokes new possibilities for the future.

Let us sign off with a quote from Julia Maria Aguirre, bringing our book full circle from preface to conclusion:

> *Know that we stand with you. Together we can dismantle racist systems in mathematics education and promote more joyful, humanizing, and just mathematics learning experiences for children and their families.*

CHAPTER 7

CREATING SOCIAL JUSTICE LESSONS FOR YOUR OWN CLASSROOM

We appreciate your interest and commitment in teaching mathematics for social justice (TMSJ). We deeply value and respect the work of the educators who submitted their work for this volume as examples of what TMSJ can look like in early childhood and early elementary contexts. This chapter is intended to provide some final suggestions for getting started, or continuing, with planning your own lessons. When teachers begin asking young children about what is important to them, there are many relevant, salient social justice issues that can be incorporated into mathematics lessons.

GETTING STARTED

If you are new to TMSJ, it may seem overwhelming to begin creating social justice mathematics lessons (SJMLs). Even for more experienced teachers, this kind of teaching is hard work. As discussed in earlier chapters, there can be many tensions in developing TMSJ lessons. However, there are many positive, affirming possibilities as well, and we believe that young children deserve time and space to explore important issues and use mathematics as a tool to understand them. The following list represents eight steps that we recommend you consider in developing SJMLs, followed by elaboration of each step:

1. Learn About Children in Your Classroom and Their World

2. Learn About Relevant Social Justice Issues

3. Identify the Mathematics

4. Establish Your Goals

5. Determine How You Will Assess Your Goals

6. Create a Social Justice Question for the Lesson

7. Design the Child Resources for the Investigation

8. Plan for Action and Reflection

Step 1: Learn About the Children in Your Classroom and Their World

At several points in this book, we have discussed that effective TMSJ in early childhood and early elementary settings builds from concerns or questions children have about their school, community, nation, or world. This is what Freire (1970/2000) refers to as generative themes. Children's questions and/or concerns create the opportunity for a problem-posing pedagogy, an instructional style that engages children in noticing and wondering about the world around them. In an ideal setting, these generative themes would drive a curriculum, and teachers could match their mathematical goals to those themes, rooted in concerns about social injustice.

Authors of the lessons in this book expressed that openly talking with children, families, and community members about issues that were important to them provides insight into potential SJMLs. For some classrooms, these conversations may come during a morning meeting time where children share happenings from their experiences outside of school. It might come through photo elicitation, where teachers ask children to bring in photos of their communities and share locations they visit, assets of these communities, and needs that they feel are important. Other times, teachers may acclimate themselves to the community in which the children live by engaging in a community tour to see and visit the places children experience as part of their lives outside of school. A common thread of all these pieces is that teachers take the time to talk to and become immersed in the community in which they work and the children in their classroom reside.

Beyond getting to know the community, listening to the children and their stories is an essential element of this work. We see that children are often positioned as naive or lacking in voice and power. From our experiences, children have a lot to say about the world. Their thoughts and ideas add value to our classroom conversations. When children are positioned at a young age to share about themselves (their identity) and see that adults are actively listening to what they say, they are more likely to share and become change agents. Here are some interview questions and prompts you might consider using:

- *Tell me about your life right now.*
    + *What makes you, you?*
    + *Who are the most important people?*
    + *What are the most important things?*
- *Tell me about your school/community.*
    + *What are your favorite things to do there?*
    + *Where are your favorite places to go?*
    + *What do you notice about your community?*
- *What are some of the best things (assets) about your school/community?*

- *What are some things you don't like (challenges)?*

- *What are some things that you wonder about your school/community?*

These are questions we have used to get to know our students, from PreK to higher education. Oftentimes children are surprised that we are asking them to share their thoughts and wonderings about their lives and communities. They may need time to think and prompts to enhance and sustain the conversations (such as photos of places, or more closed questions), but once they begin to open up and share, they always have a lot to say.

Step 2: Learn About the Relevant Social Justice Issues

Early childhood teachers have always been leaders in PreK–12 education when learning about contexts that are engaging and relevant to children and how to incorporate these in tasks, activities, and lessons. However, when TMSJ, it is also important to learn all you can about the issue of injustice that you and/or children want to explore. This is the time in which you can begin to develop your own community knowledge. Many issues will have local or community meaning or impact. Children can identify social issues and potential injustices right in your area that might directly involve them, their families, and/or community members. Consider reaching out to community members and organizations that focus on responding to the topic or issue. Attend meetings and scour their websites. Find a member of the organizations to speak with. We have rarely found it helpful to ask what mathematics they use to understand or respond to the injustice; however, your deeper understanding of the issue can help you to make that connection later. This deep understanding can also help you to prepare and respond to questions that come up from children, families, and other stakeholders during the lesson facilitation.

Of course, you can also review news and media outlets to learn what news items children may be discussing in school, with friends, or in their out-of-school lives. Whether local, national, or even international news sites, online media are often good sources to expose children to broader issues at the local, state, national, and international levels; as such, these resources can also be used as part of your lesson. Many news outlets post stories to their internet sites, which allows you to share articles and videos with your children. However, it's also important to note that sources of information come with bias, whether it be news or other forms of media or information—even community groups. (For support on examining messages and meaning of text with young children, see the work of Vivian Vasquez, 2016.)

We've encouraged you to collaborate with school colleagues to develop allies in your work. This is an excellent opportunity to involve the school librarian or other teachers (1) to learn more about bias in information sources and (2) to learn how to counteract and balance the information you receive as well as present to children. You may collaborate with others to determine relevant literature to bring into the classroom, or identify possible guest speakers to work with. School colleagues who may have been already engaged in this work may provide needed support and connection as you are building both your community knowledge and knowledge of social justice issues. They may also provide critical insight into how this work would be seen from other stakeholders, helping you proactively prepare for possible questions or backlash.

Our first step still asks you to learn about the questions and concerns of the children with whom you work. However, rather than immediately pursuing them in conjunction with your children, it is oftentimes important to learn more about the topic on your own first. Our intent is that you've identified a few potential social injustices from which to build a SJML aligned with the mathematics content you must teach.

Step 3: Identify the Mathematics

When TMSJ, the task, activity, or lesson you design must allow you to connect with mathematics that is important for children to use and learn in mathematically meaningful ways. But what mathematics is involved in the potential issues you've learned about from children in your classroom in Steps 1 and 2?

We have a few strategies that have worked for us. One strategy is to begin with the content; however, it sometimes seems harder to think with a particular standard—sometimes the mathematics is so specific, the connection is not apparent. Using the broader domain, such as number and operations, geometry, measurement, patterns and algebraic thinking, and data collection and analysis, is typically where most teachers can start. Once you know the domain where the lesson will focus, then you can dive more deeply into your grade-level standards and into thinking about what is it about the domain that you want children to learn. For example, within the number and operations domain, will they be estimating and computing with two-digit numbers or three-digit numbers?

Another approach that has worked well for us is to look at a few of our favorite well-designed tasks or task sequences such as those in this volume and in this series. Often, early childhood and elementary teachers are skilled at looking at examples and using the context of these tasks to provide insight into how they could be modified or replaced with the context of a different generative theme. Thus, much of the rich mathematical development is already in place, and we are modifying the context to match the questions or concerns children have about a social issue or injustice.

Finally, in addition to thinking about the important mathematics you will incorporate, you may want to consider other content areas or disciplines such as language arts, social studies, art, or science. Early childhood education has always been a place where interdisciplinary activities, lessons, and units have been useful. This is discussed more in Step 4.

Step 4: Establish Your Goals

When developing goals for your explorations, you should set both mathematics and social justice goals. The mathematics goals should focus on both mathematics content standards as well as the mathematical practices and processes in which children will engage. Here you should draw upon your local expectations and resources, such as district or state learning objectives or standards, as well as build on children's past experiences. You can plan your social justice goals with regard to identity, diversity, justice, and action using the Learning for Justice Social Justice Standards (Learning for Justice, 2016) for guidance (see Appendix D). The outcomes they identify for children in Grades K–2 may be especially helpful. Goals, understandings, and topics related to social justice might also be related to developing, supporting, and challenging children's understanding about the issue. Finally, you might also consider how this is situated in your classroom related to other content areas and/or routines already established in the classroom.

We encourage you to write only a small number of learning outcomes for each lesson. This will allow you to maintain focus on what children should be learning. While it can be easy to see many connections mathematically and to the Social Justice Standards, when you articulate too many goals it can be difficult to maintain focus on teaching or learning any of them.

Step 5: Determine How You Will Assess Your Goals

To help maintain your focus on children's learning outcomes, you will need to identify how you will assess how children are understanding both the mathematics and social issues in your TMSJ task, activity, lesson, or unit and how these relate to your goals. Formative assessment will be helpful in ascertaining what children already know about the social issue and their mathematical knowledge, and it will support you in connecting on and building on these understandings. You may also consider including brief check-ins throughout a lesson to check on one or more of your learning goals. Plan to pose social justice and mathematics questions to assess and advance children's thinking.

Reflection activities at the end of the experiences can also tell you whether you are reaching goals for the whole class as well as for individual children. Later (in Step 8), we also discuss having a plan for action and reflection, which is also another way you can gauge the extent to which children achieve both the mathematical and social justice learning goals in their final product.

Step 6: Create a Social Justice Question for the Lesson

Develop a central question to guide your lesson based on the social justice issue at hand. This can come from the children themselves or one you have crafted based on what you know about their questions, concerns, and the topic itself. Choosing a question should be both interesting and powerful to better explore, understand, and respond to the issue.

Remember, one central aim for your SJML is for the children in your classroom to see how mathematics can be used to help better understand the issue. The question(s) used to drive the lesson might make that explicit or be grounded in a mathematical approach to better understand the social injustice. Sometimes it may seem like the mathematics is in the foreground or background as well as integrated with other content areas, depending on the lesson.

Step: 7 Design the Resources for the Investigation

This next step can feel like a daunting task, and we don't want to minimize it. The resources you develop to support the mathematical and social justice learning outcomes for children in your classroom—through exploration driven by the social justice question—form the heart of the investigation.

You will need to identify the resources children might draw upon to learn more about the social issue—likely a few of the same that you used to better understand the issue. Materials with the following qualities are most effective. We suggest that the resources should

- Be written specifically for an early childhood and early elementary audience;

- Use various kinds of media (print resources, including text and photos, short clips of video), and you might even include guest speakers that could join the class in person or via video conference; and

- Be able to identify common assumptions and misunderstandings about the context, and be paired to offer opposing (and often nondominant) perspectives on a controversial issue.

As you will notice, in many of the lessons in this book, children's literature is a key feature of SJMLs geared toward early elementary children. Children's literature is often an excellent way for teachers to begin, continue, or end conversations about important topics as they allow children to make connections to "big ideas" in meaningful ways.

You will also need to structure the mathematical investigation of the lesson. Sometimes, we can rely on our experience with different curricula and similar mathematical tasks to identify a series of prompts or tasks that allow children to better understand the context through deepening their understanding of mathematics. We often use an approach that follows an *Introduce–Explore–Summarize* model that engages children in opportunities to explore, reason, create, justify, generalize, and/or apply, rather than having them simply recall, compute, or calculate before interpreting the meaning in the context of the lesson. The latter approach not only creates more shallow mathematical understanding, but it also causes children to lose ownership of the investigative process.

The most success we've had designing the investigation portion of the SJML is to gain inspiration from or modify strong lessons we've used in the past. And, as we have said before, we hope that you are able to use these lessons as they are written and modified to meet the needs of the children with whom you work. Using the structure and sequence of questions from an established, quality lesson is often the most reliable way to ensure that a lesson promotes reasoning, problem solving, and quality engagement of children.

When you implement tasks, ensure that there are plenty of opportunities for children to take the lead. They should be the ones doing the intellectual work of the mathematical problem solving, the work of the problem posing, the work of the child-to-child discussion. It is important for you to give many (and varied) opportunities for participation, allowing children to hear the voices of one another in the whole-group setting, in small groups, and by assigning pairs of children to work collaboratively.

As a final bit of advice: If you haven't already been developing the lessons with others, consider asking a colleague for feedback on the first draft of the resources to use with children. You might even try the activity with a small group of children and solicit their feedback.

Step 8: Plan for Action and Reflection

The final element of an effective SJML is to ensure opportunities for reflection and action. Consider the following questions: What individual, small-group, and whole-class opportunities will you provide for children to reflect on the lesson and consider possible actions they can take to address an injustice? How will children share what they have learned about the social injustice? How might they use the mathematics knowledge and skills developed in this lesson?

The lessons in this book provide different examples of how teachers engaged and supported young children in reflection and action. The Social Justice Standards Action domain also provides insight into different ways we might think of action in early childhood classrooms. For example, children might commit to stand up to the exclusion, prejudice, or bias surrounding the lesson topic. You might support them in deciding what an appropriate and effective response might be.

Better yet, ask children how they want to take action.

FINAL WORDS

If you have read to this point in the book, you have already begun your journey to integrate social justice into your classroom, and we encourage you to use and share this book with others as you engage in all phases of preparing to teach a SJML. Our hope is that this book will inspire you and others to empower children as learners and doers of mathematics who can use mathematics as a tool to explore, understand, and respond to issues of social injustice.

Each of us has a role to play in shaping the future of the mathematics education community, so connect with others who embrace TMSJ, who are using SJMLs in their classrooms, who are continuing to learn about the topics discussed in this book, who are taking action to make a difference, and who are members of a TMSJ community willing to share and learn together. We invite you to connect with us through Facebook at Math Lessons to Explore Social Injustice and Twitter @SJMathematics.

APPENDIX A: ADDITIONAL RESOURCES

Additional Examples of Social Justice Mathematics Lessons

- Chao, T., & Marlowe, M. M. (2019). Elementary mathematics and #BlackLivesMatter. *Occasional Paper Series*, 2019(41). https://educate.bankstreet.edu/occasional-paper-series/vol2019/iss41/9

- Felton-Koestler, M. D., Simic-Muller, K., & Menéndez, J. M. (2017). *Reflecting the world: A guide to incorporating equity in mathematics teacher education*. Information Age.

- Gutstein, E., & Peterson, B. (Eds.). (2013). *Rethinking mathematics: Teaching social justice by the numbers* (2nd ed.). Rethinking Schools.

- Guzmán, L. D., & Craig, J. (2019). The world in your pocket: Digital media as invitations for transdisciplinary inquiry in mathematics classrooms. *Occasional Paper Series*, 2019(41), 6. https://educate.bankstreet.edu/occasional-paper-series/vol2019/iss41/6

- Kinser, K. *STEM by the numbers*. Learning for Justice. https://www.learningforjustice.org/classroom-resources/lessons/stem-by-the-numbers

- Learning for Justice. *What do Halloween costumes say?* https://www.learningforjustice.org/classroom-resources/lessons/what-do-halloween-costumes-say

- Math and Social Justice: A Collaborative MTBoS Site: https://sites.google.com/site/mathandsocialjustice/curriculum-resources

- Mathematical Modeling With Cultural and Community Contexts: https://sites.google.com/qc.cuny.edu/m2c3/home

- Turner, B. (2019, January). Open secrets in first-grade math: Teaching about white supremacy on American currency. *Learning for Justice*. https://www.learningforjustice.org/magazine/open-secrets-in-firstgrade-math-teaching-about-white-supremacy-on-american-currency

- Ward, J. (2020). Exploring playground access with mathematics. *Mathematics Teacher: Learning and Teaching Pre-K–12*, 113(11), 887–894. https://doi.org/10.5951/MTLT.2020.0076

- Ward, J. (2021). Characters like us: Using project-based learning to advocate for representation in media. In J. S. Lee & E. Galindo (Eds.), *Project-based learning in elementary classrooms: Making mathematics come alive*. National Council of Teachers of Mathematics.

Learn More About Elements of TMSJ

- A Pathway to Equitable Math Instruction. *Dismantling racism in mathematics instruction: Exercises for educators to reflect on their own biases to transform instructional practice.* https://equitablemath.org/

- Aguirre, J., Mayfield-Ingram, K., & Martin, D. B. (2013). *The impact of identity in K–8 mathematics: Rethinking equity-based practices.* National Council of Teachers of Mathematics.

- Aguirre, J. M. & del Rosario Zavala, M. (2013). Making culturally responsive mathematics teaching explicit: A lesson analysis tool. *Pedagogies: An International Journal, 8*(2), 163–190. https://doi.org/10.1080/155480X.2013.768518

- Bartell, T. G. (2018). *Toward equity and social justice in mathematics education.* Springer.

- Benjamin Banneker Association. (2017). *Implementing a social justice curriculum: Practices to support the participation and success of African-American students in mathematics.* http://bbamath.org/index.php/2017/11/19/the-benjamin-banneker-social-justice-position-statement/

- Dingle, M., and Yeh, C. (2021). Mathematics in context: The pedagogy of liberation. *Learning for Justice.* https://www.learningforjustice.org/magazine/spring-2021/mathematics-in-context-the-pedagogy-of-liberation

- Drake, C., Aguirre, J. M., Bartell, T. G., Foote, M. Q., Roth McDuffie, A., & Turner, E. E. (2015). *TeachMath learning modules for K–8 mathematics methods courses—Teachers empowered to advance change in mathematics project.* http://www.teachmath.info

- Esmonde, I., & Caswell, B. (2010). Teaching mathematics for social justice in multicultural, multilingual elementary classrooms. *Canadian Journal of Science, Mathematics and Technology Education, 10*(3), 244–254. https://doi.org/10.1080/14926156.2010.504485

- Felton, M. D. (2010). Is math politically neutral? *Teaching Children Mathematics, 17*(2), 60–63. https://doi.org/10.5951/TCM.17.2.0060

- Gewertz, C. (2020). Teaching math through a social justice lens. *EducationWeek.* https://www.edweek.org/teaching-learning/teaching-math-through-a-social-justice-lens/2020/12

- Gutstein, E. (2006). *Reading and writing the world with mathematics.* Routledge.

- NCSM & TODOS: Mathematics for ALL. (2016). *Mathematics education through the lens of social justice: Acknowledgement, actions, and accountability.* https://www.todos-math.org/socialjustice

- Ontario Ministry of Education. (n.d.). *Teaching mathematics through a social justice lens.* https://thelearningexchange.ca/projects/teaching-mathematics-through-a-social-justice-lens/

- Stinson, D. W., & Wager, A. A. (2012). *Teaching mathematics for social justice: Conversations with educators.* National Council of Teachers of Mathematics.

- Swoveland, M. (2013). On "that's so gay" and learning math. *Learning for Justice.* https://www.learningforjustice.org/magazine/on-thats-so-gay-and-learning-math

- TODOS: Mathematics for ALL (2020). *The mo(ve)ment to prioritize anti-racist mathematics: Planning for this and every school year.* https://www.todos-math.org/statements

- Wiki for Ideas for Social Justice in Math: https://sites.google.com/site/mathandsocialjustice/curriculum-resources/wiki-for-ideas-for-social-justice-in-math

Learn More About Early Elementary Mathematics Teaching

- Borthwick, A., Gifford, S., & Thouless, H. (2021). *The power of pattern: Patterning in the early years.* Association of Teachers of Mathematics (UK). https://www.atm.org.uk

- Carpenter, T. P., Fennema, E., Franke, M. L., Levi, L., & Empson, S. B. (2015). *Children's mathematics: Cognitively guided instruction* (2nd ed.). Heinemann. (recommended for the K–2 grade band)

- Carpenter, T. P., Franke, M. L., Johnson, N. C., Turrou, A. C., & Wager, A. A. (2017). *Young children's mathematics: Cognitively guided instruction in early childhood education.* Heinemann. (recommended for the PreK–K years)

- Celadón-Pattichis, S., White, D. Y., & Civil, M. (Eds.) (2017). *Access and equity: Promoting high-quality mathematics in Pre-K–Grade 2.* National Council of Teachers of Mathematics

- Chval, K., Chavez, O., Pomerenke, S., & Reams, K. (2009). *Mathematics for every student: Responding to diversity, Grades Pre-K–5.* National Council of Teachers of Mathematics.

- Cohen, E. G., & Lotan, R. A. (2014). *Designing groupwork: Strategies for the heterogeneous classroom* (3rd ed.). Teachers College Press.

- Huinker, D., & Bill, V. (2017). *Taking action: Implementing effective mathematics teaching practices in K–Grade 5.* National Council of Teachers of Mathematics.

- National Council of Teachers of Mathematics. (2020). *Catalyzing change in early childhood and elementary mathematics: Initiating critical conversations.* Author.

- Parks, A. N. (2015). *Exploring mathematics through play in the early childhood classroom.* Teachers College Press.

- Smith, M. S., & Stein, M. K. (2018). *5 practices for orchestrating productive mathematics discussions* (2nd ed.). National Council of Teachers of Mathematics.

- Turrou, A. C., Johnson, N. C., & Franke, M. L. (2021). *The young child and mathematics.* National Association for the Education of Young Children.

- Yeh, C., Ellis, M. W., & Hurtado, C. K. (2017). *Reimagining the mathematics classroom.* National Council of Teachers of Mathematics.

Teaching for Social Justice

Publications

- Agarwal-Rangath, R. (2020). *Planting the seeds of equity: Ethnic studies and social justice in the K–2 classroom.* Teachers College Press.

- Blake, C. (n.d.). *Teaching social justice in theory and practice.* Resilient Educator. https://resilienteducator.com/classroom-resources/teaching-social-justice

- Christensen, L., Hansen, M., Peterson, B., Barbian, E., & Watson, D. (2012). *Rethinking elementary education.* Rethinking Schools.

- Cowhey, M. (2006). *Black ants and Buddhists: Thinking critically and teaching differently in the primary grades.* Stenhouse Publishers.

- Gonzalez, J. (2016, February 14). A collection of resources for teaching social justice. *Cult of Pedagogy.* https://www.cultofpedagogy.com/social-justice-resources

- Hass, C. (2020). *Social justice talk: Strategies for teaching critical awareness.* Heinemann Publishers.

- Kohl, H. (n.d.). *Teaching for Social Justice 15.2.* Rethinking Schools. https://rethinkingschools.org/articles/teaching-for-social-justice

- North, C. E. (2015). *Teaching for social justice?: Voices from the front lines.* Routledge.

- Peterson, B. (n.d.). *Teaching for Social Justice 8.3.* Rethinking Schools. https://rethinkingschools.org/articles/teaching-for-social-justice-8-3

- Picower, B. (n.d.). *Six elements of social justice pedagogy.* Using Their Words. http://www.usingtheirwords.org/6elements/

- Rodriguez, N. N., & Swalwell, K. (2021) *Social studies for a better world: An anti-oppressive approach for elementary educators.* W. W. Norton & Company.

- Sensoy, O., & DiAngelo, R. (2017). *Is everyone really equal?: An introduction to key concepts in social justice education.* Teachers College Press.

- Souto-Manning, M. (2013). *Multicultural teaching in the early childhood classroom: Approaches, strategies, and tools (preschool to 2nd grade).* Teachers College Press.

Websites and Podcasts
- Abolitionist Teaching Network: https://abolitionistteachingnetwork.org/

- Facing History and Ourselves: https://www.facinghistory.org

- Great Lakes Equity Center: https://greatlakesequity.org/

- Learning for Justice: https://www.learningforjustice.org/

- Rethinking Schools: https://www.rethinkingschools.org

- TODOS Podcast: https://www.podomatic.com/podcasts/todosmath (access through the link or subscribe anywhere you listen to podcasts)

Communities Interested in Teaching Mathematics for Social Justice

- Abolitionist Teaching Network: https://abolitionistteachingnetwork.org/

- Black Teacher Project: https://www.blackteacherproject.org/

- Education for Liberation Network: https://www.edliberation.org/

- Educators for Social Justice & Inclusive Teaching Practices—Facebook: https://www.facebook.com/groups/1136557443074208

- Equity and Social Justice in Mathematics Education—Facebook: https://www.facebook.com/groups/178344199241717

- Free Minds Free People: https://fmfp.org/

- Graphs in the World
    + Instagram: @graphsintheworld
    + Facebook: https://www.facebook.com/graphsintheworld

- National Network of Teacher Activist Groups: https://teacheractivists.org/

- Nepantla Teachers Community: https://nepantlateachers.wixsite.com/

- New York Collective of Radical Educators (NYCoRE)—Facebook: https://www.facebook.com/NYCoRE

- People's Education Movement LA
    + Online: https://peoplesed.weebly.com/
    + Twitter: @peoples_ed

- Social Justice Math—Twitter: @socjusticemath

- Teaching for Change
    + Online: https://www.teachingforchange.org
    + Facebook: https://www.facebook.com/TeachingforChange

- Teaching on Days After: Dialogue & Resources for Educating Toward Justice—Facebook: https://www.facebook.com/groups/teachingondaysafter

- Teaching Social Justice Resource Exchange—Facebook: https://www.facebook.com/groups/teachaboutjustice

- Witness for Peace Solidarity Collective: https://www.solidaritycollective.org

Resources for Building Your Own Social Justice Mathematics Lessons

- A Little Stats: https://alittlestats.blogspot.com/p/data-sources.html

- Bigelow, B. (n.d.). *Videos with a global conscience*. Rethinking Schools. https://rethinkingschools.org/books/rethinking-globalization/videos-with-a-global-conscience

- Borderlinks: https://www.borderlnks.org

- Data for Black Lives: http://d4bl.org/

- DATAJUSTICE project: https://datajusticeproject.net

- EdGap: http://edgap.org

- Gallup: https://www.gallup.com/

- Gapminder: https://www.gapminder.org

- GLSEN: https://www.glsen.org

- Mathematical Modeling with Cultural and Community Contexts: https://sites.google.com/a/uw.edu/dr-julia-aguirre/research/mathematical-modeling-with-cultural-and-community-contexts-m2c3

- Smith, D. J. (2011). *If the world were a village: A book about the world's people* (2nd ed.). Kids Can Press.

- Social Justice Books: https://socialjusticebooks.org/store/

- U.S. Census Bureau: https://www.census.gov/en.html

- What's Going on in This Graph? *New York Times*: https://www.nytimes.com/column/whats-going-on-in-this-graph

Available for download at
resources.corwin.com/TMSJ-EarlyElementary

APPENDIX B: LESSON RESOURCES

5.1 EXPLORING FAIRNESS THROUGH DATA AND NUMBERS

Website
- Collaborative for Academic, Social, and Emotional Learning: https://casel.org/

Books
- *Miss Tizzy* by Libba Moore Gray

- *Wilfrid Gordan McDonald Partridge* by Mem Fox

- *Come With Me* by Holly M. McGhee

- *All Are Welcome* by Alexandra Penfold

- *The Push: A Story of Friendship* by Patrick Gray

- *Happy in Our Skin* by Fran Manushkin

- *Giraffes Can't Dance* by Giles Andreae and Guy Parker-Rees

- *Mango, Abuela, and Me* by Meg Medina

5.2 ADDRESSING FOOD INSECURITY

Websites
- Feeding America: http://www.FeedingAmerica.org

- "Food Deserts" by the Food Empowerment Project: https://bit.ly/3I9tLc3

Blog Posts
- "Food Equity: Our Social Awakening" by Jaclyn Bowen, *Clean Label Project Blog* (https://bit.ly/3xR15zJ)

- "Food Deserts in the United States" by The Annie E. Casey Foundation, February 13, 2021 (https://bit.ly/3IczSft)

Books
- *Maddie's Fridge* by Lois Brandt

- *Lulu and the Hungry Monster* by Erik Talkin

- *Uncle Willie's Soup Kitchen* by Dyanne Disalvo-Ryan

- *The Ugly Vegetables* by Grace Lin

- *The Have a Good Day Café* by Francis Park and Ginger Park

Online Resource
- Worksheet 1: *Recording Sheet*

5.3 SAME AND DIFFERENT: AN EXPLORATION OF IDENTITY THROUGH GEOMETRY SHAPES

Books
- *Shapes That Roll* by Karen Nagel

- *Color Zoo* by Lois Ehlert

- *I'm New Here* by Anne Sibley O'Brien

- *I Am America* by Charles R. Smith Jr.

- *The All-Together Quilt* by Lizzy Rockwell

Article
- Gerardo, J. M., & Winters, H. (2018, March). Our school family: Similarities and differences. *ComMuniCator, 42*(3), 24–26, 28.

Online Resources
- Teacher Resource 1: *Pattern Blocks Template* (in English and Spanish)

- Teacher Resource 2: *Shape Portrait Template* (in English and Spanish)

- Teacher Resource 3: *Shape Portrait Examples*

- Teacher Resource 4: *Example Letters to Stakeholders*

5.4 EXAMINING AIR QUALITY

Websites
- Purple Air real-time air quality monitoring: http://www.purpleair.com

- AirNow air quality data: https://www.airnow.gov/

- California Air Resource Board, "Children's Environmental Health Protection Program": https://bit.ly/3odWpAX

- "Study finds wildfire smoke more harmful to humans than pollution from cars," NPR (https://n.pr/3d6Gr5c)

- "Long wildfire seasons also mean extended periods of dangerous air quality," NPR (https://n.pr/3rqxax0)

- "Smoky air from wildfires impacting parts of California differently," KQED (https://bit.ly/3pdt7S6) [Smoke story starts at 5 minutes]

Online Resources
- Teacher Resource 1: *Maps for Exploring Air Quality*

- Teacher Resource 2: *Three Ways to Display How Air Quality Is Measured*

- Teacher Resource 3: *Sample Family Letter on Supporting Children to Keep Exploring Air Quality*

5.5 FAMILY COUNTS! MATHEMATICS, FAMILY, AND THE DIVERSITY ACROSS OUR HOMES

Books
- *Grandma's Tiny House: A Counting Story!* by JaNay Brown-Wood

Online Resources
- Worksheet 1: *Family Member Cutouts*

- Worksheet 2: *How Many Family Members and Friends in Grandma's Tiny House?*

- Worksheet 3: *Family at Home*

5.6 LEARNING FROM OUR ANIMAL FRIENDS: MATHEMATIZING WITH THE ARTWORK OF RICARDO LEVINS MORALES

Art
- *What To Do In a Pandemic (Animals)* posters by Ricardo Levins Morales (https://bit.ly/3dajUUZ)

5.7 ACTIVISM THROUGH ART

Websites
- Black Lives Matter: https://blacklivesmatter.com/

- National Education Association Black Lives Matter at School Resources: https://bit.ly/31r5Wf2

Articles

- Learning for Justice: "Why Teaching Black Lives Matters, Part I," by Jamilah Pitts (https://bit.ly/3DfKRRV)

- Learning for Justice: "Bringing Black Lives Matter Into the Classroom, Part II," by Jamilah Pitts (https://bit.ly/3rqmcI3)

- The Verge Photo Essay: "33 Powerful Black Lives Matter Murals" (https://bit.ly/32GTmbU)

- Penn Graduate School of Education News: "Talking to children after racial incidents" (https://bit.ly/3d8tisn)

- "The 'Black Lives Matter' street art that contains multitudes," by Julia Jacobs, *New York Times*, August 4, 2020 (https://nyti.ms/3oagfNk)

Videos

- "Black Lives Matter Protests," from BrainPOP (https://bit.ly/3ocijEs)

- "Artists have two days to paint Cincinnati's 'Black Lives Matter' mural," from WCPO (https://bit.ly/3lr55ly)

Online Resource

- Teacher Resource 1: *Mural Links*

5.8 SEEING THE COLORS OF OURSELVES AND OTHERS

Books

- *The Colors of Us* by Karen Katz (multiple copies if possible)

- *I Am Human: A Book of Empathy* by Susan Verde

Journal Article

- Welch, B. (2016). The pervasive whiteness of children's literature: Collective harms and consumer obligations. *Social Theory and Practice*, 42(2), 367–388. https://www.jstor.org/stable/24871348

Websites

- Social Justice Books: https://socialjusticebooks.org. This is a good resource for more information including a list of books that more closely fit the learning needs of the children in your classroom

Online Resources

- Tasksheets 1 and 2: *Who Is In My Books?*

- Teacher Resource 1: *List of Characters and Skin Tones From* The Colors of Us

- Teacher Resource 2: *Template Letter to Families*

5.9 HUMAN DIVERSITY AND DISABILITY: DO WE ALL HAVE 10 FINGERS?

Books

- *What Happened to You?* by James Catchpole and Karen George

- *Intersectional Allies: We Make Room for All* by Chelsea Johnson, LaToya Council, and Carolyn Choi

- *The Bug Girl* by Sophia Spencer

- *Emmanuel's Dream: The True Story of Emmanuel Ofosu Yeboah* by Laurie Ann Thompson and Sean Qualls

- *Hello Goodbye Dog* by Maria Gianferrari

- *I Am Not a Label* by Cerrie Burnell

- *A Kids Book about Disabilities* by Kristine Napper

- *Mama Zooms* by Jane Cowen-Fletcher

- *Rescue and Jessica: A Life-Changing Friendship* by Jessica Kensky and Patrick Downes

- *Terry Fox and Me* by Mary Beth Leatherdale

- *All Are Welcome* by Alexandra Penfold

Chapter Books

- *Braced* by Alyson Gerber

- *Roll With It* by Jamie Sumner

Teacher Resource

- Vasquez, V. M. (2016). *Critical literacy across the K-6 curriculum.* Taylor & Francis.

Articles and Lessons

- "How to talk to your kid about disabilities," by Caroline Bologna, *Huffington Post*, March 1, 2021 (https://bit.ly/32Svi68)

- Learning for Justice, "Picturing Accessibility: Art, Activism and Physical Disabilities" (https://bit.ly/3oeLVkC)

- Learning for Justice, "What Is Ableism?" (https://bit.ly/3oe0kh9)

- Learning for Justice, "What Is a Disability?" (https://bit.ly/3lrFFUG)

5.10 FEEDING OURSELVES AND OTHERS

Book
- *Uncle Willie and the Soup Kitchen* by DyAnne DiSalvo-Ryan

5.11 REPRESENTATION MATTERS IN MATHEMATICS CLASS

Books and Position Statements
- Gustein, E. (2006). *Reading and writing the word with mathematics: Towards a pedagogy for social justice.* Routledge.

- NCSM and TODOS: Mathematics for ALL (2016). *Mathematics education through the lens of social justice: Acknowledgement, actions and accountability.* https://www.todos-math.org/assets/docs2016/2016Enews/3.pospaper16_wtodos_8pp.p

Journal Articles
- Galindo, C., Sonnenschein, S., & Montoya-Ávila, A. (2019). Latina mothers' engagement in children's math learning in the early school years: Conceptions of math and socialization practices. *Early Childhood Research Quarterly*, 47, 271–283. https://doi.org/10.1016/j.ecresq.2018.11.007

- Wang, M., & Degol, J. (2014). Staying engaged: Knowledge and research needs in student engagement. *Child Development Perspectives*, 8(3), 137–143. https://doi.org/10.1111/cdep.12073

- Yeh, C., & Otis, B. (2019). Mathematics for whom: Reframing and humanizing mathematics. *Bank Street Occasional Paper Series*, 2019(41). https://educate.bankstreet.edu/occasional-paper-series/vol2019/iss41/8

Online Resources
- Worksheet 1: *Counting Collections Recording Sheet*

- Teacher Resource 1: *Math Games Directions*

- Teacher Resource 2: *Sample Family Letter*

5.12 RESPECTING OUR HOUSE: PROTECTING OUR SALMON NEIGHBORS

Websites
- Since Time Immemorial Early Learning Curriculum offered by Washington State's Department of Children, Youth and Families: https://bit.ly/2ZKXLJP

- Northwest Indian Fisheries Commission: https://nwifc.org/

Video

- "Through Salmon Eyes," from Northwest Treaty Tribes (https://bit.ly/3G0s0fg)

5.13 EARLY ELEMENTARY MATHEMATICS TO EXPLORE PEOPLE REPRESENTED IN OUR WORLD AND COMMUNITY

Book

- *If the World Were a Village* by David J. Smith

Website

- 100 People: A World Portrait: https://www.100people.org/statistics-100-people/

Video

- "The 100 People Project: An Introduction," from 100 People (https://www.100people.org/the-100-people-project-an-introduction/)

Journal Articles and Teacher Books

- Guzmán, L. D., & Craig, J. (2019). The world in your pocket: Digital media as invitations for transdisciplinary inquiry in mathematics classrooms. *Occasional Paper Series, 2019*(41), 6. https://educate.bankstreet.edu/occasional-paper-series/vol2019/iss41/6

- Raygoza, M. C. (2016). Striving toward transformational resistance: Youth participatory action research in the mathematics classroom. *Journal of Urban Mathematics Education, 9*(2).

- Thanheiser, E., & Koestler, C. (2021). If the world were a village: Learning mathematics while learning about the world. *Mathematics Teacher Educator, 9*(3), 202–228. https://doi.org/10.5951/MTE.2020.0021

- Vasquez, V. M. (2016). *Critical literacy across the K–6 curriculum.* Taylor & Francis.

Online Resources

- Teacher Resource 1: *Supplementary Video Links With Social Characteristics in Each*

5.14 JOURNEY FOR JUSTICE: THE FARMWORKERS' MOVEMENT

Book

- *Journey for Justice: The Life of Larry Itliong* by Dawn B. Mabalon with Gayle Romasanta

Website

- United Farm Workers: https://ufw.org/

Articles

- "This Day in History: Sept. 8, 1965: Delano Grape Strike Began," from the Zinn Education Project (https://bit.ly/32F9r1N)

- "The 1965–1970 Delano Grape Strike and Boycott," by Inga Kim, *United Farm Workers*, March 7, 2017 (https://bit.ly/3xGME1a)

Video

- "The Farm Worker Movement," from PBS (https://bit.ly/2ZIjzWq)

 Available for download at **resources.corwin.com/ TMSJ-EarlyElementary**

APPENDIX C: EDUCATION OF YOUNG CHILDREN LEARNING PATHS (2010)

NAEYC's Position Statement on *Early Childhood Mathematics: Promoting New Beginnings* provides significant guidance on early childhood mathematics, especially the *Learning PATHS and Teaching STRATEGIES in Early Mathematics*. The full position statement plus additional guidance can be found at https://www.naeyc.org/resources/position-statements.

APPENDIX D: SOCIAL JUSTICE STANDARDS

Anchor Standard	Grade Level K–2 Outcome
Identity 1	I know and like who I am and can talk about my family and myself and describe our various group identities.
Identity 2	I know about my family history and culture and about current and past contributions of people in my main identity groups.
Identity 3	I know that all my group identities are part of who I am, but none of them fully describes me and this is true for other people too.
Identity 4	I can feel good about my identity without making someone else feel bad about who they are.
Identity 5	I know my family and I do things the same as and different from other people and groups, and I know how to use what I learn from home, school, and other places that matter to me.
Diversity 6	I like knowing people who are like me and different from me, and I treat each person with respect.
Diversity 7	I have accurate, respectful words to describe how I am similar to and different from people who share my identities and those who have other identities.
Diversity 8	I want to know more about other people's lives and experiences, and I know how to ask questions respectfully and listen carefully and non-judgmentally.
Diversity 9	I feel connected to other people and know how to talk, work, and play with others even when we are different or when we disagree.
Diversity 10	I know that the way groups of people are treated today, and the way they have been treated in the past, is a part of what makes them who they are.
Justice 11	I try and get to know people as individuals because I know it is unfair to think all people in a shared identity group are the same.
Justice 12	I know when people are treated unfairly, and I can give examples of prejudice in words, pictures, and rules.
Justice 13	I know that words, behaviors, rules, and laws that treat people unfairly based on their group identities cause real harm.
Justice 14	I know that life is easier for some people and harder for others based on who they are and where they were born.
Justice 15	I know about the actions of people and groups who have worked throughout history to bring more justice and fairness to the world.

(Continued)

(Continued)

Anchor Standard	Grade Level K–2 Outcome
Action 16	I pay attention to how people (including myself) are treated, and I try to treat others how I like to be treated.
Action 17	I know it's important for me to stand up for myself and for others, and I know how to get help if I need ideas on how to do this.
Action 18	I know some ways to interfere if someone is being hurtful or unfair, and will do my part to show respect even if I disagree with someone's words or behavior.
Action 19	I will speak up or do something when I see unfairness, and I will not let others convince me to go along with injustice.
Action 20	I will work with my friends and family to make our school and community fair for everyone, and we will work hard and cooperate in order to achieve our goals.

Source: Reprinted with permission of Teaching Tolerance, a project of the Southern Poverty Law Center. https://www.tolerance.org/

APPENDIX E: SOCIAL JUSTICE TOPICS AND MATHEMATICS DOMAINS

Lesson	Social Justice Topic	Suggested Grade Level	Number and Operations	Geometry	Measurement	Patterns and Algebraic Thinking	Data Collection and Analysis
5.1	Diversity and Empathy	PreK–K					X
5.2	Food Insecurity	PreK–2	X		X		X
5.3	Exploring Identity	PreK–2		X			
5.4	Air Quality	K–2	X		X		X
5.5	Family Diversity	K–2	X		X		X
5.6	Taking Care of Ourselves and Others	K–2	X				X
5.7	Activism Through Art	1–2		X			
5.8	Skin Tone Representation in Picture Books	1–2	X			X	X
5.9	Body Diversity and Disability	1–2				X	
5.10	Poverty and Homelessness	1–2				X	
5.11	Mathematical Access and Identity	1–2	X				
5.12	Protecting the Watershed	1–2	X		X		
5.13	The Diversity of the "Global Village"	2				X	X
5.14	Workers' Rights and the Delano Grape Strike	2	X				

online resources Available for download at **resources.corwin.com/TMSJ-EarlyElementary**

APPENDIX F: SOCIAL JUSTICE MATHEMATICS LESSON PLANNER

PART I

CONTEXT	
Purpose	
Audience	
Allies	
Timing	

CONTENT	
Mathematics Goal(s)	**Mathematical Content Domain**
Social Justice Topic and Brief Description	
Social Justice Outcome	

WHO	
Resources for Your Learning	Classroom Practices and Norms to Establish Social and Emotional Safety
How Your Lesson Supports Children in Recognizing Injustice at Both Individual and Institutional or Systemic Levels	

WHEN
Possible Interdisciplinary Connections

HOW
Instructional Model (e.g., Classroom Routine, Mathematics Task, Three-Act Task)

PART II

Launch	
What will the teacher do?	**What will the children do?**

Exploration	
What will the teacher do?	**What will the children do?**

Summarize	
What will the teacher do?	**What will the children do?**

Taking Action

Stakeholder Communication	
How is the teacher communicating lesson goals?	**How are the children communicating their learning?**

REFERENCES

Adair, J. K. (2015). *The impact of discrimination on the early schooling experiences of children from immigrant families.* Mitigation Policy Institute. https://www.migrationpolicy.org/sites/default/files/publications/FCD-Adair.pdf

Aguirre, J., Mayfield-Ingram, K., & Martin, D. B. (2013). *The impact of identity in K–8 mathematics: Rethinking equity-based practices.* National Council of Teachers of Mathematics.

Aguirre, J. M., & del Rosario Zavala, M. (2013). Making culturally responsive mathematics teaching explicit: A lesson analysis tool. *Pedagogies: An International Journal, 8*(2), 163–190. https://doi.org/10.1080/1554480X.2013.768518

Artiles, A. J., Klinger, J. K., & Tate, W. F. (2006). Representation of minority students in special education: Complicating traditional explanations. *Educational Researcher, 35*(6), 3–5. https://doi.org/10.3102/0013189X035006003

Association of Mathematics Teacher Educators. (2020). *Standards for preparing teachers of mathematics.* Information Age Publishing.

Banks, J. A. (2004). Multicultural education: Historical development, dimensions, and practice. In J. A. Banks & C. A. M. Banks (Eds.), *Handbook of research on multicultural education* (pp. 3–29). Jossey-Bass.

Bartell, T. B. (2013). Learning to teach mathematics for social justice: Negotiating social justice and mathematical goals. *Journal for Research in Mathematics Education, 44*(1), 129–163. https://doi.org/10.5951/jresematheduc.44.1.0129

Benjamin Banneker Association. (2017). *Implementing a social justice curriculum: Practices to support the participation and success of African-American students in mathematics.* http://bbamath.org/index.php/2017/11/19/the-benjamin-banneker-social-justice-position-statement

Bishop, R. S. (1990). "Mirrors, Windows, and Sliding Glass Doors." *Perspectives: Choosing and Using Books for the Classroom, 6*(3). http://www.rif.org/us/literacy-resources/multicultural/mirrors-windows-and-sliding-glass-doors.htm

Boaler, J. (2015). *Mathematical mindsets: Unleashing students' potential through creative math, inspiring messages and innovative teaching.* John Wiley & Sons.

Branscombe, M. V. (2019). *Teaching through embodied learning: Dramatizing key concepts from informational texts.* Routledge.

CAST. (2018). *Universal Design for Learning Guidelines Version 2.0.* Author. https://udlguidelines.cast.org/

Center for Economic and Social Justice (n.d.). *Defining economic justice and social justice.* https://www.cesj.org/learn/definitions/defining-economic-justice-and-social-justice/

Chval, K. B., Smith, E., Trigos-Carrillo, L., & Pinnow, R. J. (2021). *Teaching math to multilingual students, Grades K–8: Positioning English learners for success.* Corwin.

Collaborative for Academic, Social, and Emotional Learning. (2022). *Fundamentals of SEL.* https://casel.org

Cvencek, D., Meltzoff, A. N., & Greenwald, A. G. (2011). Math-gender stereotypes in elementary school children. *Child Development, 82*(3), 766–779. https://doi.org/10.1111/j.1467–8624.2010.01529.x

Derman-Sparks, L., Edwards, J. O., & Goins, C. M. (2020). *Anti-bias education for young children and ourselves* (2nd ed). National Association for the Education of Young Children. https://www.naeyc.org/resources/pubs/books/anti-bias-education

Dillard, C. (2019, Fall). Black minds matter: Interrupting school practices that disregard the mental health of Black youth. *Learning for Justice, 63*. https://www.learningforjustice.org/magazine/fall-2019/black-minds-matter

Dingle, M., & Yeh, C. (2021). Mathematics in context: The pedagogy of liberation. *Learning for Justice*. https://www.learningforjustice.org/magazine/spring-2021/mathematics-in-context-the-pedagogy-of-liberation

Doucet, F., & Adair, J. K. (2013). Addressing race and inequity in the classroom. *Young Children, 68*(5), 88–97.

Dunn, A. H. (2021). *Teaching on days after: Educating for equity in the wake of injustice*. Teachers College Press.

Feagin, J. R. (2001). Social justice and sociology: Agendas for the twenty-first century [Presidential address]. *American Sociological Review, 66*(1), 1–20. http://www.jstor.org/stable/2657391.

Featherstone, H., Crespo, S., Jilk, L. M., Oslund, J. A., Parks, A. N., & Wood, M. B. (2011). *Smarter together! Collaboration and equity in the elementary math classroom*. National Council of Teachers of Mathematics

Fisher, P. H., Dobbs-Oates, J., Doctoroff, G. L., & Arnold, D. H. (2012). Early math interest and the development of math skills. *Journal of Educational Psychology, 104*(3), 673. https://doi.org/10.1037/a0027756

Flores, A. (2007). Examining disparities in mathematics education: Achievement gap or opportunity gap? *High School Journal, 91*(1), 29–42. http://www.jstor.org/stable/40367921

Freire, P. (2000). *Pedagogy of the oppressed* (M. B. Ramos, Trans.). Continuum. (Original work published 1970)

Galindo, C., Sonnenschein, S., & Montoya-Ávila, A. (2019). Latina mothers' engagement in children's math learning in the early school years: Conceptions of math and socialization practices. *Early Childhood Research Quarterly, 47*, 271–283. https://doi.org/10.1016/j.ecresq.2018.11.007

Galindo, E., & Lee, J. (2018). *Rigor, relevance, and relationships: Making mathematics come alive with project-based learning*. National Council of Teachers of Mathematics.

Gay, G. (2000). *Culturally responsive teaching: Theory, research, and practice*. Teachers College Press.

Gerardo, J. M., & Winters, H. (2018, March). Our school family: Similarities and differences. *ComMuniCator, 42*(3), 24–26, 28.

Gonzalez, L. (2009). Teaching mathematics for social justice: Reflections on a community of practice for urban high school mathematics teachers. *Journal of Urban Mathematics Education, 2*(1), 22–51.

González, N., Moll, L., & Amanti, C. (Eds.). (2005). *Funds of knowledge: Theorizing practices in households, communities, and classrooms*. Erlbaum Associates.

Goodman, M. E. (1952). *Race awareness in young children*. Collier Books.

Gutstein, E. (2006). *Reading and writing the world with mathematics: Toward a pedagogy for social justice*. Routledge.

Harper, F. (2019). A qualitative metasynthesis of teaching mathematics for social justice in action: Pitfalls and promises of practice. *Journal for Research in Mathematics Education, 50*(3), 269–310. https://doi.org/10.5951/jresematheduc.50.3.0268

Katz, L. G., & Chard, S. C. (2000). *Engaging children's minds: The project approach*. Greenwood Publishing.

Koestler, C. (2012). Beyond apples, puppy dogs, and ice cream: Preparing prospective K–8 teachers to teach mathematics for equity and social justice. In A. Wager and D. Stinson, (Eds.) *Teaching mathematics for social justice: Conversations with educators* (pp. 81–98). National Council of Teachers of Mathematics.

Ladson-Billings, G. (1995). Toward a theory of culturally relevant pedagogy. *American Educational Research Journal*, 32(3), 465–491. https://doi.org/10.3102/00028312032003465

Learning for Justice. (2016). *Social justice standards: The teaching tolerance anti-bias framework*. https://www.tolerance.org/magazine/publications/social-justice-standards

Learning for Justice. (2021). *Toolkit for "Mathematics in Context": The pedagogy of liberation*. https://www.learningforjustice.org/magazine/spring-2021/toolkit-for-mathematics-in-context-the-pedagogy-of-liberation

Loveless, T. (2013). *The resurgence of ability grouping and persistence of tracking* (Part II, 2013 Brown Center Report on American Education). The Brookings Institution.

McGee, E. O. (2020). *Black, brown, bruised: How racialized STEM education stifles innovation*. Harvard Education Press.

Michaels, S., O'Connor, C., & Resnick, L. B. (2008). Deliberative discourse idealized and realized: Accountable talk in the classroom and in civic life. *Studies in Philosophy and Education*, 27(4), 283–297. http://doi.org/10.1007/s11217-007-9071-1

Mistry, R., Nenadal, L., Hazelbaker, T., Griffin, K., & White, E. (2017). Promoting elementary school-age children's understanding of wealth, poverty, and civic engagement. *PS: Political Science & Politics*, 50(4), 1068–1073. http://doi.org/10.1017/S1049096517001329

Moses, R. P., & Cobb, C. E. (2001). *Radical equations: Civil rights from Mississippi to the Algebra Project*. Beacon Press.

Murrell, P. C., Jr. (1997). Digging again the family wells: A Freirean literacy framework as emancipatory pedagogy for African-American children. In P. Freire (with J. W. Fraser, D. Macedo, T. McKinnon, & W. T. Stokes) (Ed.), *Mentoring the mentor: A critical dialogue with Paulo Freire* (pp. 19–58). Lang.

National Association for the Education of Young Children. (2002/2010). *Early childhood mathematics: Promoting good beginnings. A joint position statement of the National Association for the Education of Young Children and National Council of Teachers of Mathematics*. https://www.naeyc.org/sites/default/files/globally-shared/downloads/PDFs/resources/position-statements/psmath.pdf

National Association for the Education of Young Children. (2019). *Advancing equity in early childhood education*. https://www.naeyc.org/sites/default/files/globally-shared/downloads/PDFs/resources/position-statements/advancingequitypositionstatement.pdf

National Council of Teachers of Mathematics. (1989). *Curriculum and evaluation standards for school mathematics*. Author.

National Council of Teachers of Mathematics. (2000). *Principles and standards for school mathematics*. Author.

National Council of Teachers of Mathematics. (2014). *Principles to actions: Ensuring mathematical success for all*. Author.

National Council of Teachers of Mathematics. (2020). *Catalyzing change in early childhood and elementary mathematics: Initiating critical conversations*. Author.

National Education Association. (2015). *Research spotlight on academic ability grouping*. Author.

National Governors Association Center for Best Practices, Council of Chief State School Officers. (2010). *Common Core State Standards Mathematics*. Author.

National Research Council. (2001). *Adding it up: Helping children learn mathematics*. National Academies Press.

NCSM & TODOS: Mathematics for ALL. (2016). *Mathematics education through the lens of social justice: Acknowledgement, actions, and accountability*. https://www.todos.math.org/socialjustice

Nell, M. L., Drew, W. F., & Bush, D. E. (2013). *From play to practice: Connecting teachers' play to children's learning*. National Association for the Education of Young Children.

Nickel City Housing Coop. (n.d.). *Implicit bias discussion questions*. https://www.nasco.coop/sites/default/files/srl/Activity.Implicit%20Bias%20Discussion%20Questions.pdf

Parks, A. N. (2015). *Exploring mathematics through play in the early childhood classroom*. Teachers College Press.

Picower, B. (2012). Using their words: Six elements of social justice curriculum design for the elementary classroom. *International Journal of Multicultural Education*, *14*(1), 1–17. https://doi.org/10.18251/ijme.v14i1.484

Revised Code of Washington, Curricula—Tribal history and culture, Wash. RCW 28A.320.170 (2015). Office of Superintendent of Public Instruction in partnership with the Federally Recognized Tribes in Washington State. (2015). Since Time Immemorial Early Learning Curriculum. Retrieved May 19, 2022, from https://www.dcyf.wa.gov/tribal-relations/since-time-immemorial

Ryan, S., & Grieshaber, S. (2005). Shifting from developmental to postmodern practices in early childhood teacher education. *Journal of Teacher Education*, *56*(1), 34–45. https://doi.org/10.1177/0022487104272057

Silver, E. A., & Mills, V. L. (2018). *A fresh look at formative assessment in teaching mathematics*. National Council of Teachers of Mathematics.

Smith, D. J. (2009). *If America were a village: A book about the people of the United States* (Vol. 7). Kids Can Press.

Smith, D. J. (2011). *If the world were a village: A book about the world's people* (2nd ed.). Kids Can Press.

South Carolina School Report Card. (2022). *Lancaster County School District: 2018–2019*. https://screportcards.com/overview/academics/preparing-for-success/?q=eT0yMDE5JnQ9RCZzaWQ9MjkwMTAwMA

Steele, D. M., & Cohn-Vargas, B. (2013). *Identity safe classrooms: Places to belong and learn*. Corwin.

Stipek, D. (2019, March 25). Should children be ready for kindergarten—Or should kindergarten be ready for children? *Education Week*. https://www.edweek.org/teaching-learning/opinion-should-children-be-ready-for-kindergarten-or-should-kindergarten-be-ready-for-children/2019/03

Svinicki, M. D., & McKeachie, W. J. (2014). *McKeachie's teaching tips: Strategies, research, and theory for college and university teachers* (14th ed.). Wadsworth Cengage Learning.

Swalwell, K. (2013). *Educating activist allies: Social justice pedagogy with the suburban and urban elite*. Routledge.

Tate, W. F. (2013). Race, retrenchment, and the reform of school mathematics. In E. Gutstein & B. Peterson (Eds.), *Rethinking mathematics: Teaching social justice by the numbers* (2nd ed., pp. 42–51). Rethinking Schools.

United Nations Division for Social Policy. (2006). *Social justice in an open world: The role of the United Nations*. United Nations Publications.

University of Wisconsin–Madison. (n.d.). Cooperative Children's Book Center. https://ccbc.education.wisc.edu/.

Vasquez, V. M., (2016). *Critical literacy across the K–6 curriculum*. Taylor & Francis.

Walker, T. (2020, August 5). *Helping students and educators recover from COVID-19 trauma*. National Education Association. https://www.nea.org/advocating-for-change/new-from-nea/helping-students-and-educators-recover-covid-19-trauma

Wang, M., & Degol, J. (2014). Staying engaged: Knowledge and research needs in student engagement. *Child Development Perspectives*, 8(3), 137–143. https://doi.org/10.1111/cdep.12073

Welch, B. (2016). The pervasive whiteness of children's literature: Collective harms and consumer obligations. *Social Theory and Practice*, 42(2), 367–388. https://www.jstor.org/stable/24871348

Winkler, E. N. (2009). Children are not colorblind: How young children learn race. *PACE: Practical Approaches for Continuing Education*, 3(3), 1–8. https://inclusions.org/wp-content/uploads/2017/11/Children-are-Not-Colorblind.pdf

Yeh, C. (under review). *Towards Justice-Oriented Mathematics*.

Yeh, C., & Otis, B. (2019). Mathematics for whom: Reframing and humanizing mathematics. *Occasional Paper Series*, 2019(41). https://educate.bankstreet.edu/occasional-paper-series/vol2019/iss41/8

INDEX

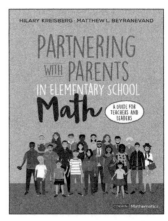

**JENNIFER M. BAY-WILLIAMS,
JOHN J. SANGIOVANNI, ROSALBA SERRANO,
SHERRI MARTINIE, JENNIFER SUH**

Because fluency is so much more
than basic facts and algorithms

Grades K–8

**KAREN S. KARP,
BARBARA J. DOUGHERTY,
SARAH B. BUSH**

A schoolwide solution for students'
mathematics success

Elementary, Middle School, High School

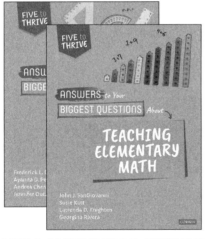

**JOHN J. SANGIOVANNI, SUSIE KATT,
LATRENDA D. KNIGHTEN, GEORGINA RIVERA,
FREDERICK L. DILLON, AYANNA D. PERRY,
ANDREA CHENG, JENNIFER OUTZS**

Actionable answers to your most pressing questions
about teaching elementary and secondary math

Elementary, Secondary

**SARA DELANO MOORE,
KIMBERLY RIMBEY**

A journey toward making
manipulatives meaningful

Grades K–3, 4–8

CORWIN

A SAGE Publishing Company

Helping educators make the greatest impact

CORWIN HAS ONE MISSION: to enhance education through intentional professional learning.

We build long-term relationships with our authors, educators, clients, and associations who partner with us to develop and continuously improve the best evidence-based practices that establish and support lifelong learning.

NATIONAL COUNCIL OF
TEACHERS OF MATHEMATICS

The National Council of Teachers of Mathematics supports and advocates for the highest-quality mathematics teaching and learning for each and every student.